GENEALOGIST'S HANDBOOK
FOR NEW ENGLAND RESEARCH

Fourth Edition

by

MARCIA D. MELNYK

NEW ENGLAND HISTORIC
GENEALOGICAL SOCIETY

1999

First edition published by the
NEW ENGLAND LIBRARY ASSOCIATION
1980

Second edition (revised) published by the
NEW ENGLAND HISTORIC GENEALOGICAL SOCIETY
1985

Third edition (revised) published by the
NEW ENGLAND HISTORIC GENEALOGICAL SOCIETY
1993

Fourth edition (revised) published by the
NEW ENGLAND HISTORIC GENEALOGICAL SOCIETY
1999

Order from:
N E H G S Sales Department
160 North Washington Street, 4th Floor
Boston, MA 02114-2120
Toll-free 1-888-296-3447

Soft-cover $19.95

Published by
The New England Historic Genealogical Society
101 Newbury St.
Boston, MA 02116

Printed by Thompson-Shore, Inc., Dexter, Michigan

PREFACE

The *Genealogist's Handbook for New England Research* was conceived as a resource for persons tracing their family roots in New England. It is not a 'how-to' book, but rather a location guide to public records, repositories, libraries, and genealogical societies in Connecticut, Maine, Massachusetts, New Hampshire, Rhode Island, and Vermont.

The first (1980) edition of the *Handbook* was compiled by the Bibliography Committee of the New England Library Association, with Marcia Wiswall Lindberg as chairperson. Six printings (6,000 copies) of this edition were sold out by 1984, when the NELA transferred copyright privileges to the New England Historic Genealogical Society. In 1985 a second edition was published by NEHGS.

The third (1993) edition was edited and prepared by Ms. Lindberg, who had overseen the preparation of the first two. Letters were sent to all agencies listed in the second edition; 97% responded with updated information for the third, which included more than 200 corrections and additions.

This, the fourth edition, was edited and prepared by Marcia D. Melnyk, and contains numerous new and updated entries – many facilities and organizations added, many entries corrected or expanded. A preliminary "New England" chapter has been added, which lists sites holding records pertaining to the whole region, not just to one of its six states.

ARRANGEMENT

After the NEW ENGLAND chapter, the reader will find chapters devoted to each of the six states (presented in alphabetical order), with the materials for each state arranged by type of record. The materials presented or discussed include:

- COUNTIES (an alphabetical list, with years of creation, *etc.*)
- TOWNS (an alphabetical list, with settlement or incorporation dates, counties, *etc.*)
- [NAME OF STATE] (general remarks on its history, *etc.*)
- VITAL RECORDS (*i.e.*, of birth, marriage, and death)
- FEDERAL CENSUS
- STATE CENSUS
- PROBATE – wills, administrations, guardianships, *etc.* – AND LAND – deeds (alphabetical by county)
- CEMETERY RECORDS
- CHURCH RECORDS
- MILITARY RECORDS (federal and state)
- IMMIGRATION AND NATURALIZATION
- NEWSPAPERS
- CIVIL AND CRIMINAL COURT RECORDS
- LIBRARIES (with unique or significant genealogical holdings; alphabetical by town)

- LDS FAMILY HISTORY CENTERS

- SOCIETIES (with a genealogical focus; alphabetical by name)

- PERIODICALS (major genealogical, focusing on state in question)

- BOOKS AND ARTICLES

GENERAL USAGE NOTES

Information of the sort published in this *Handbook* – locations, telephone numbers and Web and e-mail addresses, holdings, policies, and especially hours and fees – 'spoils' rapidly; some data asserted herein will almost certainly be obsolete even by publication. The reader is therefore advised to *call in advance* to confirm crucial information, particularly before traveling any distance to a repository whose hours or even address may have changed.

It should also be noted that the author has not been able to visit every repository in recent months; we have therefore relied, in many cases, and out of necessity, on replies to letters and e-mail of inquiry, telephone interviews, and printed and internet informational literature. Though we have tried to confirm all statements received and to clarify obscure points, this has not always been possible. The reader is urged to call errors to our attention for correction in future editions.

The *main* entry for a repository is usually in **BOLD CAPS**. When you see a repository mentioned in PLAIN CAPS, that means it has a *main* entry, with a fuller discussion, elsewhere – exactly where, should be generally clear (*e.g.*, the XYZ SOCIETY should be listed alphabetically under SOCIETIES; the CRABGRASS LIBRARY, alphabetically by town, under LIBRARIES); the STATE is mentioned in such cross-references *only* when the main entry is in some other chapter. If all else fails, there is an INDEX.

Space being at a premium, especially in tables and travel directions, a modest array of abbreviations has been used throughout. Most of these are common, if not standard, but since not every reader will necessarily recognize *every* abbreviation, the following *key* is presented to alleviate confusion.

KEY TO ABBREVIATIONS

St, Rd, Ln, Av, Blvd, Dr, Pkwy – Street, Road, Lane, Avenue, Boulevard, Drive, Parkway
Pl – in *directions*, 'Place;' in *town-lists*, 'Plantation'
Ctr, Sq, Cir – Center, Square, Circle
I-, Rte, Hwy, Tpk, Jct – Interstate, Route, Highway, Turnpike, Junction
hse, bldg, PO, El, sta – house, building, Post Office, elevated, station
light – traffic light
X – intersection
N, S, E, W – north, south, east, west (in *directions*)
N., S., E., W. – North, South, East, West (as components of *place-names*)
'til – until (in tables only)
Mon, Tue, Wed, Thu, Fri, Sat, Sun – 7 days of week
Jan, Feb, Mar, Apr, May, Jun, Jul, Aug, Sep, Oct, Nov, Dec – 12 months of year
mi, yd, yr, hr – mile, yard, year, hour
/ – 'per'
s & h – shipping and handling
SASE – self-addressed stamped envelope
VRs, TRs – vital records, town records

ID – identification

N.B. – '*nota bene,*' note well, take particular notice
i.e. – 'id est,' that is
e.g. – 'for example'
et al. – 'and others'

ACKNOWLEDGEMENTS

Appreciation and thanks are owed to:

Gary Boyd Roberts, Senior Research Scholar at NEHGS, for editing each section and guiding choice of format and presentation.

Jane Fletcher Fiske, Director of Publications for NEHGS, for editing all chapters and providing unfailing guidance during the entire project.

Aileen Novick, Editorial and Production Assistant at NEHGS, for editing of format and layout.

Dr. Ralph J. Crandall, Director of NEHGS, for agreeing to publish this edition, and offering frequent encouragement.

Numerous *public officials*, for answering our requests for updated material.

Maureen J. Taylor, former Director of the Rhode Island Historical Society Library and former Director of Library User Services at NEHGS, for reviewing the New England and Rhode Island chapters.

Jonathan Galli, NEHGS Enquiries Service Coordinator, for reviewing the Rhode Island chapter.

Ann Smith Lainhart, for reviewing the Massachusetts chapter.

Sandra (Nickerson) Frost, for reviewing the Maine chapter and preparing the LDS FAMILY HISTORY CENTER entries.

Scott Andrew Bartley, former NEHGS Curator of Manuscripts, for reviewing the chapter on Vermont.

George Freeman Sanborn Jr., Reference Librarian and Editorial and Production Assistant at NEHGS, for reviewing the chapter on N.H.

Marshall Kenneth Kirk, Reference Librarian and Editorial and Production Assistant at NEHGS, for vetting the manuscript.

Helen S. Ullmann, for reviewing the Connecticut chapter.

David C. Dearborn and *Jerome E. Anderson* of the NEHGS staff, for a variety of additions and corrections.

Thanks also to my husband, Jim, and daughters, Diana and Kate, for their continuing support.

Marcia D. Melnyk
Rowley, Mass., July 1999

*　*　*　*　*

This *Handbook* lists most – but not all – New England governmental agencies, public libraries, and historical or other societies that hold collections of interest to genealogists. For the most nearly comprehensive and up-to-date listings of these several types of facility see *American Library Directory*; Mary Bray Wheeler, *Directory of Historical Organizations in the United States and Canada;* and Mary Keysor Meyer, *Meyer's Directory of Genealogical Societies in the U.S.A. and Canada*. Please note also P. William Filby, *Directory of Libraries with Genealogy or Local History Collections.*

The reader is urged to send notice of errors, significant omissions, and obsolescences to **Jane Fletcher Fiske**, NEHGS, 101 Newbury Street, Boston, MA 02116-3007; a copy of the *Handbook*, so annotated, will be maintained to aid in the preparation of the next edition.

NEW ENGLAND

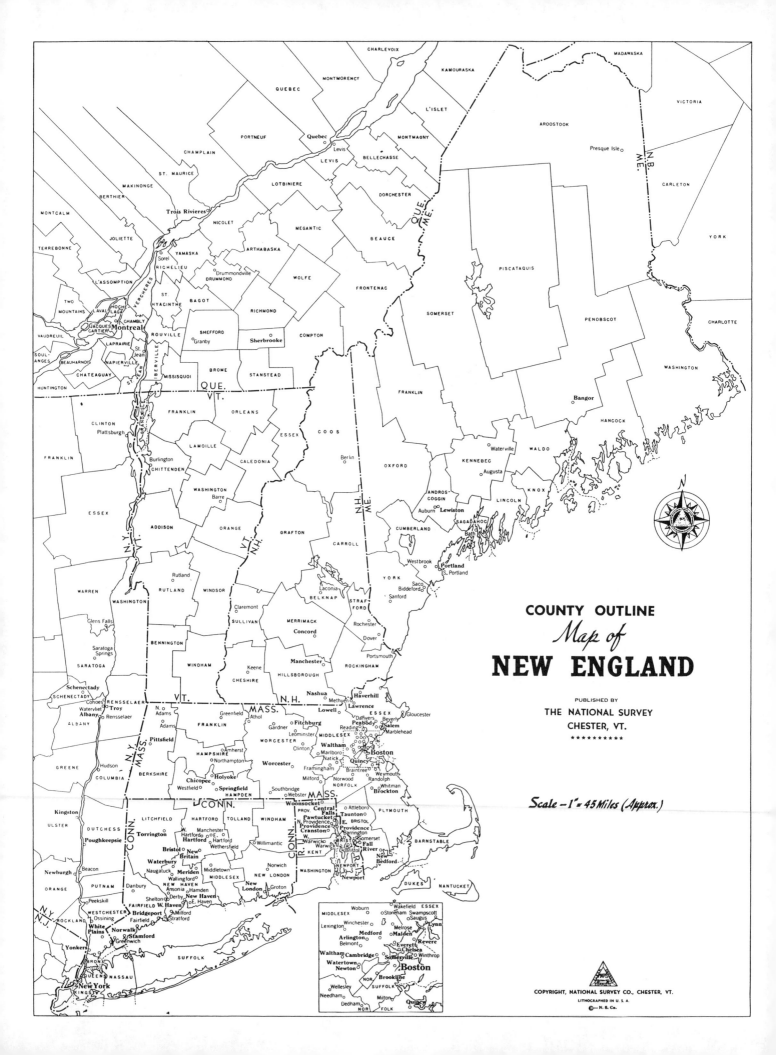

COUNTY OUTLINE
Map of
NEW ENGLAND

PUBLISHED BY

THE NATIONAL SURVEY
CHESTER, VT.

★★★★★★★★★★

Scale – 1" = 45 Miles (Approx.)

COPYRIGHT, NATIONAL SURVEY CO., CHESTER, VT.

LITHOGRAPHED IN U.S.A.

©—N. S. Co.

NEW ENGLAND

The research facilities listed in this section hold materials covering all six New England states, and in many cases, other states as well. (Please be sure to consult the section for each individual state, as well, for additional research materials.) Most 'ethnic genealogy' societies are listed here, unless their membership is specific to a single state.

NATIONAL ARCHIVES AND RECORDS ADMINISTRATION (NARA) – RENTAL

Census Microfilm Rental   [301] 604-3699
   Program
P.O. Box 30
9050 Junction Drive
Annapolis Junction, MD 20701-0030
Web: http://www.nara.gov/publications/microfilm/micrent.html

Join the Rental Program for $25, and you receive the following Startup Kit: a complete set of Federal Population Census catalogs listing all orderable film reels; catalogs for the 1790-1880 and 1900-20 censuses, the Compiled Military Service Records of Revolutionary War soldiers (which have a general index), and the Revolutionary War Pension and Bounty-Land-Warrant Application files; five 'member' film-rental order forms; two bonus coupons for free rental of your first two reels; and free lifetime membership in the Program, including an ID card with account number, with which you can order all film reels directly, and purchase a selection of National Archives and other genealogical publications at a 10% discount. 30-day rental: 1-4 reels, $3.25 each; 5-9, $2.75 each; 10 or more, $2.25 each, plus $3 s & h per order. (N.B., a $12 fee is charged for each lost or damaged reel.) Orders must specify the official reel-numbers; those for the Censuses may be ascertained from four booklets, available from the National Archives Trust Fund Board, Washington, D.C.: "Federal Population Censuses, 1790-1890," "1900 Federal Population Census," "1910 Federal Population Census," and "1920 Federal Population Census." *Please, no research requests*!

HERITAGE QUEST (formerly American Genealogical Lending Library [AGLL])

P.O. Box 329   [801] 298-5358
Bountiful, UT 84011-0329
Web: http://www.heritagequest.com/genealogy/microfilm

Heritage Quest is a 50,000-reel private microfilm library, from which individuals or institutions may borrow U.S. censuses, ship passenger lists, Revolutionary War Pension- and Bounty-Land-Warrant-Application files, and much more (check website for holdings). Initial 'membership' fee is $39.95; with it, films may be rented for $3.25/reel, or $2.75 each for 10 or more reels (plus a flat $3 per-order fee for 4th-class s & h; or $.50 more per reel for 1st-class or UPS); membership also carries subscription to *Genealogical Bulletin* (6 issues/yr), plus a coupon book ($1600 value) and 3 free mail inquiries. Per-reel *purchase* price is $17.95 for members, $24.95 for non-. For further information, send a SASE to the above address. *Mail order ONLY* – facility not open to public.

FEDERAL RECORDS

Many New England libraries with sizable genealogical collections own federal population census films for their own county and/or state. But for census films covering the entire U.S., the National Archives and Records Administration (NARA) is the place to go. There are facilities in Waltham and Pittsfield, Mass.

NARA – NORTHEAST REGION – WALTHAM

380 Trapelo Road   [781] 647-8100   From Rte 128, take Trapelo Exit E,
Waltham, MA 02154   2¾ mi. Low brick bldg on right, just
Web: http://www.nara.gov/regional/boston.html   before Fernald School.

Mon-Fri 8am-4:30pm
1ˢᵗ Sat 8am-4:30pm (*except holiday weekends – call*)

Open to all, no admission fee; about 40 film readers; 2 reader/printers, $.25/page; self-service photocopying, $.10/page. **HOLDINGS**: primarily film; all U.S. federal censuses, 1790-1880 and 1900-20 (1890 was lost to fire before filming); many printed census indexes, 1790-1860 (a few for later years). The indexes list (in alphabetical order) only heads of household and people of other surnames in each household, as well as the page of the actual census on which each name appears. "Soundexes" for 1880 (only for households with children aged 10 or under), 1900, 1910 (only for 23 states, none in New England), and 1920 are also alphabetized by head of household. Each Soundex card, however, lists every person living in that household.

The NARA facilities have film of Revolutionary War Pension- and Bounty-Land-Warrant-Application files and Revolutionary service records (plus indexes). Also on film is an index to compiled service records of volunteer soldiers during the War of 1812 and abstracts of service records of naval officers, 1798-1893. There are also indexes to pension applications for Civil War Union veterans, although the files themselves haven't been filmed and are available (as photocopies) only by mail from NARA's central facility in Washington, D.C. (NATF-80 order forms are available at the regional facilities, or by e-mail: inquire@archz.nara.gov.) Passenger lists for entry at the ports of Boston (1820-74 and 1883-1930), New Bedford, Mass. (1826-52 and 1902-42), Portland, Maine (1820-68 and 1893-1943), Providence, Rhode Island (1820-67 and 1911-43), and Galveston, Texas (1896-1948), as well as *via* the St. Albans District (1895-1954) are also available. (The St. Albans District extended along most of the U.S./Canadian border, and its records cover people who crossed into the States at any point, not just *via* Vermont).

NARA's Waltham center also holds naturalization records from federal courts in each New England state – for Mass., 1790-1966; Maine, 1790-1955; N.H., 1873-1977; Vermont, 1801-1972; Rhode Island, 1842-1950; and Conn., 1842-1973. The Maine, Mass., Rhode Island, and Vermont naturalization records have fairly complete name indexes; for N.H., you must contact the clerk of the U.S. District Court at Concord for index information. Conn.'s U.S. District Court naturalization records are only partially indexed, for recent years; contact the Court clerks at Hartford, New Haven, and Bridgeport for information from these indexes.

NARA – Waltham also holds original naturalization records (1790-1974) from a number of non-federal Conn. courts – superior, common pleas, district, and some municipal. NARA has, as well, 5 x 8" photostatic negatives ('dexigraphs') of naturalization records from federal, state, county, and municipal courts in Maine, Massachusetts, New Hampshire, Rhode Island, and Vermont, 1790-1906. These were made in the late 1930s by the WPA, which also prepared name indexes (available at NARA's Waltham and Pittsfield facilities, and at NEHGS).

Other genealogically useful NARA records include an index to applications for passports (1810-1906); registers of lighthouse keepers (1845-1912); records of appointment of postmasters (1789-1971); and lists of U.S. diplomatic and consular officers (1789-1939).

Of special interest are the following additions to NARA – Waltham's film collection:

- **M265** Index to passenger lists of vessels arriving at Boston, 1848-91
- **T518** Index to passengers arriving at Providence, 1911-64
- **T521** Index to passengers arriving at Boston, 1902-06
- **T617** Index to passengers arriving at Boston, 1906-20
- **T843** Lists of passengers arriving at Boston, 1891-1943
- **T522** Index to passengers arriving at New Bedford, 1902-54
- **T524** Index to passengers arriving at Portland, Maine, 1893-1954
- **M1321** Passengers arriving at Gloucester, Mass., Oct 1906-Mar 1942
- **T496** 1835 census of Cherokees east of the Mississippi, with index
- **T529** Final rolls of citizens and freedmfie of the Five Civilized Tribes in Indian Territory, through 1914
- **M1186** Enrollment cards for the Five Civilized Tribes, 1898-1914
- **M433** Slave-related records of the Washington, D.C., U.S. District Court, 1851-63
- **M434** *Habeas Corpus* records of the Washington, D.C., U.S. District Court, 1820-63
- **M816** Signatures of deposit, Freedmen's Savings and Trust Company, 1865-74
- **M817** Indexes to Deposit Ledgers in Branches of the Freedmen's Savings and Trust Company, 1865-1874
- **T288** Index to pension files (U.S. veterans and widows), 1861-1934
- **M535** Index to service records of volunteer Union soldiers serving from Conn.
- **M543** … from Maine
- **M544** … from Mass.
- **M549** … from N.H.
- **M555** … from Rhode Island
- **M557** … from Vermont
- **M848** War of 1812 bounty-land warrants, 1815-1939
- **M1509** World War I Draft Registration Cards, 1917-18 (New England only)
- **M1659** Service records of soldiers in the 54th Mass. Infantry Regiment (colored), 1863-6
- **M1747** Index to War of 1812 prisoners
- **M1784** Index to pension applications of remarried widows (War of 1812, Indian wars, Mexican War, and regular army before 1861)
- **M1785** … (Civil War and regular army after 1865)
- **M1786** Invalid pension payments to veterans of the Revolution and the regular army and navy, Mar 1801-Sep 1815
- **M1801** Compiled service records of volunteer Union soldiers: 55th Mass. Infantry (colored)
- **M1898** …: 54th Mass. Infantry (colored)
- **M2014** Burial registers for military posts, camps, and stations, 1768-1921
- **T1224** Census enumeration districts, 1910 and 1920

NARA – NORTHEAST REGION – PITTSFIELD

10 Conte Drive [413] 445-6885
Pittsfield, MA 01201-8230 & -7599 (FAX)
Web: http://www.nara.gov/regional/pittsfie.html
E-mail: archives@pittsfield.nara.gov

Mon, Tue, Thu, Fri 8am-4pm; Wed 8am-9pm
(*closed weekends and federal holidays*)

MA Tpk to Exit 2 (Lee); after toll on Rte 20N, right, 8 mi (Rte 20 joins Rte 7) to Dan Fox Dr; 1st right on Conte; follow signs to National Records Center and Archives.

Open to the public, no admission fee; 33 film and 3 fiche readers; 3 reader/printers, $.25/page; self-service copying, $.10/page; certified copies for a fee; mail inquiries as to holdings answered (sorry, no research requests); copies of ship manifests sent (if port and exact date of arrival are provided), $10/page; handicapped accessible; public telephones; free parking; lockers; lunchroom with fridge, microwave, and vending machines; gift shop; genealogical bookstore. **HOLDINGS**: U.S. federal census schedules, 1790-1920, with available indexes (see above, under NARA – WALTHAM); Revolutionary War service records and pension and bounty-land warrants; indexes to compiled service records of volunteer soldiers, 1784-1901; U.S. Army enlistments, 1798-1914; records of the 54th Mass. volunteer infantry (the Glory Regiment), 1863-5; indexes to pension records for regular army service, 1783-1926; World War I draft registration cards, 1917-18, for Conn., Maine, Mass., N.H., New York, and Rhode Island. Index to New England naturalization petitions, 1791-1906; index to naturalization petitions and records of Mass.'s U.S. District Court, 1906-66, and U.S. Circuit Court, 1906-29. Ship manifests of passengers into Boston (1820-1942), New York (1820-1957), Philadelphia (1800-82), and Baltimore (1820-91); indexes to same for Boston (1820-91 and 1902-20), New York (1820-46 and 1897-1948), and Philadelphia (1800-1906); arrivals at miscellaneous Atlantic and Gulf ports are also available, and Canadian arrivals for the St. Albans District (see above, under NARA – WALTHAM), 1895-1954; records of arrival at some smaller New England ports (*e.g.*, New Bedford, Providence, and Portland) are also available. Also of interest: Eastern Cherokee applications in the U.S. Court of Claims, 1906-9; enrollment cards for the Five Civilized Tribes, 1898-1914; final rolls of citizens and freedmen of the same; signatures of deposit in the Freedmen's Savings and Trust Co., 1865-74; appointment of postmasters, 1832-1950; P.O. reports of site locations; and records of Russian consulates in the U.S., 1861-1922.

Also available (on CD) are *Germans to America, The Famine Immigrants, Italians to America,* and *Emigrants from the Russian Empire.* Pittsfield's secondary sources deal with military, immigration and naturalization, and census records, and with genealogy in general; they also hold a full range of NARA publications.

LIBRARIES AND RESEARCH FACILITIES

NEW ENGLAND HISTORIC GENEALOGICAL SOCIETY (NEHGS) LIBRARY

99-101 Newbury Street	[617] 536-5740	Storrow Dr to Beacon St to Arlington
Boston, MA 02116-3007	& -7307 (FAX)	St to Newbury; bldg near corner of
Web: http://www.nehgs.org	Reference, x 234	Newbury & Clarendon Sts. 2-hr on-
	Local History, x 230	street parking; garages on Clarendon
Tue, Fri, Sat 9am-5pm	Microtext, x 239	(next to Hancock tower) & under
Wed, Thu 9am-9pm		Boston Common. Subway: Green
(*closed Sat before Mon holiday*)		line to Copley or Arlington stop;
		Orange to Back Bay.

New England's oldest and largest genealogical research facility. Open to non-members, $15/day, $10 after 5pm; annual membership $50/individual, $70/family (includes book-loan option [additional per-loan fee], the *Register* [quarterly] and *NEXUS* [five issues a year], and reduced Enquiries Service fees), and $20/student (no *Register, NEXUS,* or loan). Three individually staffed research rooms (Reference, Local History, and Microtext, each handicapped- and elevator-accessible); climate-controlled; eating area with fridge, microwave, and snack-and-soda machines (many restaurants in neighborhood). New and used bookstore. 18 film and 5 fiche readers; 5 reader/printers, $.25/page; 1 or 2 self-service copiers on each research floor, $.25/page; 3 LDS (see next section, below) and 4 'other CD' computers; computerized catalog on each research floor. Book loan: from separately housed circulating library of 25,000 volumes

($14 for any 3 books, plus postage). **HOLDINGS**: largest collection of family genealogies, local histories, relevant periodicals, and genealogical manuscripts in New England; manuscripts include the 1798 Direct Tax for Mass. and Maine; C.A. Torrey's New England Marriages to 1700; the Corbin Collection (on central and western Mass.); collections by W.C. Sprague, H.W. Welch, C.H. Abbott, and F.E. Crowell on families of Braintree, Scituate, Andover and [New Englanders in] Nova Scotia; and the papers of many leading genealogical scholars, including Torrey, G.A. Moriarty, M.L. and W.L. Holman, and J.I. Coddington.

NEHGS is currently attempting to acquire microfilm copies of *all* available vital statistics (birth, marriage, and death), town records, church registers, probate, and deeds for every New England state, county, and town. Although the process is expected to take at least two years, film is already pouring in so rapidly that any detailed listing here would be obsolete before the *Handbook* goes to press. (*Current* vital statistics coverage, however, is: *Maine* – pre-1892, 75 towns in 'state' series, plus individual TRs of several score more; county marriages only to 1892; the whole state, 1892-1954; *N.H.* – the whole state to 1900; *Vermont* – the whole state to the 1980s; *Mass.* – most towns to 1850, statewide 1840s-1905; *Conn.* – statewide to 1850; *Rhode Island* – births and marriages to 1894, deaths to 1900.) The reader is advised to call NEHGS Microtext (see above) for current film holdings.

Some major holdings – many fairly recent – that fall outside the above parameters include: film of the Hale Collection of Conn. gravestones, vital records from newspapers, and probate information; an index to New England naturalizations through 1906; indexes to ship-passenger arrivals at Boston, 1848-91 and 1902-20; the John H. Cook collection of books and manuscripts on Continental European genealogy; many Canadian books and microforms, including all censuses through 1901 (New Brunswick through 1921) and the Loiselle and Drouin (Catholic) marriage indexes; a broad range of resources on Atlantic Canada – Nova Scotia, New Brunswick, and most notably Prince Edward Island; virtually all N.H. town records through 1850 or so; U.S. federal censuses for all of New England, 1790-1910 (N.H., to 1920), with Soundexes for 1880 and 1900; federal censuses for many states outside New England; the three major Irish census substitutes (Spinning Wheel Survey of 1796, Griffith's Valuation, and the Tithe Applotment Books for both north and south); a broad miscellany of pedigree files, vital records, census indexes, and less briefly characterizable compilations on CD; and – also on CD – the 1996 edition of the LDS Family Search program. (In 1996, NEHGS became an LDS Family History Center library [for more on which, see below], and patrons can now order microfilm from Salt Lake City through the Society.) Since the first edition of the *Handbook*, NEHGS has become a major New England center not only for New England and British, but also Canadian, Irish, and Continental European genealogy, as well as ethnic genealogy sourcebooks.

N.B., the library underwent a major renovation in 1996-9, and now has lockers, restrooms, and photocopiers on each of three research floors. Various finding aides and indexes have been prepared by staff and are available at each reference desk.

CHURCH OF JESUS CHRIST OF LATTER-DAY SAINTS (LDS) FAMILY HISTORY CENTERS

The Family History Library (FHL) in Salt Lake City, Utah, started filming the world's records in 1938, and now has the world's largest collection, by far, of genealogies and relevant source materials. A system of branch libraries was established in 1964, and more than 2,000 Family History Centers (FHCs) are now located in 60 countries. To locate the FHCs in each New England state, go to the chapter on that state, and consult the subsection on LDS FAMILY HISTORY CENTERS. FHCs are open to the public free of charge, staffed by volunteers, and all contain the same basic materials:

FAMILY HISTORY LIBRARY CATALOG (FHCL) – A catalog, on fiche, of the holdings of the FHL in Salt Lake City; lists over 1.8 million reels of film, 385,000 fiche, and 250,000 books. It is divided into four sections: Locality, Surname, Subject, and Author/Title. Almost any FHL film can be ordered and viewed in your local FHC.

INTERNATIONAL GENEALOGICAL INDEX (IGI) – A CD index to births, christenings, and/or marriages (but not deaths) of nearly 300 million people in 90 countries, from the early 1500s to about 1900. Entries name parents or spouse, as applicable (and if stated in the original record), and the date and place of the event.

PARISH AND VITAL RECORDS LIST – Fiche list of countries, states, counties (outside U.S.), parishes, and towns for which birth, christening, and/or marriage records have been, or are currently being, extracted and indexed for the IGI. Alphabetical, entries also give range of years covered and call number of FHL source.

ACCELERATED INDEXING SYSTEM (AIS) U.S. CENSUS INDEXES – These fiche list heads of household in the federal censuses, 1790-1850. (Some earlier tax rolls and other miscellaneous records are also included, as are some records after 1850.) Alphabetical within each time period and locality, the AIS indexes can help you quickly 'track down' fast-moving ancestors.

PERIODICAL SOURCE INDEX (PERSI) – A fiche subject index to over half a million articles in over 2,000 English-language and French-Canadian genealogical journals; arranged by locality, surname, and research methodology. PERSI doesn't index every name in an article, nor queries, ancestor charts, family-group sheets, book reviews, society officers, membership lists, surname journals or newsletters; nor are page numbers provided. In two sets: 1857-1985 and 1986-93.

SCOTTISH OLD PAROCHIAL REGISTERS (OPR) INDEX – Fiche index of over 6 million christenings and 2.2 million marriages in the Church of Scotland (Presbyterian), up to 1855, when Civil Registration began. Arranged by county, it includes all surviving registers, with starting dates ranging from 1553 to the early 1800s. Batch/Serial Numbers identify the FHL source. An "Instructions" fiche gives further information.

RESEARCH OUTLINES – Available so far for the U.S., all individual states, U.S. military records, tracing immigrant ancestors, Hamburg (Germany) passenger lists, Canada, most Canadian provinces, England, Ireland, Wales, Denmark, Norway, Sweden, and several other areas of the world. These outlines describe research strategies, terminology, and availability and content of major classes of record, with addresses, book titles, other sources, and – if at the FHL – film or fiche order number.

GENEALOGICAL WORD LISTS – These helpful booklets include words you'll find in foreign-language records, with English translations; also number, date, and time designations. Booklets now available include Danish, Dutch, French, German, Italian, Latin, Norwegian, Polish, Portuguese, Spanish, and Swedish.

BOOK COLLECTIONS – FHCs usually have only a few basic reference and how-to books and some of local-research interest. Books are not available from the FHL on interlibrary loan.

VIDEOS – Ask to see any of the following: *Using a Family History Center* – this 15-minute video should be viewed the first time you visit an FHC. *How to Use the U.S. Census* – a 13-minute overview of censuses through 1910, and how to use them. *How to Use the Family History Library Catalog* – a 24-minute key to obtaining FHL records.

FAMILY SEARCH COMPUTER SYSTEM – A collection of genealogical databases on CD, 'read' by software search-engines. At most FHCs, you must sign up ahead for an appointment to use a computer. FAMILY SEARCH is now available in some libraries (*e.g.*, NEHGS in Boston and the Berkshire Athenaeum), but not yet sold to individuals. FAMILY SEARCH comprises 5 databases:

- **FHLC** (Family History Library Catalog) – locality and surname sections only from fiche version, but has been updated several times.
- **IGI** (International Genealogical Index) – see above. Searchable by country or region; "parent search" gives possible family groups, including children born in different towns and states.
- **Social Security Death Index** – over 40 million U.S. Social Security recipients whose deaths – mainly 1962-95 – were reported to the SSA. Not searchable by Social Security #; no middle names or initials.
- **U.S. Military Death Index** – soldiers who died in the Korean or Vietnam conflicts, 1950-75.
- **Ancestral File** – a growing compilation of pedigrees, family group sheets, and descendancies submitted by researchers worldwide; currently contains over 15 million linked names. (Like all genealogical data, only as accurate as the submitter.) Ask for the brochure, "Contributing Information to the Ancestral File," if you wish to submit your own. Your name and address will be included in the file, and you will be asked to agree to answer correspondence on your research.

CEMETERY RECORDS

ASSOCIATION FOR GRAVESTONE STUDIES (AGS)

278 Main Street, Suite 207   [413] 772-0836   I-91 to Exit 26; bldg nearby. Buses
Greenfield, MA 01301   from Springfield to town ctr.
Web: http://www.berkshire.net/ags
E-mail: ags@javanet.com

Mon-Fri 9am-2pm

Open to public, free; no mail-in research inquiries accepted; no records may be photocopied; mail-order lending library for members ($2 per-loan processing fee, plus $1.13-3.83 for 1-way postage). Membership: $30/individual, $25/senior or student, $35/institution, $40/family; members receive *AGS Quarterly* and discounts on AGS publications and conferences. **HOLDINGS**: books, papers, theses, and original works concerning, and photographs of, gravestones (international scope). You are advised to call 2 weeks in advance for an appointment with the archivist. AGS also publishes *Markers: The Journal of the Association for Gravestone Studies* (an annual featuring scholarly articles on all aspects of gravestone research), as well as detailed books and leaflets on gravestone preservation and restoration, and other works describing methods and techniques for recording cemetery data, photographing stones, and preparing legislation to protect graveyards from vandalism, theft, and demolition. Guides, bibliographies, slide and video shows, and instructional leaflets on a wide range of topics – such as gravestone rubbing and gravestones as an educational resource – are also available. Among the Association's major focuses is the neglected cemetery and stone. A complete list of publications is available from the AGS office. AGS holds an annual conference the fourth week in June, at a different location each year, featuring lectures, demonstrations, exhibits, conservation workshops, classes, slide presentations, and informal guided cemetery tours. Contact the office for details.

SOCIETIES

ACADIAN CULTURAL SOCIETY

P.O. Box 2304
Fitchburg, MA 01420-8804
Web: http://www.angelfire.com/ma/1755

Founded in 1985 to preserve and promote the Acadian heritage and facilitate the exchange of Acadian information, both old and current. Publishes a quarterly newsletter, *Le Réveil Acadien* (The Acadian Awakening), whose aim is to encourage those of Acadian ancestry "to share their rich history, culture, music, language, recipes, and literature by researching their family genealogies." **HOLDINGS**: in the Willis Room at the Fitchburg Public Library. N.B., write to the Society for membership information.

AMERICAN-CANADIAN GENEALOGICAL SOCIETY (for library see NEW HAMPSHIRE – LIBRARIES – MANCHESTER)

P.O. Box 668   [603] 622-1554
Manchester, NH 03105-0668
Web: http://www.acgs.org

Founded in 1973 "to acquire … materials on Canadian and American genealogy; to encourage members to research their family lineage and contribute a duplicate to the library; to encourage the gathering of civil, church, newspaper records, *etc.* for publication and research." Membership: annually, $20/person; for family, $20, plus $10 for each additional person in household; life, $300/person, plus $150 for spouse; all memberships include *American-Canadian Genealogist* (quarterly). Twice-yearly meetings in Manchester, one weekend in spring and fall.

AMERICAN-FRENCH GENEALOGICAL SOCIETY (see RHODE ISLAND – SOCIETIES)

AMERICAN-JEWISH HISTORICAL SOCIETY (see MASSACHUSETTS – LIBRARIES – WALTHAM)

FRENCH-CANADIAN GENEALOGICAL SOCIETY OF CONNECTICUT (see CONNECTICUT – SOCIETIES)

GENERAL SOCIETY OF MAYFLOWER DESCENDANTS

4 Winslow Street   [508] 746-3188   Rte 3S to Plymouth, Exit 6 to Rte
Plymouth, MA 02360   44E, to 1st light. Right on Court St, 4
Mail: P.O. Box 3297   blocks to No. St. Left, 1 block to
Plymouth, MA 02361   Winslow. Left, 1st driveway. Museum
Web: http://www.mayflower.org   at front, library at rear.

Mon-Fri 10am-3:30pm

Founded in 1847; conducts research into descendants of Pilgrims through 5th generation. Publications: *The Mayflower Quarterly*; *Mayflower Families Through Five Generations* (18 volumes to date); *Mayflower Ancestral Index* (1981); *Mayflower Families in Progress* (4- or 5-generation paperbacks, over a dozen to date). Library in Plymouth has 3,500 books or microforms of Mayflower interest; $2.50

admission for non-members; staff photocopying, $.25/page (books), $.75/page (films or fiche); 1 film reader/printer; 2 fiche readers. Fifty state chapters, plus D.C. and Royal Canadian; 24,000 members, restricted to persons descended from a Mayflower passenger (on the 1620 voyage to Plymouth). Members join state chapters, which contribute 'assessments' to the General Society. Triennial (*i.e.*, third-year) meetings, usually at Plymouth.

POLISH GENEALOGICAL SOCIETY OF CONNECTICUT (see CONNECTICUT – SOCIETIES)

THE IRISH ANCESTRAL RESEARCH ASSOCIATION (TIARA)

Department W
P.O. Box 619
Sudbury, MA 01776
Web: http://world.std.com/~ahern/TIARA.html

Founded in 1983 to provide educational programs and exchange information relating to Irish genealogical research, both Catholic and Protestant, in Dublin, Belfast, and North. TIARA does not undertake research. Membership non-denominational; annually, $15/person or organization, $22.50/family (Canadian, add $5; overseas, $10). Meets second Friday of each month (except Jul and Aug), 7:30pm, at Boston College, Higgins Hall, Room 307. Quarterly newsletter with queries; brochure available.

MILITARY RECORDS – FEDERAL

Military Service Branch (NNMS) / General Service Branch (NNRG)
National Archives and Records Administration
8th and Pennsylvania Avenue, NW
Washington, DC 20408
E-mail: inquire@arch2.nara.gov

All requests for records of military and naval service from Revolutionary War up to (but not including) World War I must be made on NATF Form 80 (free at NEHGS and NARA [see above]). Send to above address, Room 5E, with fee – currently (Mar 1999) $10/file.

National Personnel Records Center
Military Personnel Records
9700 Page Avenue
St. Louis, MO 63132-5100
Web: www.nara.gov/regional/mpr.html
E-mail: center@stlouis.nara.gov

Mon-Fri 7:30am-3:45pm
closed weekends and federal holidays

MPR facility in Overland, MO (suburb of St. Louis), 10 mi WNW of Gateway Arch. I-170 to Page Av, W 1 mi, left at Spencer Av light, into Federal Records Center complex **OR** I-170 to Page, E 4 mi, right at Spencer light. Consult guard at gate. Navy research room at E end of Bldg 100.

E-mail may be used to contact MPR facility *only* as to proper method of submitting written requests for information in military personnel records. The Privacy Act of 1974 (5 U.S.C. 552a) and Dept. of Defense directives require a written request, signed and dated, to access information from personnel records. Please consult the above Web site before contacting the Center. *No E-mail requests for records or record information will be accepted.*

Records Information: Air Force: [314] 538-4243; Army: [314] 538-4261; Navy, Marine Corps, & Coast Guard: [314] 538-4141; FAX: [314] 538-4175

Records-information numbers are for voice-mail; leave your name and address – center will mail necessary request form. Or, FAX a request (signed and dated) to this number – center will mail reply. Ask for Standard Form 180 (Request Pertaining to Military Records) for a genealogical search. There may be a nominal fee. NA Form 13043 (Genealogical and Public Access to Records) is an information sheet, not needed to request records.

BOOKS AND ARTICLES

Bentley, Elizabeth Petty, *County Court House Book* (2nd ed., 1995: Baltimore, Genealogical Publishing Co.).

_____, *Genealogists' Address Book* (4th ed., 1998: Baltimore, Genealogical Publishing Co.).

Carmack, Sharon DeBartolo, *The Genealogy Sourcebook* (1997: Los Angeles, Lowell House).

Hone, E. Wade, *Land and Property Research in the United States* (1997: Salt Lake City, Ancestry Publishing).

Humling, Virginia, *U.S. Catholic Sources: A Diocesan Research Guide* (1995: Salt Lake City, Ancestry Publishing).

Kemp, Thomas Jay, *International Vital Records Handbook* (3rd ed., 1994: Baltimore, Genealogical Publishing Co.).

Lainhart, Ann Smith, *Digging for Genealogical Treasure in New England Town Records* (1996: Boston, NEHGS).

_____, *State Census Records* (1992: Baltimore, Genealogical Publishing Co.).

National Archives and Records Administration, *Guide to Genealogical Research in the National Archives* (1985: Washington, DC, NARA).

Neagles, James C., *U.S. Military Records: A Guide to Federal and State Sources* (1994: Salt Lake City, Ancestry Publishing).

Saldana, Richard H., ed., *A Practical Guide to the "Misteaks" Made in Census Indexes* (1997: Salt Lake City, the author).

Sanborn, Melinde Lutz, *Supplement to Torrey's New England Marriages Prior to 1700* (1991: Baltimore, Genealogical Publishing Co.).

_____, *Second Supplement to Torrey's New England Marriages Prior to 1700* (1995: Baltimore, Genealogical Publishing Co.).

_____, *Third Supplement to Torrey's New England Marriages Prior to 1700* (to appear, from Genealogical Publishing Co.).

Schaefer, Christina K., *The Center: A Guide to Genealogical Research in National Capital Area* (1996: Baltimore, Genealogical Publishing Co.).

Strangstad, Lynette, A *Graveyard Preservation Primer* (1995: Walnut Creek, AltaMira Press).

Szucs, Loretto Dennis and **Luebking, Sandra Hargreaves**, *The Source: A Guidebook of American Genealogy* (rev. ed., 1997: Salt Lake City, Ancestry Publishing).

Tepper, Michael, *American Passenger Arrival Records* (1993: Baltimore, Genealogical Publishing Co.).

Torrey, Clarence Almon, *New England Marriages Prior to 1700* (1992: Baltimore, Genealogical Publishing Co.). NEHGS is preparing a CD-ROM ed., with Torrey's source citations.

United States Department of Commerce, *200 Years of Census Taking: Population and Housing Questions, 1790-1990* (1992).

CONNECTICUT

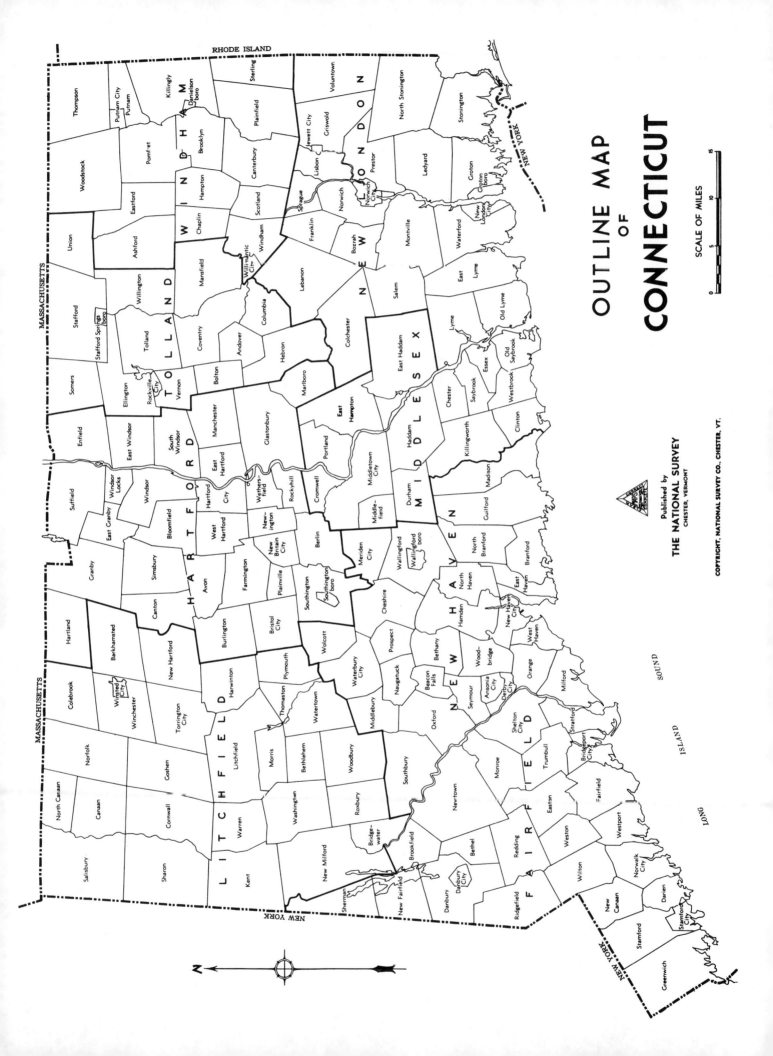

OUTLINE MAP
OF
CONNECTICUT

SCALE OF MILES

Published by
THE NATIONAL SURVEY
CHESTER, VERMONT

COPYRIGHT, NATIONAL SURVEY CO. CHESTER, VT.

COUNTIES

County	Formed	Parent(s)
Fairfield	1666	-----
Hartford	1666	-----
Litchfield	1751	Fairfield & Hartford
Middlesex	1785	Hartford & New Haven
New Haven	1666	-----
New London	1666	-----
Tolland	1785	Windham
Windham	1726	New London

TOWNS

The following table lists each town; the year it was founded; the town(s) – if any – from which it was set off; its county (for census and Superior Court records); its current probate district (for wills, administrations, *etc.*); the year in – and district(s) from – which that probate district was created; and any earlier names for the town.

Town	Est'd	Parent(s)	County	Probate Dist	Est'd	Parent Dist	Alias(es)
Anderson *(see Middlebury)*							
Andover	1848	Coventry & Hebron	Tolland	Andover	1851	Hebron	
Ansonia	1889	Derby	New Haven	Derby	1858	New Haven	
Ashford	1714		Windham	Ashford	1830	Pomfret	
Avon	1830	Farmington	Hartford	Avon	1844	Farmington	
Barkhamsted	1779		Litchfield	Barkhamsted	1834	New Hartford	
Beacon Falls	1871	Bethany, Naugatuck, Oxford, & Seymour	New Haven	Naugatuck	1863	Waterbury	
Berlin	1785	Farmington, Middletown, & Wethersfield	Hartford	Berlin	1824	Farmington, Hartford, & Middletown	Great Swamp, Kensington, & Worthington
Bethany	1832	Woodbridge	New Haven	Bethany	1854	New Haven	
Bethel	1855	Danbury	Fairfield	Bethel	1859	Danbury	
Bethlehem	1787	Woodbury	Litchfield	Woodbury	1719	Hartford, Fairfield, & New Haven	
Bloomfield	1835	Farmington, Hartford, Simsbury, & Windsor	Hartford	Hartford	1666		
Bolton	1730		Tolland	Andover	1851	Hebron	

23

Town	Est'd	Parent(s)	County	Probate Dist	Est'd	Parent Dist	Alias(es)
Bozrah	1786	Norwich	New London	Bozrah	1843	Norwich	Norwich Farms
Branford	1639	Guilford	New Haven	Branford	1850	Guilford	
Bridgeport	1821	Fairfield & Stratford	Fairfield	Bridgeport	1840	Stratford	Newfield, Pequonnock, & Stratford
Bridgewater	1856	New Milford	Litchfield	New Milford	1787	Woodbury, Danbury, & Sharon	
Bristol *(see also Middlebury)*	1785	Farmington	Hartford	Bristol	1830	Farmington	West Farms
Brookfield	1788	Danbury, New Milford, & Newtown	Fairfield	Brookfield	1850	Newtown	
Brooklyn	1786	Canterbury & Pomfret	Windham	Brooklyn	1833	Pomfret & Plainfield	
Burlington	1806	Bristol	Hartford	Burlington	1834	Farmington	
Canaan	1739		Litchfield	Canaan	1846	Sharon	
Canada Parish *(see Hampton)*							
Canterbury	1703	Plainfield	Windham	Canterbury	1835	Plainfield	
Canton	1806	Simsbury	Hartford	Canton	1841	Simsbury	W. Simsbury
Chaplin	1822	Hampton, Mansfield, & Windham	Windham	Chaplin	1850	Windham	Suffrage
Chatham *(see E. Hampton)*							W. Farms & E. Hampton
Cheshire	1780	Wallingford	New Haven	Cheshire	1829	Wallingford	
Chester	1836	Saybrook	Middlesex	Saybrook	1780	Guilford	
Clinton	1838	Killingworth	Middlesex	Clinton	1862	Killingworth	
Colchester	1698		New London	Colchester	1832	E. Haddam	
Colebrook	1779		Litchfield	Winchester	1838	Norfolk	Coldbrook
Columbia	1804	Lebanon	Tolland	Andover	1851	Hebron	
Cornwall	1740		Litchfield	Cornwall	1847	Litchfield	
Coventry	1712		Tolland	Coventry	1849	Hebron	
Cromwell	1851	Middletown	Middlesex	Middletown	1752	E. Haddam, Guilford, & Hartford	
Danbury	1685		Fairfield	Danbury	1744	Fairfield	
Darien	1820	Stamford	Fairfield	Darien	1921	Stamford	
Deep River	1635		Middlesex	Deep River	1949	Saybrook	Saybrook 'til 1947
Derby	1675		New Haven	Derby	1858	New Haven	
Durham	1704		Middlesex	Middletown	1752	E. Haddam, Guilford, & Hartford	
E. Farms *(see N. Canaan)*							
Eastford	1847	Ashford	Windham	Eastford	1849	Ashford	
E. Granby	1858	Granby & Windsor Locks	Hartford	E. Granby	1865	Granby	
E. Greenwich *(see Warren)*							
E. Haddam	1734	Haddam	Middlesex	E. Haddam	1741	Hartford	
E. Hampton	1767	Middletown	Middlesex	E. Hampton	1824	E. Haddam & Middletown	Chatham 'til 1915
E. Hartford	1783	Hartford	Hartford	E. Hartford	1887	Hartford	Podunck
E. Haven	1785	New Haven	New Haven	E. Haven	1955	New Haven	
E. Lyme	1839	Lyme & Waterford	New London	E. Lyme	1843	New London	

Town	Est'd	Parent(s)	County	Probate Dist	Est'd	Parent Dist	Alias(es)
Easton	1875	Weston	Fairfield	Trumbull			
(annexed to Bridgeport, 1878)							
E. Windsor	1768	Windsor	Hartford	E. Windsor	1782	Hartford & Stafford	
Ellington	1786	E. Windsor	Tolland	Ellington	1826	E. Windsor	Stafford
Enfield	1683		Hartford	Enfield	1831	E. Windsor	Freshwater
(part of Mass. 'til 1749)							
Essex	1852	Saybrook	Middlesex	Essex	1853	Saybrook	
(originally Old Saybrook;				*(Old Saybrook 'til 1859;*			
renamed Essex in 1854, when new town				*became Essex)*			
of Old Saybrook set off)							
Fairfield	1639		Fairfield	Fairfield	1666		
Farmington	1645		Hartford	Farmington	1769	Hartford	
Franklin	1786	Norwich	New London	Norwich	1748	New London	
Freshwater *(see Enfield)*							
Glastonbury	1693	Wethersfield	Hartford	Glastonbury	1975	Hartford	
Goshen	1739		Litchfield	Torrington	1847	Litchfield	New Bantum
Granby	1786	Simsbury	Hartford	Granby	1807	Hartford & Simsbury	
Great Swamp *(see Berlin)*							
Great Plain *(see Plainville)*							
Greenwich	1665	Stamford	Fairfield	Greenwich	1853	Stamford	
(under jurisdiction of New Amsterdam Dutch, 1642-56)							
Griswold	1815	Preston	New London	Griswold	1979	Norwich	
Groton	1705	New London	New London	Groton	1839	Stonington	
Guilford	1639		New Haven	Guilford	1719	New Haven & New London	
Haddam	1668		Middlesex	Haddam	1830	Chatham & Middletown	
Hamden	1786	New Haven	New Haven	Hamden	1945	New Haven	New Haven
Hampton	1786	Brooklyn, Canterbury, Pomfret, Windham, & Mansfield	Windham	Hampton	1836	Windham	Canada Parish, Kennedy, & Windham Village
Hartford	1635		Hartford	Hartford	1666		
Hartland	1761		Hartford	Hartland	1836	Granby	
Harwinton	1737		Litchfield	Harwinton	1835	Litchfield	
Hebron	1708		Tolland	Hebron	1789	E. Windsor	
Huntington *(see Shelton)*				Huntington *(see Shelton)*			
Kenellworth *(see Killingworth)*							
Kennedy *(see Hampton)*							
Kensington *(see Berlin)*							
Kent	1739		Litchfield	Kent	1831	New Milford	
Killingly	1708		Windham	Killingly	1830	Pomfret & Plainfield	Scatacook
Killingworth	1667		Middlesex	Killingworth	1834	Saybrook	Kenellworth
Lebanon	1700		New London	Lebanon	1826	Windham	
Ledyard	1836	Groton	New London	Ledyard	1837	Stonington	
Lisbon	1786	Norwich	New London	Norwich	1748	New London	
Litchfield	1719		Litchfield	Litchfield	1742	Hartford, New Haven, & Woodbury	New Bantum
Lyme	1665	Saybrook	New London	Lyme	1869	Old Lyme	
				(called Lyme "old district" 'til 1868)			

Town	Est'd	Parent(s)	County	Probate Dist	Est'd	Parent Dist	Alias(es)
Madison	1826	Guilford	New Haven	Madison	1834	Guilford	
Manchester	1823	E. Hartford	Hartford	Manchester	1850	E. Hartford	
Mansfield	1702	Windham	Tolland	Mansfield	1831	Windham	
Marlborough	1803	Colchester, Glastonbury, & Hebron	Hartford	Marlborough	1846	Colchester	
Meriden	1806	Wallingford	New Haven	Meriden	1836	Wallingford	
Middlebury	1807	Southbury, Waterbury, Woodbury	New Haven	Waterbury	1779	Woodbury	Anderson, Bristol, & W. Farms
Middlefield	1866	Middletown	Middlesex	Middletown	1752	E. Haddam, Guilford, & Hartford	
Middletown	1651		Middlesex	Middletown	1752	E. Haddam, Guilford, & Hartford	
Milford	1639		New Haven	Milford	1832	New Haven	
Milltown *(see N. Stonington)*							
Monroe	1823	Huntington	Fairfield	Trumbull	1959	Bridgeport	
Montville	1786	New London	New London	Montville	1851	New London	
Morris	1859	Litchfield	Litchfield	Litchfield	1742	New Haven, Hartford, & Woodbury	S. Farm
Naubuc *(see Glastonbury)*							
Naugatuck	1844	Bethany, Oxford, & Waterbury	New Haven	Naugatuck	1863	Waterbury	
New Bantum *(see Goshen & Litchfield)*							
New Britain	1850	Berlin	Hartford	Berlin	1824	Farmington, Hartford, & Middletown	
Newbury *(see Bristol)*							
New Canaan	1801	Norwalk & Stamford	Fairfield	New Canaan	1937	Norwalk	
New Fairfield	1740		Fairfield	New Fairfield	1975	Danbury	
Newfield *(see Bridgeport)*							
New Hartford	1738		Litchfield	New Hartford	1825	Simsbury	
New Haven	1638		New Haven	New Haven	1666		
New Haven Village *(see Wallingford)*							
Newington	1871	Wethersfield	Hartford	Newington	1975	Hartford	
New London	1646		New London	New London	1666		
New Milford	1712		Litchfield	New Milford	1787	Danbury, Sharon, & Woodbury	
Newtown	1711		Fairfield	Newtown	1820	Danbury	
Norfolk	1758		Litchfield	Norfolk	1779	Litchfield & Simsbury	
N. Branford	1831	Branford	New Haven	N. Branford	1937	Guilford & Wallingford	N. Farms
N. Canaan	1858	Canaan	Litchfield	Canaan	1846	Sharon	E. Farms
N. Farms *(see N. Branford)*							
N. Haven	1786	New Haven	New Haven	N. Haven	1955	New Haven	
N. Stonington	1807	Stonington	New London	N. Stonington	1835	Stonington	Milltown

Town	Est'd	Parent(s)	County	Probate Dist	Est'd	Parent Dist	Alias(es)
Norwalk	1651		Fairfield	Norwalk	1802	Fairfield & Stamford	
Norwich	1659		New London	Norwich	1748	New London	
Norwich Farms *(see Bozrah)*							
Old Lyme	1665	Lyme & Saybrook	New London	Old Lyme *(was Lyme "old district" 'til 1868)*	1830	New London	S. Lyme 'til 1857
Old Saybrook	1854	Essex	Middlesex	Old Saybrook *(i.e., Essex, q.v.)*	1853	Essex	
Orange	1822	Milford & New Haven	New Haven	Orange	1975	New Haven	
Orford *(see Manchester)*							
Oxford	1798	Derby & Southbury	New Haven	Oxford	1846	New Haven	New Haven
Pequonnock *(see Bridgeport)*							
Plainfield	1699		Windham	Plainfield	1747	Windham	
Plainville	1869	Farmington	Hartford	Plainville	1909	Farmington	Great Plain
Plymouth	1795	Watertown	Litchfield	Plymouth	1833	Waterbury	
Podunck *(see E. Hartford)*							
Pochaug *(see Westbrook)*							
Pomfret	1713		Windham	Pomfret	1752	Plainfield & Windham	
Portland	1841	Chatham	Middlesex	Portland	1913	Chatham	
Preston	1687		New London	Norwich	1748	New London	
Prospect	1827	Cheshire & Waterbury	New Haven	Cheshire	1829	Wallingford	
Putnam	1855	Killingly, Pomfret, & Thompson	Windham	Putnam	1856	Thompson	
Redding	1767	Fairfield	Fairfield	Redding	1839	Danbury	
Ridgefield	1708		Fairfield	Ridgefield	1841	Danbury	
Rippowam *(see Stamford)*							
Rocky Hill	1843	Wethersfield	Hartford	Newington	1975	Hartford	
Roxbury	1796	Woodbury	Litchfield	Roxbury	1842	Woodbury	
Salem	1819	Colchester, Lyme, & Montville	New London	Salem	1841	Colchester & New London	
Salisbury	1741		Litchfield	Salisbury	1847	Sharon	
Saybrook *(see Deep River)*				Saybrook *(serves only Chester)*	1780	Guilford	
Scatacook *(see Kent)*							
Scotland	1857	Windham	Windham	Windham	1719	Hartford & New London	
Seymour	1850	Derby	New Haven	Derby	1858	New Haven	
Sharon	1739		Litchfield	Sharon	1755	Litchfield	
Shelton	1789	Stratford	Fairfield	Shelton *(Huntington 'til 1919)*	1889	Bridgeport & Derby	
Sherman	1802	New Fairfield	Fairfield	Sherman	1846	New Milford	
Simsbury	1670		Hartford	Simsbury	1769	Hartford	
Somers *(part of Mass. 'til 1749)*	1734	Enfield	Tolland	Somers	1834	Ellington	
Southbury	1787	Woodbury	New Haven	Southbury	1967	Woodbury	
Southington	1779	Farmington	Hartford	Southington	1825	Farmington	
S. Farm *(see Morris)*							

Town	Est'd	Parent(s)	County	Probate Dist	Est'd	Parent Dist	Alias(es)
S. Windsor	1845	E. Windsor	Hartford	E. Windsor	1782	Hartford & Stafford	
Sprague	1861	Franklin & Lisbon	New London	Norwich	1748	New London	
Spruce Swamp *(see Torrington)*							
Stafford	1719		Tolland	Stafford	1759	Hartford & Pomfret	
Stamford	1641		Fairfield	Stamford	1728	Fairfield	Rippowam
Sterling	1794	Voluntown	Windham	Sterling	1852	Plainfield	
Stonington	1649		New London	Stonington	1766	New London	
Stratford	1639		Fairfield	Stratford	1782	Fairfield	
(see also Bridgeport)							
Suffield	1674		Hartford	Suffield	1821	Granby & Hartford	
(part of Mass. 'til 1749)							
Suffrage *(see Canton)*							
Thomaston	1875	Plymouth	Litchfield	Thomaston	1882	Waterbury	
Thompson	1785	Killingly	Windham	Thompson	1832	Pomfret	
Tolland	1715		Tolland	Tolland	1830	Stafford	
Torrington	1740		Litchfield	Torrington	1847	Litchfield	Spruce Swamp
Trumbull	1797	Stratford	Fairfield	Trumbull	1959	Bridgeport	
Union	1734		Tolland	Stafford	1759	Hartford & Pomfret	
Vernon	1808	Bolton	Tolland	Ellington	1826	E. Windsor & Stafford	
Volunteers' Town *(see Voluntown)*							
Voluntown	1721		New London	Norwich	1889	Voluntown	
Wallingford	1670		New Haven	Wallingford	1776	New Haven & Guildford	New Haven & Guilford Village
Warren	1786	Kent	Litchfield	Litchfield	1742	Hartford, New Haven, & Woodbury	
Washington	1779	Litchfield Kent, New Milford, & Woodbury	Litchfield	Washington	1832	Litchfield & Woodbury	
Waterbury	1686		New Haven	Waterbury	1779	Woodbury	
Waterford	1801	New London	New London	New London	1666		
Watertown	1780	Waterbury	Litchfield	Watertown	1834	Waterbury	
(see also Wethersfield)							
Wellington *(see Willington)*							
Westbrook	1840	Saybrook	Middlesex	Westbrook	1854	Old Saybrook	Pochaug
W. Farms *(see Bristol, Chatham, Middlebury, & W. Haven)*							
W. Hartford	1854	Hartford	Hartford	Hartford	1666		
W. Haven	1921	Orange	New Haven	W. Haven	1921	New Haven	
Weston	1787	Fairfield	Fairfield	Westport *(Weston dist estab'd 1832 from Fairfield; annexed by Westport, 1875)*	1835	Fairfield, Norwalk, & Weston	
Westport	1835	Fairfield	Fairfield, Norwalk, & Weston	Westport	1835	Fairfield, Norwalk, & Weston	
W. Simsbury *(see Canton)*							
Wethersfield	1634		Hartford	Newington	1975	Hartford	Watertown

Town	Est'd	Parent(s)	County	Probate Dist	Est'd	Parent Dist	Alias(es)
Willington	1727		Tolland	Tolland	1830	Stafford	Wellington
Wilton	1802	Norwalk	Fairfield	Norwalk	1802	Fairfield & Stamford	
Winchester	1771		Litchfield	Winchester	1838	Norfolk	
Windham	1692		Windham	Windham	1719	Hartford & New London	
Windham Village (see Hampton)							
Windsor	1633		Hartford	Windsor	1855	Hartford	
Windsor Locks	1854	Windsor	Hartford	Windsor Locks	1961	Hartford	
Wolcott	1796	Southington & Waterbury	New Haven	Waterbury	1779	Woodbury	
Woodbridge	1784	Milford & New Haven	New Haven	New Haven	1666		
Woodbury	1673		Litchfield	Woodbury	1719	Fairfield, Hartford, & New Haven	
Woodstock	1686		Windham	Woodstock	1831	Pomfret	

(part of Mass. 'til 1749; New Roxbury 'til 1690)
Worthington *(see Berlin)*

N.B., for more information on Conn. towns and their records, see (under BOOKS AND ARTICLES) Betty Jean Morrison, *Connecting To Connecticut*, and Thomas Jay Kemp, *Connecticut Researcher's Handbook*.

CONNECTICUT

Conn. is a gold mine for genealogists and local historians – a small, compact state whose records have been generally well preserved from earliest days. For the genealogist, the place to start is the STATE LIBRARY in Hartford, which has thousands of historical and genealogical reference books and periodicals, and houses the STATE ARCHIVES as well. The genealogical records and indexes there are among the best and most centralized in the country.

STATE HOLIDAYS PECULIAR TO CONNECTICUT – REPOSITORIES MAY BE CLOSED – CALL

Celebrates *both* Lincoln's *and* Washington's Birthdays, separately; Good Friday (Fri before Easter)

VITAL RECORDS

From settlement to mid-1800s: each town kept its own VRs in the town hall (and still does). As an alternative to consulting town clerks, most pre-1850 Conn. VRs were abstracted onto slips as the "Barbour Collection." This comes in two forms: (a) as separate bound books for each town, with that town's records of birth, marriage, and death alphabetized by last and first name; and (b) as a slip file, likewise alphabetized by name but covering the whole state at once, which is now at the STATE LIBRARY (and also on film at NEHGS). The years covered by the Barbour Collection vary from town to town; some go through the 1860s; Bozrah, through 1871. With permission from the STATE LIBRARY, institutions may buy the filmed Collection as a whole, or reel by reel, from the Latter-day Saints' Family History Library (see under NEW ENGLAND chapter). N.B., the VRs of some Conn. towns, most notably New Haven, have been published separately, and are not part of the Barbour Collection.

End of "Barbour" to 1897: from the point at which the Barbour records leave off (1850 or a bit later) to 1897 (when centralized state recording begins), there is no statewide index to Conn. VRs. They may be consulted *via* town clerks, or on film (to 1900) at the STATE LIBRARY, or at LDS FHCs.

1897 to present: VRs are still recorded and kept by the towns, but also centralized at …

STATE OF CONNECTICUT – DEPARTMENT OF PUBLIC HEALTH

Vital Records Section
410 Capitol Avenue, 1st Floor
P.O. Box 340308, MS #11 VRs
Hartford, CT 06134-0308

Mon-Fri 7:45am-4:30pm

[860] 509-7896

From I-91N: Capitol Area Exit (left) to Elm St; at end, left on Trinity St to Capitol Av; pass Legislative Office Bldg & State Armory; thru light (corner of Broad St & Capitol); DPH is 3rd bldg on right. From I-91S: Capitol Av Exit (right), then same directions.

Certified copies, $5, payable to Connecticut Department of Health Services.

N.B., in 1996, Connecticut Public Act 96-258 clarified the rules governing access to vital records. Anyone may receive, read, and copy all marriage and death records, no matter how recent; and all birth records a century or more old. Access to more recent birth records is limited to those named in the record itself and their spouses, guardians, and grandparents; municipal officers and their delegates; directors of health, attorneys at law, and title examiners; and members of legally incorporated genealogical societies authorized to do business in Conn. – including the CONN. SOCIETY OF GENEALOGISTS, CONN. ANCESTRY SOCIETY, FRENCH-CANADIAN GENEALOGICAL SOCIETY OF CONN., JEWISH GENEALOGICAL SOCIETY OF CONN., POLISH GENEALOGICAL SOCIETY OF CONN., KILLINGLY HISTORICAL AND GENEALOGICAL SOCIETY, LANCE GENEALOGICAL RESEARCH SOCIETY, and MIDDLESEX GENEALOGICAL SOCIETY.

"Access" means full physical access at the town halls. You are advised, however, to call ahead for an appointment, as space is often limited. (N.B., access to Conn. VRs *doesn't* include permission to *publish* the data they contain.)

IMPORTANT NOTE: the Vital Records section is currently (April 1999) filming its records, a process it expects to complete in about 18 months. Meanwhile, researchers are urged to consult town clerks and the STATE LIBRARY for VRs. The clerks and Library, however, lack the Vital Records section's *statewide* indexes to post-1897 Conn. VRs, which will apparently be unavailable for the duration.

FEDERAL CENSUS

The 1790-1880 and 1900-20 federal censuses of Conn. are extant and open to the public. (The 1890 census burned.) The STATE LIBRARY has a card index to all Conn. returns, 1790-1850, as well as the 1880, 1900, and 1920 Soundexes for Conn.; indexes to Conn. returns through 1860 have also been published as books and/or CDs by commercial firms, such as Accelerated Indexing Systems of Bountiful, Utah – these are at the STATE LIBRARY and HISTORICAL SOCIETY, the NATIONAL ARCHIVES (see NEW ENGLAND chapter) – which has all federal schedules for all states – NEHGS in Boston, and other large libraries. The 1910 census is not indexed.

STATE CENSUS

Conn. has never conducted a state census. However, town tax lists, state militia rolls, and other records, from colonial times on, may serve much the same purpose. Also, the Connecticut State Military Preparedness Census of 1917 – unique in the nation – is a detailed record of 491,000 individuals, officially including all males, 20 to 30 (as well as many, 16 to 19), friendly and enemy aliens, nurses, and automobile owners, in addition to agricultural statistics. The original is in the STATE ARCHIVES (Record Group 29) at the STATE LIBRARY. (See Thomas Jay Kemp, *Connecticut Ancestry,* 22:3[Feb 1980], 117-22 for details of this census.)

PROBATE AND LAND

Probate documents – wills, administrations, and the like – are recorded by the court of the local probate district. Until about 1698, probate and county courts were not separate. In 1719, the four original probate districts were first divided; this fissioning process has continued ever since, with Conn.'s 169 towns now being covered by 131 probate districts. Some have been abolished, or their boundaries repeatedly altered. The STATE LIBRARY has on deposit most pre-1850 probates, statewide, and Hartford probates to 1900; most are indexed by decedent, with the statewide and Hartford-district indexes on film. Pre-1880 estate papers are also on film. In addition, the STATE LIBRARY has films of pre-1900 probate record books. Later records of both types – files and record books – are still at the courts, but many of the books to *ca.* 1915 are on film at the STATE LIBRARY and *via* the LDS.

Deeds and the like have always been recorded by the town clerks and kept in the town halls (with indexes). The STATE LIBRARY has film of deeds, mortgages, releases, and other land records for most Conn. towns to *ca.* 1900; grantor/grantee indexes are included for each town, but there is no statewide index. The staff does not copy filmed records; see the STATE LIBRARY entry for information on professional researchers.

CEMETERY RECORDS

Among Conn.'s excellent indexed genealogical resources are its cemetery records. In the 1930s, Charles R. Hale directed a WPA transcription of tombstones in 2,269 Conn. cemeteries; these records were then merged into a master name-index (which includes newspaper death notices). The STATE LIBRARY has 59 typescript volumes of Hale transcripts – which often give a bit more information such as place of death – and several hundred file-card drawers. There is also a Hale Collection file of newspaper marriage notices – a statewide slip file, and separate volumes for each newspaper. The collection is also on film at NEHGS in Boston and *via* the LDS. Many cemetery transcripts have also appeared in the *New England Historical and Genealogical Register, Connecticut Ancestry, The Connecticut Nutmegger,* and other genealogical journals. Many historical societies, as well, have transcribed their local cemeteries (see CONNECTICUT GRAVESTONE NETWORK).

CHURCH RECORDS

Under the direction of State Librarian George S. Goddard, churches across Conn. were urged to deposit their original records at the STATE LIBRARY. Many of these have been filmed; about 25% – mainly Congregational – have been indexed in over 100 volumes, and as a statewide alphabetical slip index (both on film at NEHGS). (For Quaker records, see RHODE ISLAND HISTORICAL SOCIETY LIBRARY).

In addition, the Colonial Dames have copied the records of about 100 churches, and deposited the transcripts with the CONNECTICUT HISTORICAL SOCIETY. Other copies are at the OLD COLONY HISTORICAL SOCIETY (New Haven).

MILITARY RECORDS

Conn. has been called the "Provision State" in honor of its military contribution There are printed lists of Conn. soldiers in most colonial wars, and numerous Civil War regimental histories. Note especially the *Record of Service of Connecticut Men in the* [1] *War of the Revolution* [2] *War of 1812* and [3] *Mexican War* (1889). The STATE ARCHIVES has an index to Revolutionary state papers.

IMMIGRATION AND NATURALIZATION

Immigration to New England falls, in a rough and ready way, into three eras. For the first – from 1620 to, say, 1680 or '90 – virtually all 'immigration' was necessarily trans-Atlantic, and primarily to Mass.; the modest roster of passenger lists that survive (covering, probably, fewer than 10% of all colonists) have all been published, often several times over. For these early lists, see Charles E. Banks, *The Planters of the Commonwealth* (1930: Boston, Houghton Mifflin) and, much more recently, the various '*Emigrants*' books by Peter W. Coldham.

For the second period – from the late 1600s to 1819 –very little by way of passenger lists survives. What there is may be tracked down *via* P. William Filby and Mary K. Meyer, *Passenger and Immigration Lists Index*, 24 vols. and counting (1981+: Detroit, Gale).

The third, or 'modern,' period begins in 1820 with passage of a Federal law requiring ports of entry to keep records of ship-passenger arrivals. Most of what survives for New England ports, up and into the 20th century, should be found at NARA – WALTHAM (see NEW ENGLAND chapter).

All Conn. naturalization records from federal courts, 1842-1973, and non-federal, 1790-1974, are at the NATIONAL ARCHIVES (see NEW ENGLAND chapter), which has a Soundex on cards. This index is also on film at the STATE LIBRARY. (NEHGS has the index on film through 1906.)

NEWSPAPERS

Charles R. Hale compiled marriage and death notices from Conn. newspapers, 1755-1865, and a statewide card index for the set. This collection is at the STATE LIBRARY and on film at NEHGS. *A Preliminary Checklist of Connecticut Newspapers 1775-1975* (prepared by the State Library) is a useful guide to the newspapers and their repositories. The STATE LIBRARY has a collection of original and filmed Conn. newspapers; use of the former is subject to strict archival rules. The HISTORICAL SOCIETY owns Doris Cook's original card index to the *Connecticut Courant*, 1754-1820.

CIVIL AND CRIMINAL COURT RECORDS

Most pre-1850 Conn. civil and criminal court records are at the STATE LIBRARY. Other legal records may be found at the Judicial District Superior Courts, geographical area courts, and town clerks' offices. Records at the STATE LIBRARY are described in *Guide to the Records of the Judicial Department:*

State Archives Record Group No. 3 (1997), by the Office of the Public Records Administrator and State Archives.

LIBRARIES

All Conn. towns have public libraries, whose holdings vary greatly. Most have small collections, which may or may not include items of genealogical interest. Many are open 12 hours a week or less and undertake no research. For a list of all libraries, with hours, consult the *American Library Directory* in most large libraries. The CONNECTICUT SOCIETY OF GENEALOGISTS also has a list of genealogical libraries and local collections, with hours and telephone numbers.

BRIDGEPORT – BURROUGHS LIBRARY BUILDING

925 Broad Street
Bridgeport, CT 06604

[203] 576-7417

Rte I-95 to Exit 27 (Lafayette St); right on State St; right on Broad. Parking at Crossroads Mall.

Tue, Wed 10am-8pm; Thu-Sat 9am-5pm
(*summer*: closed Sat, but open Mon 9-5)

Copying, $.15/page (by mail, $5 minimum); film reader; reader/printer, $.25/page (by mail, $.30, with $5 minimum). **HOLDINGS**: covering Bridgeport, Conn., and New England; federal censuses of Conn. (1800-1920) on film; Bridgeport-area obituary index (1978-97); cemetery records (Hale Collection for Bridgeport, Fairfield, and Stratford); city directories for Bridgeport (1855 to present) and most other Conn. cities (*ca.* 1935 to present); local newspapers (on film, 1861 to present); Barbour Collection of VRs (on film); coats-of-arms index; *Boston Transcript* on microcards; *American Genealogical & Biographical Index*; DAR lineage books; periodicals; maps and atlases; LDS Family Search (see under NEW ENGLAND chapter).

FAIRFIELD HISTORICAL SOCIETY LIBRARY (FHS)

636 Old Post Road
Fairfield, CT 06430

[203] 259-1598

From Rte I-95S, Exit 22, left to Rte 1; right; 1 block; left on Beach Rd; 1 block; right on Old Post. FHS is 2nd bldg on left.

Tue-Fri 9:30am-4:30pm; Sat 10am-4:30pm
Sun 1-4:30pm

Open to public; fee for preliminary research, $10/query; copying, $.25/page plus $1.50 for postage & handling; books do not circulate; limited interlibrary loan; mail inquiries accepted. **HOLDINGS**: local histories; sermons; monographs; genealogies; biographies; maps; manuscripts; photos; Fairfield County genealogical and biographical reference works; genealogical and shipping research papers; almanacs; city directories; church, cemetery, court, school, and tax records; diaries.

GRANBY – SALMON BROOK HISTORICAL SOCIETY (SBHS)

208 Salmon Brook Street
Granby, CT 06035
Carol Laun, Curator

[860] 653-3965

Route I-91 to Rte 20, thru E. Granby to Granby. Left on Rte 10/202 (Salmon Brook); ½ mi; SBHS on left. Ample parking.

Thu 9-noon (*or by appointment – desired*)

No fee (donations welcome); no copier or film/fiche reader; appointment (1 week in advance) desired; mail inquiries *re*: local genealogy only, $15/hour plus expenses; staff copying (done offsite), $.25/page. **HOLDINGS**: genealogical files on families of Granby, Simsbury, and area; published genealogies and local histories; manuscript research; private papers, diaries, and letters; Granby census and cemetery, church, town, and vital records; local account books; Civil War letters; military documents; local photos. Some records have been filmed by LDS.

HARTFORD – CONNECTICUT HISTORICAL SOCIETY LIBRARY (CHS)

1 Elizabeth Street Hartford, CT 06105 Tue-Sat 9am-4:45pm *(closed, major holidays)*	[860] 236-5621 x 230	Rte 84 to Exit 46 (Sisson Av); right at end of ramp on Sisson St. At 2nd light, left on Farmington Av; 1 short block; right on Girard. At 2nd X, right on Elizabeth. Free parking, 2nd driveway on right.

Free admission for members, children under 5, and students with valid ID; $3 for non-members (includes admission to museum); film and fiche readers and reader-printers; microprint opaque viewer; copying, $.25/page, some restrictions; restaurants within walking distance. The CHS library has a collection of duplicate town histories and genealogies, for 1-month loan to members of the CHS or the Conn. chapter of the Society of Mayflower Descendants ($4/volume, limit of 3, plus return postage; catalog, $7, including postage – Conn. residents add sales tax). Volunteers will research specific individuals in library resources – $15/query for members, $25, non- (plus copying fee and postage). Call or write for details and query form. **HOLDINGS**: 100,000 volumes; 3,000 linear feet of manuscripts; 3,500 bound volumes of newspapers; maps, atlases, and broadsides; covering Conn. and New England history and genealogy, early 17th century to present, Americana. Special collections include Conn. imprints; local histories; city directories; trade catalogs; Conn. almanacs and sermons; early American children's books; periodicals; Conn. newspapers; personal and business papers; town and tax records (including Conn. sections of the 1798 Direct Tax); account books and diaries; genealogical reference books, periodicals, and indexes; printed and manuscript genealogies; federal censuses of Conn.; Mass. vital records; church records by town (including Colonial Dames transcripts of about 100 churches); working papers of many noted Conn. genealogists, especially Donald Lines Jacobus, and David W. Patterson on E. Haddam families.

HARTFORD – CONNECTICUT STATE LIBRARY (CSL)

History and Genealogy Unit (HGU) 231 Capitol Avenue Hartford, CT 06106 **Web**: http://www.cslib.org Mon-Fri 9am-5pm	[860] 566-3692, -3690, & -2133 (FAX)	I-84E to Exit 48 (Capitol) **OR** I-84W to Exit 47 (Sigourney St), left under I-84 to I-84E; 1st Exit (48, Capitol). CSL across from Capitol bldg **OR** I-91N or S to Exit 29A (Capitol area); move to 1 of 2 left lanes; at rotary take Elm St; west to light, left on Trinity St; 1 block to CSL. (See below for parking.)

Open to public; open stacks and card indexes; archives pass (available from librarian) required for use of manuscripts or original records. Self-service copying, $.10/page (copying card, $.50; rechargeable with $1s, $5s, $10s, or $20s); film reader/printers, $.25/page; change machines. Cafeteria open 9:30am-2pm, or bring own food. No eating or drinking in reading room or stacks; no smoking in building. Small lockers for personal items. Metered on-street parking on Oak, Russ, Lafayette, and Buckingham; all-day free parking on Hungerford (one-way south), one block west of (and parallel to) Oak; parking garages on Buckingham and Oak. To arrange handicapped parking and building access, call the Security Office – [860] 566-4452 – in advance.

In response to *mail queries*, staff will search the following indexes (one individual only) for ½ hour: Barbour Collection (Conn. VRs, beginnings to *ca.* 1850); Bible and Family Records; federal censuses of Conn. (1790-1850, excluding New London County for 1790); Connecticut Newspaper Marriage and Death Notice Abstracts (1755-*ca.* 1865); Hale Collection of Connecticut Cemetery Inscriptions (1600s-*ca.* 1934); Connecticut Church Records Abstracts (name index for roughly 25% of church records – mainly Congregational – in State Archives [1600s-*ca.* 1900]); Connecticut Probate Estate Papers to *ca.* 1880. Copies will be made if specific citations are furnished. Research fees: Conn. non-residents, $15 per ½ hr; residents, $5 per ½ hr; plus $.25/page (8 ½ x 11"), $.50/page (11 x 17"). Photographic copies of maps, drawings, plans, mss., *etc.*, $10/page (12 x 18"), $13/page (18 x 24"). Add postage to fees, or pick up in person. Reply time 4-6 weeks.

Other Holdings: local histories and genealogies, emphasizing Conn. and New England; federal censuses (on film) of Conn. (1790-1920) and other New England states, New York, Pennsylvania (1790-1850), and Ohio (1820-50); vital, land, and probate record books (1600s-early 1900s; on film) for most Conn. towns; New England Naturalization Papers Index (film); records from hundreds of Conn. churches (mainly film); atlases and maps of Conn., New England, and other states and countries (1600s-present); Conn. city directories (mostly *ca.* 1870 to present); published passenger lists, other immigration records, and indexes; filmed passenger lists for Boston, New York, and some other ports (*ca.* 1790-1850); genealogical research guides for other states and countries; the Ancestral File, International Genealogical Index, and Social Security Death Index (LDS); other CDs. Manuscripts include: Barbour's *Families of Early Hartford, Connecticut* (1977); Talcott's *Families of Early Guilford, Connecticut* (1984); Charles Dyer Parkhurst's 36 volumes on New London-area families; and Jonathan Clarke's two volumes on Windham and Hampton families.

STATE ARCHIVES: archival records, manuscripts, Special Collections items, and original newspapers are retrieved *twice daily* (10:30am and 2pm). Patrons must obtain archives pass and submit call slips *at least 15 minutes* before scheduled retrieval time. There is a variety of finding aids; archivists or HGU librarians will interpret them, and answer any questions regarding unprocessed records, restrictions and confidentiality, loan of archival records, and copying of fragile items. Holdings include manuscripts; original probate records; unpublished genealogies; Fairchild and Robinson aerial photographs; tax abstracts and other town records; state court records; military rolls and other records; pictorial archives; and diaries. Call or write the HGU in advance about application and rules governing use and copying of archival material.

HARTFORD – WATKINSON LIBRARY

Trinity College	[860] 297-2268	From Capitol Av, Hartford, W to
300 Summit Street		Broad St, left to college; enter S end
Hartford, CT 06106		of campus; past gym & around arts
		ctr. Red brick Gothic bldg w/
hours vary, especially in summer; call ahead		granite annex opposite arts ctr.
		Parking at rear, & rear of arts ctr.

Free and open to public; copying, $.25/page; film reader. **HOLDINGS**: large British collection, including references, printed parish registers, town and county histories and gazetteers, *etc.*

MIDDLETOWN – GODFREY MEMORIAL LIBRARY

134 Newfield Street	[860] 346-4375	Rte 91 to Exit 22S to Rte 9S. Exit
Middletown, CT 06457	[860] 347-9874	15 to Rte 66W (Washington St). At
E-mail: office@godfrey.com		5th light, right on Rte 3 (Newfield).
Web: http://www.godfrey.org		Library ½ mi on right.

Mon 9am-8pm; Tue-Fri -4pm

Copying, $.10/page; film/fiche reader/printer; staff will answer brief mail queries; no interlibrary loan. **HOLDINGS**: 17,000 volumes in three main categories: family histories/genealogies; biographies; and local histories covering New England, New York, Pennsylvania, and many Southern states. Most information is pre-1850. Publishes *American Genealogical & Biographical Index (AGBI)*, 2nd series.

MIDDLETOWN – RUSSELL LIBRARY

Middletown Room	[860] 347-2520	I-91 to Rte 9S to Middletown ctr;
123 Broad Street		right on Rte 66 (Washington St),
Middletown, CT 06457		2 blocks; left on Broad; library on right.

winter: Mon-Thu 9am-9pm; Fri noon-9pm
    Sat 9am-5pm; Sun 1pm-5pm
summer: same, except Sat -1pm, closed Sun

Free and open to public; self-service copying, $.10/page (fragile books with red dots on spine may not be copied); no loan; staff will answer brief mail queries; users must register and leave ID to use materials. **HOLDINGS**: architectural surveys; atlases and maps; cemetery records; city directories; ephemera-clippings and pamphlet files; genealogical periodicals; genealogies; high school yearbooks; state, county, and town histories; land records; mayoral scrapbooks; naturalization indexes; newspapers; oral histories; passenger lists; regimental histories and military service records; Social Security death index; vital records.

NEW CANAAN HISTORICAL SOCIETY LIBRARY

13 Oenoke Ridge	[203] 966-1776	Merritt Parkway to Exit 37N; left
New Canaan, CT 06840		on Rte 124; 2.5 mi **OR** I-95 to Exit
		15 to New Canaan Av in Norwalk;
Tue-Sat 9:30am-12:30pm & 2-4:30pm		N to New Canaan; left on East Av;
(may be closed Sat; call)		right on Main St; to Oenoke Ridge. RR Station: Metro No.

Open to public; donations suggested; appointment desired as far in advance as possible; mail inquiries accepted (more than ½ hour billed); copier, film reader; most records copyable. **HOLDINGS**: covering New Canaan, Fairfield County, and New England.

NEW HAVEN COLONY HISTORICAL SOCIETY – WHITNEY LIBRARY

114 Whitney Avenue   [203] 562-4183   Rte 91 to Exit 3 (Trumbull St).
New Haven, CT 06510   Right at 2nd light on Whitney.
Parking on S side of bldg.

Tue-Fri 10am-5pm; Sat, Sun 2-5pm

Non-members, $2/day; mail inquiries accepted – staff research, $20/hour; film/fiche reader/printer; copying, $.50/page; no interlibrary loan; Photo Archives by appointment only. **HOLDINGS**: books; pamphlets; broadsides; maps; manuscripts; microforms; pictorial records of New Haven history, 1683 to date; genealogies and family histories; vital records; city directories; church and cemetery; New Haven city and county (1636-1901); New Haven Superior Court (1789-1905); military; schools; harbor and maritime; political; benevolent societies, correctional institutions, local businesses; military; census; probate (film); ethnic, including Afro-American. The museum has permanent and changing exhibits. The former concern New Haven's long-time maritime connections; a collection of ceramic, pewter, silver, and glass tableware; furniture, including a Herter Brothers cabinet and a curious fan chair, as well as a nearly complete Federal-style set; and important paintings of New Haven history.

NEWTOWN – CYRENIUS H. BOOTH LIBRARY

25 Main Street   [203] 426-4533   I-84 to Exit 10; W on Churchill Rd
Newtown, CT 06470   to flagpole (Main); left on Main;
2nd bldg on right. Parking in rear.

Mon-Thu 10am-8pm; Fri noon-5pm
Sat 10am-5pm; Sun 1-5pm (*summer*: closed Sun)

Donations welcome; genealogical collection on main floor, handicapped-accessible; 2 self-service copiers, $.10/page; mail inquiries accepted (brief staff research and referrals to professionals). **HOLDINGS**: Julia Brush collection of published genealogies and local histories (see *Connecticut Nutmegger* 25[1992-3]:13 for list); manuscript collection on Newtown/Danbury-area families. *Newtown Bee* (weekly newspaper), indexed by subject and VRs, 1890 to present; other local materials and standard genealogical works.

SIMSBURY – LANCE GENEALOGICAL RESEARCH LIBRARY (DeLores L. Dupuis, owner/president)

64 West Street   [203] 658-5024   I-84 to Rte 10N; left on Rte 167
P.O. Box 366   (Simsbury), 1 block. Small brick
Simsbury, CT 06070-1366   bldg on right.

Wed-Sat 10am-4pm

Three copiers, $.10/page; 2 film/fiche reader/copiers, $.10/page. Membership $15/year; $5/day for nonmembers. **HOLDINGS**: 3,000 volumes; Conn. histories and genealogies; Quebec books and film/fiche; Family Search program (LDS); Barbour Collection of Conn. vital records.

SOUTHPORT – PEQUOT LIBRARY

720 Pequot Avenue   [203] 259-0346   I-95 to Exit 19 (Center St); right on
Southport, CT 06490   Pequot. 3rd bldg on right. Ample
parking.

Oct-Apr: Mon, Wed 9am-8:30pm; Tue, Thu, Fri
     9am-5:30pm; Sat 9am-5pm; Sun 1-5pm
May-Sep: Wed 9am-8:30pm; Mon, Tue, Thu, Fri 9am-5:30pm; Sat 9am-1pm

Free and open to public; 1 copier, \$.15/page; 1 film/fiche reader/printer; mail inquiries accepted. **HOLDINGS**: local history and genealogy, focusing on New England, Conn., Fairfield County, and nearby New York; 200 volumes of family-name files.

STAMFORD – FERGUSON LIBRARY

One Public Library Plaza   [203] 964-1000   I-95 to Atlantic St Exit; Atlantic for
Stamford, CT 06904   6 lights. Library on corner of Bed-
E-mail: comments@ferglib.ct.us   ford & Broad Sts (Atlantic *becomes*
Web: http://www.ferglib.org/ferg   Bedford at Library corner), next to
Caldor's. Parking garage behind
Mon-Thu 10am-9pm; Fri 10am-6pm   stores, across Bedford.
Sat, Sun 10am-5pm (Sun, *Sep to mid-May only*)

Copying, \$.10/page; film readers; reader/printers, \$.10/page. Interlibrary loan for *Stamford residents only*. *Limited* mail inquiries accepted (must enclose SASE; minimum for copies, \$1). **HOLDINGS**: local history and genealogy, focusing on Stamford, state of Conn., and New England area; family histories and genealogies, especially local; genealogical periodicals; obituary index for local newspapers (obits may be copied).

TOLLAND – FRENCH-CANADIAN SOCIETY LIBRARY (see under SOCIETIES)

WETHERSFIELD HISTORICAL SOCIETY LIBRARY

150 Main Street   [860] 529-7656   I-91 to Exit 26 (Marsh St); left on
Wethersfield, CT 06109   Main; ¼ mi. Library in Old Acad-
Web: http://www.harborside.com/home/p/p2242/sbhs.html   emy Museum. Some parking.

Tue-Fri 10am-4pm; Sat 1-4pm (*& by appointment*)

Donations welcome. Staff copying, \$.25/page; no film or fiche; mail inquiries accepted (limited to Wethersfield, Granby, East Granby, Simsbury, and Windsor names; \$15/hr plus expenses). **HOLDINGS**: focus on Wethersfield; printed genealogies, ship logs, diaries, letters, account books, photos, family charts (6 file drawers), VRs books, military histories, church records for Hartland, Wintonbury (old name for Bloomfield), and E. Granby, Conn., and Granville, Mass., Conn. state and town histories, Mass. town histories, Ohio histories, Indian materials, and Civil War books.

WINDSOR HISTORICAL SOCIETY

96 Palisado Avenue   [860] 688-3813   I-91 to Exit 37 (Rte 305/Bloomfield
Windsor, CT 06095   Av); E 1 mi to Windsor center; N on
Rte 159 (Palisado); cross Farming-
Apr-Oct: Tue-Sat 10am-4pm   ton River bridge). Next right on
Nov-Mar: Mon-Fri 10am-4pm   No. Meadow Rd to WHS; parking.

Donations requested. Copying, $.10/page; no film or fiche; mail inquiries – 1 or 2 questions each – accepted. **HOLDINGS**: focus on founders of Windsor and passengers on *Mary and John*; printed genealogies, family-file folders and manuscripts, diaries, account books, *etc*.

LDS FAMILY HISTORY CENTERS

Bloomfield – 100 Mountain Road; [203] 242-1607; Tue-Fri 10am-2pm; Tue, Wed 7-9pm; Sat 9am-5pm

Madison – 275 Warpas Road; [203] 245-8267; Tue 10am-2pm; Wed 7-9pm; Sat 10am-2pm

Mystic – 1230 Flanders Road; [860] 536-5102; Mon 10am-1pm; Tue, Thu 10am-1pm & 7-9pm; Wed 1-4pm & 7-9pm; Sat 10am-2pm

New Canaan – 682 South Avenue; [203] 966-9511; *call for current hours*

Woodbridge – 990 Racebrook Road / Route 114; [203] 387-2012; Mon noon-4pm; Tue, Wed 10am-1pm & 7-9pm

(See NEW ENGLAND chapter for FHC holdings.)

SOCIETIES

CONNECTICUT ANCESTRY SOCIETY

P.O. Box 249
Stamford, CT 06904-0249

Founded in 1954 to promote and assist genealogical research, primarily on southwest Conn. Dues, $25/year. Meets monthly, Sep-May, at various locations. Three fall and three spring workshops, each with speakers, at different area libraries. Annual meeting in May. **HOLDINGS**: ancestral charts, manuscripts, and periodicals from corresponding societies held at Stamford's Ferguson Library. Publishes *Connecticut Ancestry* (quarterly, 1958+; prints queries).

CONNECTICUT GRAVESTONE NETWORK (CGN)

Ruth Shapleigh-Brown,   [860] 643-5652
    Executive Director
135 Wells Street
Manchester, CT 06040
E-mail: JJSRUNS@COURANT.INFINET

Founded in 1995 to make the public aware of the importance of preserving historic graveyards, and to coordinate the efforts of Conn.'s preservation groups. Mail queries accepted with SASE. Annual dues, $10 (includes quarterly newsletter). CGN sponsors tours through the warm months, holds an annual symposium, and presents an educational slide show.

CONNECTICUT HISTORICAL SOCIETY (see also under LIBRARIES – HARTFORD)

1 Elizabeth Street   [860] 236-5621
Hartford, CT 06105

Founded in 1825. Dues: individual, $30; family, $45; senior citizen, $25 (with spouse, $40); out-of-staters and historical societies, $25. The CHS museum, which displays permanent and temporary exhibits on Conn. history, is open Tue-Sun, noon-4:45pm (children under 18, students with ID, and CHS members, free; otherwise, $3; free to all, 1st Sun of month). CHS publishes monographs and sponsors events and activities, including lectures, workshops, family programs, performances, and trips.

CONNECTICUT SOCIETY OF GENEALOGISTS

Office: 175 Maple Street   [860] 569-0002   I-84 to Rte 2E to Exit 5C (Maple);
East Hartford, CT   left; ½ mi. Office & library on right.
Mail: P.O. Box 435
Glastonbury, CT 06033-0435

Mon-Fri 9:30am-4pm (*office*)

Dues: $35/individual or couple, $38/Canadian (both include $3 registration fee). Seven meetings/year (3rd Sat of month, Sep-May, except Dec and Jan). Publishes *The Connecticut Nutmegger* (1968+; all volumes available from CSG office), $12/year, libraries and institutions (or free with membership); queries accepted from members only – each may submit 2 free queries per issue. Library houses Ancestry Service, an indexed set of members' ancestor charts (500+ volumes); also has printed genealogies, town histories, VRs, *etc.* Copying, $.15/page. CSG sponsors annual literary award – $500 – for best-written New England genealogy (either ancestors or descendants of a New England resident); entry forms available from office, due by 15 Feb.

DESCENDANTS OF THE FOUNDERS OF ANCIENT WINDSOR

P.O. Box 39
Windsor, CT 06095

Annual dues, $7/individual or couple. Open to all, but focus on descendants of pre-1640 Windsor residents. Two meetings a year, in Windsor. Quarterly newsletter.

FRENCH-CANADIAN GENEALOGICAL SOCIETY OF CONNECTICUT

53 Tolland Green (*library*)   [860] 872-2597   I-84 to Exit 68 (U Conn/Rte 195);
or P.O. Box 928 (*society*)   ¼ mi to library.
Tolland, CT 06084-0928

Mon 1-8pm; Wed 4-8pm; Sat 9-4pm; Sun 1-4pm

Founded in 1981 to encourage research by Conn. residents into their French ancestry and heritage. Annual dues: individuals, $20; $10 for each additional family member; full-time students, $10; includes *Connecticut Maple Leaf* (semiannual, 1983+) and newsletter. Regular meetings, cultural activities, and genealogy workshops. Library staffed by volunteers; nonmembers, $5/day. **HOLDINGS:** 3,500 volumes; periodicals, card files, CD databases, and microforms. Major French-Canadian/Acadian genealogical references and indexes include Tanguay, Jetté, Drouin and Loiselle marriages, PRDH (new CD – all Québec Catholic baptisms, marriages, and burials, 1766-99), Arsenault, and Bergeron; Canada, New England and New York marriage *répertoires*; family and local histories; biographies; some 20th-century New England city directories and other references; IGI and Ancestral File; U.S. census and Social Security death indexes, and telephone listings, on CD. Unique to this collection are the Acadian papers of Fr. Hector Hebert, including a large card-file of VRs, New England parish records, and family data sheets and correspondence – some concerning research duplicated nowhere else.

NEW HAVEN COLONY HISTORICAL SOCIETY (see also under LIBRARIES – NEW HAVEN)

114 Whitney Avenue New Haven, CT 06510	[203] 562-4183	I-91 to Exit 3 (Trumbull St); at 2nd light, right on Whitney. 100 yds on left.

Thu, Fri 10am-5pm; Sat, Sun 2-5pm

Founded in 1862. Dues: $30/individual, $40/family, $15/library. Monthly member meetings (Sep-May) include exhibit openings, lunch lectures, and courses and workshops (including genealogy). Publishes historical monographs and genealogies; *Papers* (10 volumes); *Journal* (Mar 1952+; volumes 1-16 indexed); occasional newsletters and special announcements.

POLISH GENEALOGICAL SOCIETY OF CONNECTICUT (Jonathan D. Shea, president)

8 Lyle Road   [860] 223-5596
New Britain, CT 06053-2104
E-mail: pgsconnie@aol.com (*financial matters only*); PGSNE2@aol.com (*all other correspondence*)
Web: http://www.members.aol.com/PGSNE2

Mon 10am-2:30pm (*or by appointment*)
Archive and Resource Center (*by appointment only*)

Dues: $15/year, or $27 for two years; members throughout U.S., Canada, and Europe. Focus on Polish immigration to New England, New York, New Jersey, and Pennsylvania. Library free and open to public; appointment required (at least 1 day in advance); mail inquiries accepted; copying, $.10/page. **HOLDINGS:** gravestone inscriptions from Polish cemeteries in region, and in northeast Poland. The **Archive and Resource Center** (278 Broad Street, New Britain) has books on Polish genealogical research, immigration, and language; dictionaries; anniversary booklets; histories of Polish-American parishes; addresses of Catholic, Orthodox, and Lutheran churches in Poland; regional Polish obits (1979+); databases of Polish marriages for several northeastern states; of birthplaces of Polish immigrants to Conn., Mass., and New Jersey; and of cemetery inscriptions (fee required to use databases). The Society has a list of local researchers for hire. Publishes *Pathways and Passages* (semiannual).

The **Bialystok-Lomza Genealogical Study Group** (which has its own quarterly) collects and shares historical and genealogical information on this area of northeast Poland, and maintains a Bialystok-Lomza ancestor card file.

The Society has published Polish cemetery inscriptions from Vermont and N.H.; *Cemetery Inscriptions, St. Stanislaus Cemetery, Dabrowa Bialstocka, Poland*; *Directory of Polish Roman Catholic Parishes in the Territory of the Former Russian Partition*; *Catholic Parishes in the Territory of the Former Austrian Partition – Galicia*; *Address List of Polish Archival Repositories*; and *A Listing of Localities in the Diocese of Lomza and Their Parish Churches*. Mass. and Conn. cemetery transcriptions are underway. N.B., an indexing project using LDS films from Komza Province is also underway, and needs volunteers.

The Society also sponsors genealogical tours to Poland, including visits to major tourist attractions, regions that sent large numbers of immigrants to the U.S., and participants' ancestral villages; time is allotted for research.

PERIODICALS

THE CONNECTICUT NUTMEGGER (quarterly; see under CONNECTICUT SOCIETY OF GENEALOGISTS; for an index, see under BOOKS AND ARTICLES – Ullmann, Helen S.).

CONNECTICUT ANCESTRY (quarterly; see under CONNECTICUT ANCESTRY SOCIETY).

For 'ethnic' periodicals, see under SOCIETIES.

The first 8 volumes of what is now *The American Genealogist*, published by Donald L. Jacobus as the *New Haven Genealogical Magazine* (1922-32), consist entirely of Jacobus' massive compiled genealogies – extending in many cases down to and past 1800 – of "Families of Ancient New Haven;" under which title they have been reprinted, as a 3-volume set, by Genealogical Publishing Co. (Baltimore).

BOOKS AND ARTICLES

Abbe, Elizabeth, "Connecticut Genealogical Research: Sources and Suggestions," *NEHGR*, 134[1980]:3-26; also in Ralph J. Crandall, ed., *Genealogical Research in New England* (1984: Baltimore, Genealogical Publishing Co.).

Connecticut Society of Genealogists, *Researcher's Guide to 99 Libraries and Local Collections within Connecticut* (1992: Glastonbury, The Society).

Gannett, Henry, *A Geographic Dictionary of Rhode Island and Connecticut* (repr. ed., 1978: Baltimore, Genealogical Publishing Co.).

Hughes, Arthur H. and **Morse S. Allen**, *Connecticut Place Names* (1976: Hartford, Connecticut Historical Society).

Kemp, Thomas Jay, *Connecticut Researcher's Handbook* (1981: Detroit, Gale Research Co.).

Morrison, Betty Jean, *Connecting to Connecticut* (1995: East Hartford, Connecticut Society of Genealogists).

Parks, Roger N., ed., *Connecticut: A Bibliography of its History* (1986: Hanover, NH, University Press of New England).

Roberts, Gary Boyd, "Some Reflections on Modern Connecticut Genealogical Scholarship," *Connecticut Nutmegger*, 12[1979-80]:371-85.

Schnare, Robert E., Jr., *Local Historical Resources in Connecticut: A Guide to Their Use* (1975: Connecticut League of Historical Societies).

Sperry, Kip, *Connecticut Sources for Family Historians and Genealogists* (1980: Logan, UT, Everton Publishers).

Ullmann, Helen S., *Nutmegger Index, Volumes 1-28* (1996: Camden, ME, Picton Press).

Wright, Norman Edgar, *Genealogy in America, Volume 1: Massachusetts, Connecticut, and Maine* (1968+: Salt Lake City, Deseret Book Co.).

MAINE

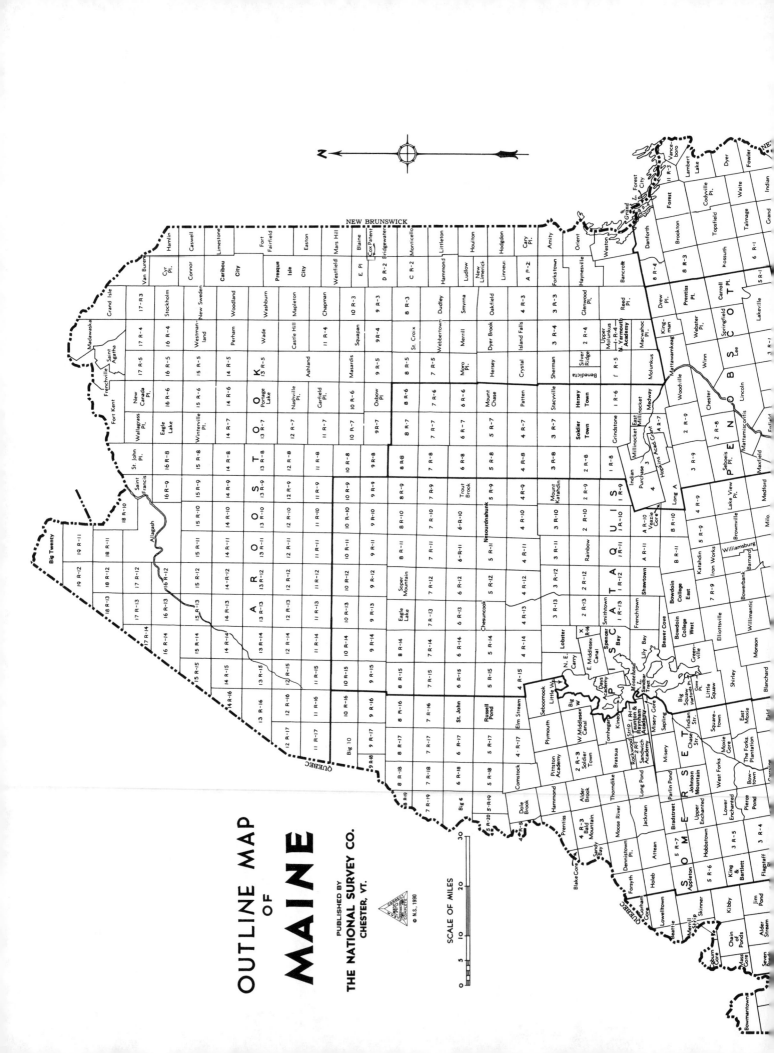

OUTLINE MAP
OF
MAINE

PUBLISHED BY
THE NATIONAL SURVEY CO.
CHESTER, VT.

© N.S. 1990

SCALE OF MILES

0   5   10   20   30

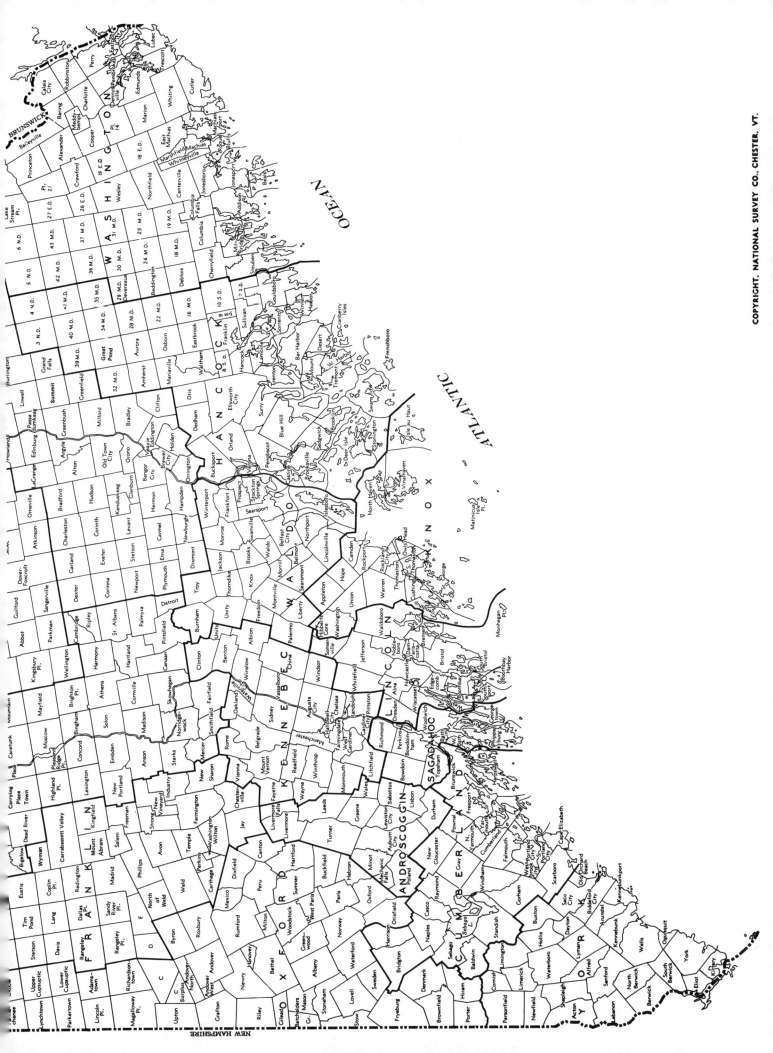

COUNTIES

Abbrev	County	Estab'd	Parent(s)	Deed Dist
AND	Androscoggin	1854	CUM, LNC, OXF & KEN	AND
ARO	Aroostook	1839	PEN & WAS	Southern & Northern Reg'ies
CUM	Cumberland	1760	YRK	CUM
FRA	Franklin	1838	KEN, OXF, & SOM	FRA
HAN	Hancock	1789	LNC	HAN
KEN	Kennebec	1799	CUM & LNC	KEN
KNX	Knox	1860	LNC & WAL	KNX
LNC	Lincoln	1760	YRK	LNC
OXF	Oxford	1805	CUM & YRK	Eastern & Western Reg'ies
PEN	Penobscot	1816	HAN	PEN
PIS	Piscataquis	1838	PEN & SOM	PIS
SAG	Sagadahoc	1854	LNC	SAG
SOM	Somerset	1809	KEN	SOM
WAL	Waldo	1827	HAN	WAL
WAS	Washington	1789	LNC	WAS
YRK	York	1652	-----	YRK

TOWNS

CODES: **F** (some loss by fire within dates shown); **Inc** (incomplete records); **Ind** (records indexed); **L** (in NEHGS Circulating Library); **MT** (in NEHGS microtext department); **MSA** (microfilm at Maine State Archives); **RB** (rare book at NEHGS); **V** (in book form at NEHGS).

N.B., Maine's pre-1892 vital records are, for the most part, in the town halls. About 75 towns sent their pre-1892 records to the state registry – these are in **bold type**, below. (The 75 are drawn from a 1998 list provided by the registry, which *supersedes* the old.)

Town	Org'd	Cty	TRs	VRs	Codes	NEHGS
Abbott	1827	PIS	1900	1900	F	
Acton	1830	YRK		1892-	Ind	RB
				1830-92	MSA/Inc	
Adams *(see Crawford)*						
Addison	1797	WAS	1824-	1834	F/Ind	
				1853-71	MSA	
Albany	1803	OXF		-1892	MSA	MT
Albion *(Fairfax -1821; Ligonia -1824)*	1804	KEN	1700s	1700s		
				1802-91	MSA	MT, V
Alexander	1825	WAS	1975-	1975-	F	
				1784-1926	MSA	
Alfred	1808	YRK	1824-	1890	F/Ind	MT
				1803-92		
Allagash Pl	1885	ARO	1892-	1892-	F/Ind	
Alna *(New Milford -1811)*	1794	LNC	1855-	1892-	F	
			1795-1891	1795-1891	MSA	MT
Alton	1844	PEN	1800s	1894	F/Ind	
				1859-1940	MSA	
Amherst	1831	HAN	1850-	1856-	F/Ind	
				1783-1891	MSA	MT
Amity	1836	ARO	1960-	1893	F	
				1862-92	MSA	
Andover *(E. Andover -1820)*	1804	OXF	1800s-	1800s-	Inc	
				1795-1891	MSA	
Anson	1798	SOM	1899-1913	1822-	F	
			1931-			
			1798-1855	1798-1890	MSA	
Appleton	1829	KNX	1820-	1700s-	Inc/Ind	
				1774-1892	MSA	MT
Argyle Pl *(disincorporated 1937)*	1839	PEN				
Arrowsic	1841	SAG	1892	1860-		
				1741-1891	MSA	
Arundel *(N. Kennebunkport -1957; name of present Kennebunkport, 1719-1821)*	1915	YRK	1916-	1916-	Ind	
			1678-1892	1678-1892	MSA	
Ashland *(named 1876; formerly Dalton)*	1862	ARO		1863-	Ind	
Athens	1803	SOM	1900-	1900-	F/Ind	
Atkinson	1819	PIS	1888-	1900-	Inc	
				1766-1901	MSA	MT
Auburn *(see Danville)*	1842	AND	1840-	1700s	Ind	
				1751-1954	MSA	MT
Augusta *(briefly Harrington, 1797)*	1797	KEN	1900-	1930-	Inc	
				1780-1896	MSA/Inc	MT, L
Aurora *(Hampton -1833)*	1831	HAN		1945-	F	
Avon	1802	FRA	1917-	1892-	F	
				1766-1850	MSA	MT
Baileyville	1828	WAS		1861-1939	MSA	
Baldwin	1802	CUM	1790s-	1790s-		
			1802-46	1802-92	MSA	
Bancroft	1889	ARO	1910-	1892-		

Town	Org'd	Cty	TRs	VRs	Codes	NEHGS
Bangor	1791	PEN	1812-	1800-	Ind	
				1775-1892	MSA/Inc	MT
Bar Harbor	1796	HAN	1892-	1892-	F/Ind	
(Eden -1918)			1798-1884	1796-1848	MSA	
Baring Pl	1825	WAS	1892-1931	1892-1931	Ind	
				1941		
Barnard Pl	1834	PIS	1921-	1921-	F	
Bath	1781	SAG	1753-	1892-	Ind	
				1757-1892	MSA	
Beals	1925	WAS	1925-	1925-		
Beaver Cove Pl	1975	PIS	1975-	1975-		
Beddington	1833	WAS	1844-	1882-	Ind	
				1792-1892	MSA	
Belfast	1773	WAL	1853-	1892-	Ind	
			1773-1903	1773-1903	MSA	L, V
Belgrade	1796	KEN	1906-	1770s	F	
				1758-1892	MSA	MT
Belmont	1814	WAL	1800s	1892-	F/Ind	
				1855-83	MSA	
Benedicta	1873	ARO	1949-	1928	F	
Benton	1842	KEN		1892-	Ind	
(Sebasticook -1850)				1841-91	MSA	MT
Berwick	1713	YRK	1700-	1700-		
			1701-1892	1701-1892	MSA	MT, V
Bethel	1796	OXF	1796-	1867-	Ind	
				1745-1923	MSA	MT
Biddeford	1653	YRK	1872-	1872-	F/Ind	
			1653-1786	1653-1923	MSA	
Bingham	1812	SOM	1812-	1812-	Ind	MT
Blaine	1874	ARO	1942-	1892-	F	
Blanchard	1831	PIS	1800s	1800s	F	
			1831-1959		MSA	MT
Blue Hill	1789	HAN	1789-	1700-	Inc	
				1785-1890		
				1892-1923	MSA	
Boothbay	1764	LNC	1763-	1763-	Ind	
				1796-1892	MSA	
Boothbay Harbor	1889	LNC	1889-	1889-		
				1763-1891	MSA	
Bowdoin	1788	SAG	1788-	1892-	F	
				1763-1891	MSA	L
Bowdoinham	1762	SAG	1900	1725-	F/Ind	
				1776-1891	MSA	
Bowerbank	1839	PIS	1966-	1966-		
(earlier records at Town Hall; permission				1832-1932	MSA	
needed to search)						
Bradford	1831	PEN		1862-	Inc	
			1819-54	1863-1940	MSA	
Bradley	1835	PEN	1770-	1770-		
				1805-93	MSA	MT
Bremen	1828	LNC	1828-	1828-		
				1756-1892	MSA	V, L

Town	Org'd	Cty	TRs	VRs	Codes	NEHGS
Brewer	1812	PEN	1812-	1770- Ind		
			1743-1859	1806-1943	MSA	
			(lineage books)			
Bridgewater	1858	ARO	1950s	1894	F/Ind	
Bridgton	1794	CUM	1794-	1794-	Ind	
				1785-1865	MSA	
Brighton Pl	1816	SOM	1800s	1892-		
(N. Hill -1827)			1816-37	1840-1918	MSA	MT
Bristol	1765	LNC	1765-	1892-		
			1765-1900	1765-1900	MSA	V, L
Brooklin	1849	HAN	1849-	1849-		
(earlier, Port Washington)			1849-98	1835-1936	MSA	MT
Brooks	1816	WAL	1930-	1892-	F	MT
Brooksville	1817	HAN	1966-	1817-	F	
				1818-1940	MSA	
Brownfield	1802	OXF	1800s	1802	F	
Brownville	1824	PIS		1824-	Ind	
				1812-68	MSA	
Brunswick	1737	CUM	1830s	1830s	Ind	
			1735-1872	1735-1910	MSA	
Buckfield	1793	OXF	1797-	1782-	Ind	
(formerly Buckstown)				1700-1891	MSA	MT
Bucksport	1792	HAN	1800-	1800-		
				1775-1920	MSA	MT
Burlington	1832	PEN	1840-	1840-		
				1769-1891	MSA	
Burnham	1824	WAL	1824-	1892-	F/Ind	
				1821-91	MSA	
Buxton	1772	YRK	1740-	1790-	Ind	
				1773-1890	MSA	MT
Byron	1833	OXF	1874-	1880-		
			1814-92	1814-92	MSA	MT
Calais	1809	WAS	1809-	1890-	F/Ind	
				1824-1911	MSA	MT
Cambridge	1834	SOM	1834-	1800-	Ind	
				1792-1896	MSA	
Camden	1791	KNX	1891-	1891-	Ind	
(split into Camden &			1783-1892	1783-1891	MSA	MT
Rockport)						
Canaan	1788	SOM	1880-	1700s-	F/Ind	
				1776-1910	MSA	MT
Canton	1821	OXF		1818-66; 1891	F	
Cape Elizabeth	1775	CUM	1903-	1903-	Ind	
(a district, 1765)			1765-1876	1765-1891	MSA	
Cape Porpus *(former name of Kennebunkport, 1653-1719)*						
Caratunk Pl	1840	SOM	1854-	1854-		
				1854-1904	MSA	
Caribou	1859	ARO	1859-	1892-		
(Lyndon -1877)			1848-1929	1848-1929	MSA	
Carmel	1811	PEN	1964-	1850s	F	
				1760-1891	MSA	
Carrebassett Valley	1972	FRA	1972-			
Carroll Pl	1845	PEN	1928-	1928-	F	

Town	Org'd	Cty	TRs	VRs	Codes	NEHGS
Carthage	1826	FRA	1826-	1828-		
				1812-82	MSA	
Cary Pl	1858	ARO	1972-		F	
(org'd 1858, ratif'd 1878)				1862-82	MSA	
Casco	1841	CUM	1873-	1920-	F	
				1841-92	MSA	
Castine	1796	HAN	1796-	1800-		
			1796-1891	1796-1891	MSA	
Castle Hill	1903	ARO	1940s	1892-	Ind	
				1855-92	MSA	
Caswell Pl	1879	ARO	1945-	1898-	F	
Centerville	1842	WAS		1800s	F	
				1770-1865	MSA	
Chandlerville *(see Detroit)*						
Chapman	1824	ARO		1868-	Ind	
(org'd 1824, ratif'd 1879, incorp'd 1915)				1868-91	MSA	
Charleston	1811	PEN	1811-	1811-	Ind	
			1809-97	1809-97	MSA	
Charlotte	1825	WAS	1821-	1821-	Ind	
				1816-92	MSA	
Chelsea	1850	KEN	1851-	1851-	Ind	
				1782-92	MSA	
Cherryfield	1816	WAS	1842-	1845-	Inc	
				1854-1939	MSA	MT
Chester	1834	PEN	1862-	1835-	Inc	
				1788-1943	MSA	MT
Chesterville	1802	FRA	1900-	1785-		
				1788-1907	MSA	
China	1796	KEN	1797-	1892-		
(Harlem -1818)			1785-1891	1785-1891	MSA	MT
Clifton	1848	PEN	1860-	1892-	Ind	
				1848-92	MSA	MT
Clinton	1795	KEN	1892-	1892-		
				1797-1898	MSA	MT, V, L
Codyville Pl	1845	WAS	1922-	1892-	Inc	
Columbia	1796	WAS	1796-	1892-	Inc	
			1752-1860	1752-1860	MSA	MT
Columbia Falls	1863	WAS	1796-	1860-		
				1863-91	MSA	
Connor	1877	ARO				
(org'd 1877, ratif'd 1883, incorp'd 1913)						
Cooper	1822	WAS	1907-	1892-	F	
				1878-1930	MSA	
Coplin Pl	1895	FRA		1895-		
Corinna	1816	PEN		1892-	Ind/Inc	
				1797-1891	MSA	
Corinth	1811	PEN	1811-40	1811-40		
			1865-	1865-	Ind	
				1785-1895	MSA	
Cornish	1794	YRK		1857-	F/Ind	
Cornville	1798	SOM	1794-	1794-	Ind	
				1772-1891	MSA	MT
Coxhall *(see Lyman)*						

Town	Org'd	Cty	TRs	VRs	Codes	NEHGS
Cranberry Isles	1830	HAN	1830-	1830-		
				1783-1890	MSA	
Crawford	1828	WAS	1901-	1890-	F	
				1827-1900	MSA	
Crystal	1901	ARO	1923-	1800s	F/Ind	
(org'd 1840, ratif'd 1878, '95, incorp'd 1901)				1854-96	MSA	
Cumberland	1821	CUM	1821-	1700s	Ind	
				1720-1892	MSA	
Cushing	1789	KNX	1845-	1818-	Ind	
				1735-1920	MSA	
Cutler	1826	WAS	1843-9	1900-	F	
			1900-	1844-96	MSA	MT
Cyr Pl	1870	ARO	1892-	1892-	Ind	
Dallas Pl	1845	FRA	1921-	1892-		
Dalton (see Ashland)						
Damariscotta	1848	LNC	1864-	1892-	Ind	
				1848-91	MSA	V, L
Danforth	1860	WAS	1936-	1892-	Ind	
				1860-91	MSA	
Danville	1802	AND				
(Pejepscot -1818; now part of Auburn)						
Dayton	1854	YRK	1854-	1854-	Ind	
			1832-99	1832-99	MSA	MT
Deblois	1852	WAS	1852-	1855-		
Dedham	1837	HAN	1932-	1820-	Ind/Inc	
				1787-1940	MSA	
Deer Isle	1789	HAN	1789-1853	1786-	F	
			1958			
				1768-1940	MSA	
Denmark	1807	OXF	1807-	1807-		
Dennistown Pl	1895	SOM	1910-	1900-		
			1614-1938	1840-1940	MSA	
(Trickey Family Records)						
Dennysville	1818	WAS	1818-	1818-	Ind	
				1790-1917	MSA	
Detroit	1828	SOM	1816-	1802-		
(Chandlerville -1841)			1780-1892	1780-1892	MSA	MT
Dexter	1816	PEN	1816-	1802-	Ind/Inc	
				1761-1897	MSA	MT
Dickeyville (see Frenchville)						
Dixfield	1803	OXF	1803-	1804-	Ind/Inc	
			1803-92	1803-92	MSA	
Dixmont	1807	PEN	1906	1821-	Ind	
				1800-94	MSA	
Dover (see Dover-Foxcroft)						
Dover-Foxcroft	1812	PIS	1800s-	1800s-		
(towns merged, 1915)				1792-1894	MSA	
Dresden	1794	LNC	1794-	1892-	Ind	
			1771-1906	1771-1906	MSA	MT
Drew Pl	1921	PEN		1850s-		
				1853-1928	MSA	
Durham	1789	AND	1961-	1774-1865		
				1892-		
				1744-1892	MSA	MT

Town	Org'd	Cty	TRs	VRs	Codes	NEHGS
Dutton *(see Glenburn)*						
Dyer Brook	1891	ARO		1895-	Ind	
E. Pl	1898	ARO	1966-			
Eagle Lake	1870	ARO	1890-	1892-	Inc	
				1867-1950	MSA	
E. Andover *(see Andover)*						
E. Livermore *(see Livermore Falls)*						
E. Machias	1826	WAS	1823-	1796-	Ind	
				1709-1900	MSA	
E. Millinocket	1907	PEN	1907-	1907-		
E. Thomaston *(see Rockland)*						
Eastbrook	1837	HAN	1892-	1892-		
Easton	1865	ARO	1896-	1892-	Ind	
Eastport	1798	WAS	1700s-	1700s-	F/Ind	
				1778-1904	MSA	MT
Eddington	1811	PEN	1805-	1802-	F/Ind	
				1802-1922	MSA	
Eden *(see Bar Harbor)*						
Edgecomb	1774	LNC	1774-	1774-	Ind	
			1774-1892	1774-1892	MSA	MT
Edinburg	1835	PEN		1872-	F	
				1835-99	MSA	
Eliot	1810	YRK	1810-	1892-		
			1810-1901	1810-92	MSA	MT
Elliotsville Pl	1835	PIS	1960-	1913-		
Ellsworth	1800	HAN	1933-	1800s	F/Ind	
Embden	1804	SOM	1820-	1892-	Inc	
			1783-1892	1782-1892	MSA	
Enfield	1835	PEN	1940-	1857-	F	
Etna	1820	PEN	1900s	1800s		
				1742-1910	MSA	
Eustis	1871	FRA		1872-		
				1871-92	MSA	MT
				(marriages)		
Exeter	1811	PEN	1950-	1950-	F	
			1808-93	1808-93	MSA	
Fairfax *(see Albion)*						
Fairfield	1788	SOM	1788-	1788-	F/Ind	
				1788-1867	MSA	MT
Falmouth	1718	CUM	1718-73	1712-	Inc	
			1850	1718-73		
			1718-73	1784-1892	MSA	
Farmingdale	1852	KEN	1852-	1855-	Ind	
				1852-91	MSA	MT
Farmington	1794	FRA	1794-	1792-	Ind	
				1741-1891	MSA	MT
Fayette	1795	KEN	1795-	1892-	F/Ind	
				1785-1952	MSA	
Forks Pl	1895	SOM		1800s		
Fort Fairfield	1858	ARO	1858-	1892-	Ind	
				1847-92	MSA	
Fort Kent	1869	ARO	1900-	1892-	Ind	
Fox Isle *(see N. Haven)*						
Foxcroft *(see Dover-Foxcroft)*						

Town	Org'd	Cty	TRs	VRs	Codes	NEHGS
Frankfort	1789	WAL	1934-	1903-	F/Ind	
Franklin	1825	HAN	1813-	1813-	Ind	
Freedom	1813	WAL	1813-	1834-	Ind	
				1777-1892	MSA	MT
Freeport	1789	CUM	1789-	1789-	Ind	
				1795-1892	MSA	MT
Frenchville	1869	ARO	1900s-	1880-	F/Ind	
(Dickeyville -1871)			1869-92	1869-92	MSA	
Friendship	1807	KNX	1824-	1824-	F/Ind	
				1769-1889	MSA	
Fryeburg	1777	OXF	1773-	1777-	Ind	
			1777-1892	1777-1892	MSA	MT
Gardiner	1803	KEN		1892-	Ind	
				1800-91	MSA	MT, V, L
Garfield Pl	1895	ARO	1958-	1892-		
Garland	1811	PEN	1936-	1859-	F/Ind	
				1854-1950	MSA	
Georgetown	1716	SAG	1716-	1750-	Ind	
			1757-1940	1757-1940	MSA	MT
Gilead	1804	OXF	1800s-	1700s-	Ind	
				1757-1892	MSA	
Glenburn	1822	PEN	1822-	1892-	F	
				1800-88	MSA	
Glenwood Pl	1867	ARO	1866-	1866-	F	
Gorham	1764	CUM	1807-	1750-	F/Ind	
			1733-1879	1721-1880	MSA	MT
Gouldsboro	1789	HAN	1789-	1792-	F	
			1772-1898	1772-1898	MSA	MT
Grand Falls Pl	1878	PEN				
Grand Isle	1869	ARO	1869-	1892-	Ind	
Grand Lake Stream Pl	1897	WAS				
Gray	1778	CUM	1778-	1700s	F/Ind	
Great Pond Pl	1895	HAN	1950-	1894-	Ind	
Greenbush	1834	PEN		1910-	Ind	
				1774-1931	MSA	
Greene	1788	AND	1788-	1788-		
				1748-1891	MSA	MT
Greenfield	1834	PEN	1848-	1850s-	F/Ind	
Greenville	1836	PIS	1831-	1883-		
				1820-92	MSA	
Greenwood	1816	OXF	1898-	1816-	F	
			1813-1920	1797-1926	MSA	
Guilford	1816	PIS	1816-	1892-	Ind	
				1770-1932	MSA	MT
Hallowell	1771	KEN		1700s-		
			1761-1812	1761-1812	MSA	MT, V, L
Hamlin	1870	ARO		1892-		
Hammond Pl	1886	ARO	1885-	1885-		
				1864-1954	MSA	MT
Hampden	1794	PEN	1794-	1892-	F/Inc	
Hampton (see Aurora)						
Hancock	1828	HAN	1917-	1890-	Ind	
			1828-91	1828-91	MSA	MT

Town	Org'd	Cty	TRs	VRs	Codes	NEHGS
Hanover	1843	OXF		1791-		
				1807-92	MSA	MT
Harlem *(see China)*						
Harmony	1803	SOM	1804-	1800-50, 1890-		
			1764-1864	1764-1864	MSA	MT
Harpswell	1758	CUM	1900s-	1740s-		
				1769-1892	MSA	MT
Harrington	1797	WAS	1837-	1771-	F/Ind	
(see Augusta)				1851-92	MSA	
				(delayed births)		
Harrison	1805	CUM	1820s-	1806-	F/Inc	
			1805-1919	1805-1919	MSA	
Hartford	1798	OXF	1798-	1892-		
				1800-91	MSA	MT
Hartland	1820	SOM	1820-	1894-	F/Ind	
				1772-1891	MSA	
Haynesville	1876	ARO		1892-		
Hebron	1792	OXF	1792-	1792-		
			1700-1893	1700-1893	MSA	MT
Hermon	1816	PEN		1930-	F	
				1872-91	MSA	
				(marriages)		
Hersey	1873	ARO	1873-	1890-		
			1862-1914	1862-1914	MSA	MT
Hibberts Gore		LNC				
Highland Pl	1871	SOM	1972-	1972-	F	
Hiram	1814	OXF	1804-	1892-		
				1815-64	MSA	
				(marriages)		MT
Hodgdon	1832	ARO	1950-	1800s-	Ind	
				1837-1940	MSA	
Holden	1852	PEN	1852-	1852-		
				1756-1945	MSA	
Hollis	1798	YRK	1798-	1892-	Inc	
			1781-1892	1781-1892	MSA	MT
Hope	1804	KNX		1740-		
				1795-1925	MSA	MT, V, L
Houlton	1831	ARO	1923-	1892-	F/Inc	
Howard *(see Willimantic)*						
Howland	1826	PEN	1911-	1892-	Ind/Inc	
				1798-1937	MSA	MT
				(births & deaths)		
Hudson	1825	PEN	1887-	1856-	Ind/Inc	
				1856-92	MSA	
Huntressville *(see Lowell)*						
Indian Island	1962?	PEN	1940s-	1962-	F	
Reservation						
Indian Township		WAS		1970-		
Pasamaquoddy Reservation						
Industry	1803	FRA	1803-	1892-	Ind	
				1738-1891	MSA	MT
Island Falls	1872	ARO	1910-	1910-	F	
Islandport *(see Long Island Pl)*						
Isle au Haut	1874	KNX	1951-	1875-	F	

Town	Org'd	Cty	TRs	VRs	Codes	NEHGS
Islesboro	1789	WAL	1789-	1789-		
Jackman	1895	SOM	1883-	1892-		
Jackson	1818	WAL	1818-	1809-	F/Inc	MT, V, L
Jay	1795	FRA	1865-	1700s-	Ind	
			1779-1891	1779-1891	MSA	
Jefferson	1807	LNC	1960s-	1770s-		
			1757-1891	1757-1891	MSA	MT
Jonesboro	1809	WAS	1918-	1892-	F/Ind	
				1766-1890	MSA	MT
Jonesport	1832	WAS	1854-	1872-	F/Ind	
Joy *(see Troy)*						
Kenduskeag	1852	PEN	1852-	1852-		
				1852-91	MSA	MT
Kennebec *(see Manchester)*						
Kennebunk	1820	YRK	1850-	1739-	Ind	
				1729-1892	MSA	MT
Kennebunkport	1653	YRK	1837-	1856-	Ind	
			1678-1892	1678-1892	MSA	MT
Kilmarnock *(see Medford)*						
Kingfield	1816	FRA	1816-	1892-	Ind	
			1816-62	1816-68	MSA	MT
Kingsbury Pl	1836	PIS	1892-	1892-	F	
			1836-68	1836-68	MSA	MT
Kingville *(see Troy)*						
Kirkland *(see Hudson)*						
Kittery	1652	YRK	1800s-		Ind	
			1648-1896	1674-1892	MSA	MT, V, L
Knox	1819	KNX	1820-	1700s-	Inc/Ind	
				1777-1896	MSA	MT
Lagrange	1832	PEN	1832-	1892-		
				1833-91	MSA	
Lake View Pl	1892	PIS	1905-	1892-		
Lakeville Pl	1868	PEN	1940-	1880-	Inc	
				1862-1955	MSA	
Lamoine	1870	HAN	1870-	1890-		
				1849-1935	MSA	MT
Lebanon	1767	YRK	1969-	1892-		
			1765-1898	1765-1898	MSA	MT, V, L
Lee	1832	PEN	1900-	1870-	F	
			1780-1945	1780-1945	MSA	
Leeds	1801	AND	1801-	1801-		
				1785-1891	MSA	MT
Levant	1813	PEN	1920-	1872-		
				1769-1917	MSA	
Lewiston	1795	AND	1795-	1830-		
			1801-39	1750-1900	MSA	
Liberty	1827	WAL	1856-	1856-	Ind	
				1864-91	MSA	
Ligonia *(see Albion)*						
Limerick	1787	YRK			Inc	V, L
Limestone	1869	ARO	1861-	1892-	F	
				1862-1935	MSA	
				(births)		

Town	Org'd	Cty	TRs	VRs	Codes	NEHGS
Limington	1792	YRK	1792- 1792-1898	1800- 1792-1892	Ind MSA	 V
Lincoln	1829	PEN	1829-	1856 1829-92 *(index to)*	Ind MSA	
Lincoln Pl	1875	OXF	1875-	1890s-		
Lincolnville	1802	WAL	1802-	1802- 1786-1892	F/Ind MSA	 MT, V, L
Linneus	1836	ARO	 1840-92	1840- 1784-1892	 MSA	
Lisbon	1799	AND	1799-	1782- 1782-1893	F/Ind MSA	 MT, V, L
Litchfield	1795	KEN	1922- 1785-1952	1700s- 1785-1952	Ind MSA	 MT
Littleton	1856	ARO		1892-	Ind	
Livermore	1795	AND	1795-	1795- 1762-1891	 MSA	 MT
Livermore Falls	1843	AND	1844-	1892-	Ind	
Long Island Pl	1857	HAN	1900-	1900-	F	
Lovell	1800	OXF	1800-	1800- 1785-1892	Ind MSA	 MT
Lowell	1837	PEN	1900-	1892- 1854-1939	F/Ind MSA	
Lubec	1811	WAS	1820-	1820- 1819-92	Ind MSA	 MT
Ludlow	1864	ARO	1840-	1840-		
Lyman	1778	YRK	1780- 1850-92	1780- 1850-92	F MSA	
Lyndon *(see Caribou)*						
Machias	1784	WAS	1931- 1773-1891	1790- 1773-1892	Ind MSA	
Machiasport	1826	WAS	1966-	1790- 1773-1892	F MSA	
Machisses *(see E. Machias)*						
Macwahoc Pl	1851	ARO	1850- 1851-96	1892- 1851-96	F MSA	
Madawaska	1869	SOM	1869-	1871-	Ind	
Madison	1804	FRA	1892-	1892- 1939-56 *(marriages)*	F	
Madrid	1836	OXF	1956-	1892- 1789-1891	F MSA	 MT
Magalloway Pl	1883	OXF	1952-	1952-	F	
Maine *(see Clifton)*						
Manchester	1850	KEN	1850-	1850- 1808-1908	 MSA	
Mansel *(see Tremont)*						
Mapleton	1878	ARO		1892- 1864-91	 MSA	
Mariaville	1836	HAN	1836-	1875-	Ind	
Marshfield	1846	WAS	1846-	1700s- 1821-91	 MSA	

Town	Org'd	Cty	TRs	VRs	Codes	NEHGS
Mars Hill	1867	ARO	1880s-	1900s-		
				1786-1892	MSA	
Masardis	1839	ARO	1930-	1818-	Ind/F	
Matinicus Isle Pl	1840	KNX	1889-	1818-	Ind/F	
			1840-99	1891-	MSA	
Mattawamkeag	1860	PEN	1860	1865-	Ind	
				1860-91	MSA	
Maxfield	1824	PEN	1962-	1971-	Ind/F	
			1825-91	1825-91	MSA	
Mechanic Falls	1893	AND	1893-	1893-		
Meddybemps	1841	WAS	1946-	1936-	Ind/F	
Medford	1824	PIS		1844-91	MSA	
				(marriage intentions)		
Medway	1875	PEN	1875-	1850s-		
				1850-1940	MSA	
				(marriage intentions)		
Mercer	1804	SOM		1769-1891	MSA/F	
				(marriage intentions)		
Merrill	1895	ARO	1938-	1893-	Ind	
Mexico	1818	OXF	1818-	1883-	Ind/F	
				1818-92	MSA	MT
Millbridge	1848	WAS	1848-	1892-	Ind	
			1848-91	1848-91	MSA	MT
Milburn *(see Skowhegan)*						
Milford	1833	PEN	1952-	1864-	F	
				1864-91	MSA	
				(marriage intentions)		
Millinocket	1901	PEN	1901-	1898-		
Milo	1823	PIS	1823-	1823-	Ind	
				1802-91	MSA	
Minot	1823	AND	1802-	1795-		
				1786-1891	MSA	MT
Monhegan Pl	1839	LNC	1840s-	1900-	Inc	
			1841-89	1841-89	MSA	MT, V, L
Monmouth	1792	KEN	1888-	1800s-	Ind/F	
Monroe	1818	WAL	1820-	1812-	Ind	
				1778-1892	MSA	MT, V, L
Monson	1822	PIS	1920-	1911-	Ind/F	
				1635-1890	MSA	MT
Montgomery *(see Troy)*						
Monticello	1846	ARO		1892-		
			1860-96	1860-96	MSA	MT
Montville	1807	WAL	1802-	1807-	Ind	
			1785-1891	1785-1891	MSA	MT
Moose River	1852	SOM	1900-	late 1800s		
Moro Pl	1850	ARO	1922-	1896-		
Morrill	1855	ARO	1855-	1855-	Ind	
				1781-1891	MSA	MT
Moscow	1816	SOM	1816-	1850-		
				1771-1892	MSA	MT
Mount Chase Pl	1864	PEN	1951-	1871-	Ind	
Mount Desert	1789	HAN	1900-	1894-		
				1806-1932	MSA	V, L

60

Town	Org'd	Cty	TRs	VRs	Codes	NEHGS
Mount Vernon	1792	KEN	1797-	1892- 1775-1903	F MSA	
Naples	1834	CUM	1834-	1892- 1834-91	MSA	MT
Nashville Pl	1889	ARO	1889-	1889-		
New Canada	1881	ARO	1892-	1892-		
New Charleston (see Charleston)						
New Gloucester	1774	CUM	1700-	1700- 1771-1892	Ind MSA	MT
New Limerick	1837	ARO	1861-	1892-		
New Milford (see Alna)						
New Portland	1808	SOM	1836-	1892- 1770-1892	F MSA	
New Sharon	1794	FRA	1800s-	1891- 1797-1953	Ind/F MSA	MT
New Sweden	1895	ARO		1895- 1872-1900	F MSA	MT
New Vineyard	1802	FRA		1892-	F	MT
Newburgh	1819	PEN	1814-	1814- 1828-1939	F MSA	
Newcastle	1753	LNC	1892- 1754-1891	1892- 1754-1891	Ind MSA	
Newfield	1794	YRK	1900-	1897-	Ind/F	
Newport	1814	PEN	1835-50 1866	1892- 1858-91	Ind/Inc MSA	
Newry	1805	OXF	1805- 1805-94	1810- 1805-94	MSA	MT
Nobleboro	1788	LNC	1788-	1914-	Ind/F	V, L
Norridgewock	1788	SOM	1950s- 1674-1892	1620- 1674-1892	Ind MSA	MT
N. Berwick	1831	YRK	1831- 1831-92	1892- 1831-92	MSA	MT, V, L
N. Haven	1846	KNX	1846- 1802-91	1892- 1802-91	MSA	
N. Hill (see Brighton Pl)						
N. Kennebunkport (see Arundel)						
N. Yarmouth	1732	CUM	1732-	1720-	Ind/Inc	V, L
Northfield	1838	WAS	1938-	1838- 1789-1907	F MSA	
Northport	1796	WAL		1896-	Ind/F	V, L
Norway	1797	OXF	1856-	1890- 1700-1892	F MSA	MT
Number 14 Pl	1895	WAS		1875-	Ind	
Number 21 Pl	1895	WAS	1899-	1892-		
Oakfield	1897	ARO	1897-	1892- 1882-91	Ind MSA	MT
Oakland	1873	KEN	1873-	1873-		
Ogunquit	1980	YRK		1871-92	MSA	
(formerly part of Wells)						
Old Orchard Beach	1883	YRK	1883-	1883-	Ind/Inc	
Old Town	1840	PEN	1840-	1820- 1820-91	Ind MSA	MT
Orient	1856	ARO		1892-	F	

Town	Org'd	Cty	TRs	VRs	Codes	NEHGS
Orland	1800	HAN	1792-	1770-	Inc	
				1765-1920	MSA	MT
Orono	1806	PEN	1806-	1806-	Ind/F	
			1806-1907	1806-1907	MSA	MT
Orrington	1788	PEN	1788-	1700s	Ind	
			1643-1887	1643-1893	MSA	MT
Osborn	1895	HAN		1938-		
Otis	1835	HAN	1962-	1898-	Inc	
			1835-1955	1835-1955	MSA	
Otisfield	1798	CUM	1798-	1798-		MT, V, L
Owl's Head	1921	KNX	1921-	1921-		
Oxbow Pl	1895	ARO	1940-	1940-	F	
Oxford	1829	OXF	1892-	1892-	Ind/F	
				1829-1957	MSA	MT
Palermo	1804	WAL	1831-	1908-	Ind/F	
Palmyra	1807	SOM	1807-	1892-		
				1800-92	MSA	
Paris	1793	OXF	1829-	1700-	Ind	
			1793-1906	1795-1902	MSA	MT
Parkman	1822	PIS	1822-	1822-		
				1782-1891	MSA	MT
Parsonsfield	1785	YRK	1785-	late 1700s-		
			1774-1969	1762-1948	MSA	
Passadumkeag	1835	PEN	1935-	1890-	Ind	
				1844-1954	MSA	
Patten	1841	PEN	1841-	1860s-	Ind/F	
				1821-1918	MSA	MT
Pejepscot	1764	AND				
(see also Danville)						
Pembroke	1832	WAS	1832-	1892-	Ind/F	
				1831-92	MSA	
Penobscot	1787	HAN	1880-	1892-		
				1732-1892	MSA	V
Pepperellborough *(see Saco)*						
Perham	1878	ARO	1897-	1897-		
				1855-91	MSA	
Perry	1818	WAS	1965-	1818-	Ind	
				1780-1891	MSA	
Peru	1821	OXF	1821-	1812-		
				1813-97	MSA	MT
Phillips	1812	FRA	1812-	1762-	Ind/Inc	
				1763-1891	MSA	
Phillipsburg *(see Hollis)*						
Phippsburg	1814	SAG	1814-	1807-		
				1825-91	MSA	MT
Pittsfield	1819	SOM	1819-80	1816-	Ind	
			1900-			
			1815-91	1815-91	MSA	MT, V
Pittston	1779	KEN	1777-	1777-	Ind/F	
			1785-1841	1785-1914	MSA	MT, V, L
Pleasant Point		WAS				
Indian Reservation *(part of Perry)*						
Pleasant Ridge Pl	1895	SOM	1852-	1892-	F	
			1852-97	1852-97	MSA	

Town	Org'd	Cty	TRs	VRs	Codes	NEHGS
Plymouth	1826	PEN	1932-	1823-	F	
				1795-1891	MSA	
Poland	1795	AND		1700-	Ind	
			1734-98	1780-1937	MSA	MT
			(proprietors' records)			
Port Watson *(see Brooklin)*						
Portage Lake	1895	ARO	1909-	1892-		
			1875-92	1875-92	MSA	MT
Porter	1807	OXF	1829-	1892		
Portland	1786	CUM	1786-	1714-	Ind	
			1786-1882	1712-1904	MSA	MT
Pownal	1808	CUM	1808-	1808-	Ind/Inc	
			1800-92	1800-92	MSA	
Pownalborough *(see Wiscasset)*						
Prentiss Pl	1858	PEN	1900s-	1880s-	F	
				1841-1939	MSA	MT
Presque Isle	1859	ARO	1892-	1892-	Ind/F	
				1859-92	MSA	MT
Princeton	1832	ARO	1960s-	1892-	F	
				1861-89	MSA	
Prospect	1794	WAL	1889-	1832-	Ind/F	
				1756-1891	MSA	MT
Putnam *(see Washington)*						
Randolph	1887	KEN	1922-	1898-	Ind	MT, V, L
Rangeley	1855	FRA	1855-	1892-	Ind	
				1795-1892	MSA	MT
Rangeley Pl	1895	FRA	1900-	1910-		
Raymond	1803	CUM	1803-	1800-	Ind/F	
				1745-1916	MSA	MT
Readfield	1791	KEN	1790s-	1791-		
				1777-1892	MSA	
Reed Pl	1878	ARO	1800-	1892-		
Richmond	1823	SAG	1823-	1892-	Ind	
				1782-1892	MSA	MT
Ripley	1816	SOM	1892-	1892-	Ind/F	
				1783-1892	MSA	
Rockabema *(see Moro Pl)*						
Robbinston	1811	WAS	1886-	1886-	Ind	
				1857-1937	MSA	
Rockland	1848	KNX	1854-	1892-	Ind	
				1803-92	MSA	MT, V
Rockport	1891	KNX	1791-	1791-	Ind/Inc	
			1783-1892	1783-1892	MSA	MT
Rome	1804	KEN			F	
			1776-1892	1776-1892	MSA	
Roque Bluffs	1891	WAS	1891-	1892-		
Roxbury	1835	OXF		1892-		
Rumford	1800	OXF	1800-	1800-	Ind	
				1800-92	MSA	MT
Sabattus	1840	AND	1700s-	1892-		MT
Saco	1762	YRK	1867-	1762-1867	Ind	
				1717-1898	MSA	
St. Agatha	1899	ARO	1889-	1889-	Ind	

Town	Org'd	Cty	TRs	VRs	Codes	NEHGS
St. Albans	1813	SOM	1914-	1813-	Ind/F	
				1785-1892	MSA	MT
St. Francis	1870	ARO	1892-	1892-		
St. George	1803	KNX	1803-	1700-		
				1737-1891	MSA	MT
St. John Pl	1870	ARO	1950-	1885-		
Sandy River Pl	1905	FRA	1905-	1895-		
Sanford	1768	YRK	1877-	1892-		
			1661-1907	1769-1907	MSA	MT
Sangerville	1814	PIS	1814-	1814-		
				1793-1885	MSA	
Scarborough	1658	CUM	1681-	1700s-	Ind	
			1725-1893	1725-1891	MSA	
Searsmont	1814	WAL	1854-	1854-	Ind/F	
				1854-91	MSA	
Searsport	1845	WAL	1845-	1892-	Ind	
				1801-1939	MSA	MT, V, L
Sebago	1826	CUM		1892-	F	
Sebasticook *(see Benton)*						
Sebec	1812	PIS	1794-	1811-	Ind/Inc	
				1813-53	MSA	
Sebois Pl	1895	PEN	1890-	*ca.* 1890-		
Sedgwick	1789	HAN	1789-	1789-	Ind/F	
				1792-1927	MSA	MT
Shapleigh	1785	YRK	1785-	1785-1873		
				1892-		
			1784-1896	1784-1896	MSA	MT
Sherman	1862	ARO	1904-	1862-	Ind/F	
				1800-92	MSA	
Shirley	1834	PIS	1896-	1890-	Ind/F	
				1797-1883	MSA	
Sidney	1792	KEN	1700-	1800s-	F	
				1772-1892	MSA	V
Skowhegan	1823	SOM	1814-	1780-1	Ind/F	
				1803-1953	MSA	
				(index to births)		
Smithfield	1840	SOM	1850-	1775-	Ind/F	
			1775-1898	1775-1898	MSA	MT
Smyrna	1839	ARO	1866-	1895-	Ind	
			1869-1909	1869-1909	MSA	
Solon	1809	SOM	1804-	1700-		
				1764-1916	MSA	MT
Somerville	1858	LNC	1853-	1883-		
				1798-1892	MSA	
Sorrento	1895	HAN	1940s-	1859-	Ind	
S. Berwick	1814	YRK	1814-	1814-	F	
			1763-1892	1763-1892	MSA	V, L
S. Bristol	1915	LNC	1916-	1916-		MT, V, L
S. Portland	1895	CUM	1933-	1761-	Ind	
			1748-1865	1748-1865	MSA	
S. Thomaston	1848	KNX	1848-	1893-	Ind	
			1780-1893	1780-1893	MSA	MT
Southport	1842	LNC	1842-	1892-	F	
			1842-92	1842-92	MSA	MT

Town	Org'd	Cty	TRs	VRs	Codes	NEHGS
Southwest Harbor	1905	HAN	1905-	1905-	Ind	
Springfield	1834	PEN	1834-78 1903	1898-	Inc	
				1834-97	MSA	
Stacyville	1883	PEN	1874- 1860-76	1872- 1860-76	F MSA	
Standish	1785	CUM	1785- 1785-1892	1790- 1770-1939	Ind/Inc MSA	
Starks	1795	SOM	1796-	1796- 1787-1892	MSA	
Stetson	1831	PEN	1900-	1800s- 1803-94	Ind/F MSA	
Steuben	1795	WAS	1795-	1795-1868 1893- 1769-1900	Ind/Inc MSA	MT
Stockholm	1911	ARO	1891-	1897-	Ind	
Stockton Springs	1857	WAL	1857-	1857- 1832-91	MSA	MT
Stoneham	1834	OXF	1912-	1892- 1837-90	F MSA	MT
Stonington	1897	HAN	1897-	1897-	Ind	
Stow	1833	OXF	1830-	1830-	Ind	
Strong	1801	FRA	1801- 1779-1892	1767- 1779-1892	MSA	
Stroudwater *(see Westbrook)*						
Sullivan	1789	HAN	1795- 1745-1891	1892- 1745-1891	Ind MSA	MT
Sumner	1798	OXF		1833- 1733-1892	MSA	MT
Surry	1803	HAN	1800s-	1700s- 1790-1938	Ind MSA	MT
Swan's Island	1897	HAN	1839-	1850-	Ind/Inc	
Swanville	1818	WAL	1814-	1800s- 1812-91	MSA	MT, V
Sweden	1813	OXF	1953-	1953-	F	MT
Talmadge	1875	WAS	1850-	1850- 1850-93	MSA	
Temple	1803	FRA	1803-	1803- 1784-1892	Ind MSA	MT
Thomaston	1777	KNX	1776-	1776- 1775-1893	Ind MSA	V
Thompsonborough *(see Lisbon)*						
Thorndike	1819	WAL	1819-	1892- 1776-1894	Ind/Inc MSA	
Topsfield	1838	WAS	1860-	1860- 1834-92	Inc MSA	
Topsham	1764	SAG	1826-	1892-	Inc	V, L
Townsend *(see Southport)*						
Tremont	1848	HAN	1848-	1853- 1825-92	Ind MSA	
Trenton	1789	HAN	1901- 1786-1891	1900- 1786-1891	MSA	

Town	Org'd	Cty	TRs	VRs	Codes	NEHGS
Troy	1812	WAL	1812-	1812-		
				1840-91	MSA	MT, V, L
Turner	1786	AND	1785-	1776-	Ind	
			1787-1892	1776-1896	MSA	MT
				1740-1955	MSA	
				(index to VRs)		
Union	1786	OXF	1788-	1795-	Ind/F	
				1789-1914	MSA	
Unity	1804	WAL	1804-	1790-		
				1797-1864	MSA	V, L
Upton	1860	OXF	1830s-	1892-		
Usher *(see Stoneham)*						
Van Buren	1881	ARO	1881-	1838-	Ind/F	
				1838-93	MSA	
Vanceboro	1874	WAS	1938-	1814-	Inc	
Vassalboro	1771	KEN	1700-	1815-	Ind	
			1764-1892	1764-1892	MSA	
Veazie	1853	PEN	1853-	1850-	Ind	
				1852-94	MSA	
Verona	1861	HAN	1955-	1900-	F	
Vienna	1802	KEN	1802-	1802-		
				1752-1893	MSA	
Vinalhaven	1789	KNX	1789-	1790-	Ind	
			1785-1892	1785-1892	MSA	V, L
Wade	1913	ARO	1949-	1899-	Ind/Inc	
Waite	1876	WAS		1892	Ind/Inc	
Waldo	1845	WAL		1892-	Ind/F	MT
Waldoboro	1773	LNC	1773-	1892-		
			1773-1892	1778-1892	MSA	MT
Wales	1816	AND	1836-58	1730s-	Ind/F	
			1921-			
				1759-1900	MSA	
Wallagrass Pl	1870	ARO	1838-	1892-	F	
			1866-1894	1866-1894	MSA	
Waltham	1833	HAN	1890-	1850-		
Warren	1776	KNX	1776-	1845-	Ind	
				1795-1938	MSA	
Warsaw *(see Pittsfield)*						
Washburn	1861	ARO	1912-	1898-	Ind/F	
Washington	1811	KNX	1811-	1812-	Ind/F	
			1800-91			MT
Waterboro	1787	YRK	1787-	1860-	Ind/F	
			1787-1876	1787-1891	MSA	
Waterford	1797	OXF	1798-	1762-	Inc	MT
				1762-1859	MSA	
Waterville	1802	KEN	1802-	1830s-	Ind	
				1813-93	MSA	
				1830-1943	MSA	
				(index to VRs)		
Wayne	1798	KEN	1819-	1770-	F	
			1773-1900	1773-1900	MSA	
Webster *(see Sabattus)*						
Webster Pl	1856	PEN	1920-	1892-		
				1840-91	MSA	

Town	Org'd	Cty	TRs	VRs	Codes	NEHGS
Weld	1816	FRA	1844-	1761-	Ind	
				1766-1895	MSA	
Wellington	1828	PIS	1828-	1898-	Ind/F	
			1823-92	1823-92	MSA	MT
Wells	1653	YRK	1700s-	1600s-	Ind/F	
				1695-1900	MSA	MT
Wesley	1833	WAS	1832-	1776-		
				1887-91 *(births & deaths)*		
				1840-6 *(marriages)*		
W. Bath	1844	SAG	1914-	1845-	Inc	
				1845-1936	MSA	
W. Forks Pl	1893	SOM	1898-	1898-	F	
W. Gardiner	1850	KEN		1850-	Ind	V, L
				1848-92	MSA	
W. Paris	1957	OXF	1958-	1958-	Ind	MT
W. Pittston *(see Randolph)*						
W. Waterville *(see Oakland)*						
Westbrook	1814	CUM	1718-	1892-	Ind	
				1800-92	MSA	
Westfield	1905	ARO	1894-1904	1892-	Ind/Inc	
			1912-			
Westmanland Pl	1895	ARO	1940s	1892-		
Weston	1835	ARO	1835-	1835-	Ind	
				1814-92	MSA	
Westport	1828	LNC		1892-	F	
			1761-1945	1761-1945	MSA	
Whitefield	1809	LNC	1791-	1700s	Ind/F	
			1748-1892	1748-1892	MSA	
Whiting	1825	WAS	1817-	1820s-		
				1814-91	MSA	
Whitneyville	1845	WAS	1890-	1890-	Ind/F	
				1861-91	MSA	
Williamsburg *(see note at end of this table)*						
Willimantic	1881	PIS	1881-	1800s		
Wilton	1803	FRA	1949-	1783-	Ind/Inc	
			1765-1891	1765-1891	MSA	
Windham	1762	CUM	1762-	1837-	Ind/Inc	
			1823-92	1789-1921	MSA	
Windsor	1809	KEN	1894-	1870-	Ind/F	
			1797-1834	1797-1892	MSA	
Winn	1857	PEN	1892-	1872-	Inc	
				1872-1917	MSA	
Winslow	1771	KEN	1771-	1759-	Ind/Inc	
			1771-1891	1771-1891	MSA	V, L
Winter Harbor	1895	HAN	1895-	1895-	Ind	
Winterport	1860	WAL	1860-	1860-	Ind/Inc	
				1860-94	MSA	
Winterville Pl	1895	ARO	1884-	1883-		
				1876-1949	MSA	
Winthrop	1771	KEN	1800s-	1890-	Ind	
				1720-1908	MSA	
Wiscasset	1760	LNC	1760-	1790-	Ind	
			1752-1945	1752-1945	MSA	MT

Town	Org'd	Cty	TRs	VRs	Codes	NEHGS
Woodland	1880	ARO	1875-	1875-	Ind/F	
				1874-91	MSA	
Woodstock	1815	OXF	1815-1908	1815-1908	MSA	MT
Woodville	1895	PEN	1930-	1900-	F	
Woolwich	1759	SAG	1871-	1752-	Ind	
			1760-1828	1756-1895	MSA	
Yarmouth	1849	CUM	1800s-	1815-	Ind	
			1849-92	1830-1910	MSA	
York	1652	YRK	1897-	1832-	Ind	
				1715-1877	MSA	V, L

N.B., although Williamsburg is listed as having submitted its pre-1892 records to the state, it appears on no other list of Maine towns. *The Length and Breadth of Maine* (see BOOKS AND ARTICLES) calls it an unorganized town in Piscataquis County. Settled in 1806 and incorporated in 1820 as the 237th Maine town, the incorporation was repealed in 1939. Part of Williamsburg was set off to Barnard in 1834.

MAINE

The 'District of Maine' was part of Mass. until 1820. Centralized recording of vital records began in 1892. Because the state is so large, it is wise to concentrate on major genealogical research centers, such as the MAINE HISTORICAL SOCIETY LIBRARY in Portland, and the MAINE STATE ARCHIVES and MAINE STATE LIBRARY in Augusta.

STATE HOLIDAYS PECULIAR TO MAINE – REPOSITORIES MAY BE CLOSED – CALL

Patriots' Day (usually 3rd Mon in Apr)

VITAL RECORDS

To 1955:

MAINE STATE ARCHIVES (MSA)

State House Station #84	[207] 287-5795	ME Tpk to Exit 15; Rte 202 toward
Augusta, ME 04333		Augusta; right at rotary on Rte 27
		(State St); 1st driveway past Capitol.
Mon-Fri 8-11:30am & 12:30-4pm		Archives & Library on left.

Open to public; must register; self-service copying (except for fragile originals, by staff) – $.15/page, reader/printer copies, $.50/page; photographic duplication on request; 13 film readers, 2 reader/printers; limited service by mail. **HOLDINGS**: non-current state and municipal records; pre-1930 Superior and Supreme Judicial Court records (originals, except for Lincoln County – film only, originals still at Wiscasset); Civil War records of the Office of the Adjutant General (and some War-of-1812 transcripts from Mass. Archives); Maine Land Office records; Maine county marriage returns (except for Cumberland, Lincoln, Oxford, and Franklin); graves-registration index for veterans (Revolution through World War I); original federal census returns, 1850-80 (with social, agricultural, industrial, and mortality schedules); many town records (see TOWNS, above; vital statistics and town meetings). MSA also has a set of pre-1892 VRs for 75 Maine towns, and films of the entire state's vital statistics for four time periods: 1892-1907, 1908-22, 1923-36, and 1937-55, as well as a Brides index (1892-1991), Grooms and Death indexes (1956-91), and a Divorce index (1892-1983). Filmed census holdings include the 1880, 1900, and 1920 Soundexes, all federal censuses of Maine, 1790-1920 (for 1890, veterans' census only); the 1798 Direct Tax of Maine; Land Office plans (useful for finding pioneers in unorganized areas); deeds for the counties of Oxford (1800-62, western and eastern registries), Somerset (1809-61), Piscataquis (1838-62), Knox (1836-60, transcripts from Lincoln); and Kennebec (1799-1872 – no index); passenger arrivals at Maine ports, 1907-19; Maine Federal Extension records, 1915-48; Board of Assessors' maps; legislative Acts and Resolves, 1820-1967; probate for Aroostook Co. (1840-1900) and Somerset Co. (with index from formation to 1970s); death records of WWI soldiers.

1955 to Present:

STATE OF MAINE – DEPARTMENT OF HUMAN SERVICES

Office of Vital Statistics	[207] 287-3181	See above.
State House Station #11	*(general info)*,	
221 State Street	-3184 *(ordering records)*,	
Augusta, ME 04333-0011	& -1907 (FAX)	

Mon-Fri 8am-5pm

No self-service – all records must be pulled by staff; first 5 free, then $2/book. Mail search, 1 name only, for specific year: $6 plus copies, $6/each; certified, $10/each. Search for 2 years before and after stated date of event, $10 (includes 1 certified copy of record, if located; $4/each additional certified copy) – N.B., *fee is payable whether or not a record is found.* **HOLDINGS**: births, deaths, and marriages, 1923 to present (pre-1923 records at MAINE STATE ARCHIVES); divorces, 1892 to present. Town clerks also have copies of VRs.

FEDERAL CENSUS

All Maine returns, 1790-1920, are on film at the MAINE STATE ARCHIVES; originals, 1850-80, are there as well. (1880 originals are shown only when the film is illegible). Maine returns to 1900 are also on film at the MAINE STATE LIBRARY. The MSA has typescript indexes for Waldo Co. and many other towns; the Waldo indexes are also at the BELFAST PUBLIC LIBRARY. (All federal census schedules for the entire U.S., including Maine, are on film at the NATIONAL ARCHIVES [see NEW ENGLAND chapter].)

STATE CENSUS

The only state census was taken in 1837; little survives. The schedules for Bangor, Portland, and unorganized townships are at the MAINE STATE ARCHIVES; for Eliot, at the MAINE HISTORICAL SOCIETY.

PROBATE AND LAND

These records are held at the county seat. Offices are generally open Mon-Fri 8:30am-5:00pm, but check each entry.

ANDROSCOGGIN COUNTY

Court House
2 Turner Street
Auburn, ME 04210

ME Tpk to Exit 12 into Auburn. Court-house at corner of Court & Turner Sts. When crossing bridge from Lewiston to Auburn, bldg on right at 2nd light.

Probate   [207] 782-0281   See above.
Mon-Fri 8:30am-5pm

Free and open to public; mail inquiries accepted (no extensive research; copies $1/page). **HOLDINGS**: Probate files, 1854 to present (indexed) – wills, administrations, guardianships, conservatorships, changes of name, and adoptions.

Deeds   [207] 782-0191   See above.
Mon-Fri 8am-5pm

Free and open to public; mail inquiries accepted (no extensive research; copies $1/page). **HOLDINGS**: deeds, 1854 to present, and some other documents relating to land (*e.g.*, divorces, lawsuits). Some records have been filmed by LDS.

AROOSTOOK COUNTY

Probate Court   [207] 532-1502   I-95N to Houlton Exit; right on No.
26 Court Street, Suite 103   St; 1 mi to & thru town sq; right; bldg
Houlton, ME   on left.

Mon-Fri 8am-4:30pm

Mail inquiries accepted (copies $1/first page, $.50/each additional; prepayment required). **HOLDINGS**: probates, 1840 to present (indexed). N.B., all post-1953 adoptions are confidential.

TWO AROOSTOOK COUNTY DEED DISTRICTS

Southern – all Aroostook County towns *except* those listed below.

Northern – Allagash Pltn., Caswell Pltn., Connor, Cyr Pltn., Eagle Lake, Fort Kent, Frenchville, Grand Isle, Hamlin, Madawaska, New Canada, St. Agatha, St. Francis, St. John Pltn., Stockholm, Van Buren, Wallagrass Pltn., Westmanland Pltn., Winterville Pltn.

Southern Registry of **Deeds**   [207] 532-1500   Same as above.
26 Court Street, Suite 102
Houlton, ME 04730

Mon-Fri 8am-4:30pm

Free and open to public; mail inquiries accepted (no searches; mailed copies $1/page). In-house copying: self-service, $.25/page; staff, $.50/page. **HOLDINGS:** deeds for southern Aroostook Co., 1808 to present; also, copies of all pre-1808 Washington Co. deeds to land in what became Aroostook Co.

Northern Registry of **Deeds** 13 Hall Street Fort Kent, ME 04743	[207] 834-3925	Take Elm St past Valley Auto to X of Elm & Hall; red brick bldg on corner.

Mon-Fri 8am-4:30pm

Free and open to public; mail inquiries accepted (1-year search only); copying, $1/page. **HOLDINGS:** deeds for northern Aroostook Co., 1846 to present (indexed).

CUMBERLAND COUNTY

Court House 142 Federal Street Portland, ME 04101-4196		ME Tpk N to Exit 6A (I-295); 295 to Exit 7 (Franklin St); right at 4th light on Congress St; left at 1st light on Pearl St; left again. Registry on 1st floor.
Probate Mon-Fri 8:30am-4:30pm	[207] 871-8383	See above.

Free and open to public; mail inquiries accepted; copying, $1/page. **HOLDINGS:** probates (on film), 1908 to present (earlier records destroyed by fire), with index.

Deeds Mon-Fri 8:30am-4:30pm	[207] 871-8389	See above.

Free and open to public; mail inquiries accepted (copies only, no research); staff copying, $1/page. **HOLDINGS:** deeds, 1760 to present, indexed and filmed.

FRANKLIN COUNTY

Court House 38 Main Street Farmington, ME 04938		I-95 to Exit 34 (Waterville); Rt 139 to Norridgewock; Rte 2 to Farmington & Rte 27 (which is Main).
Probate Mon-Fri 8:30am-4pm	[207] 778-5888	See above.

Free and open to public; *simple* mail inquiries accepted; copying, $1/page. **HOLDINGS:** probates, 1838 to present (indexed).

Deeds Mon-Fri 8:30am-4pm	[207] 778-5889 & -5899 (FAX)	See above.

Free and open to public; mail and FAX inquiries accepted (mail: $.75/page plus $1 postage; FAX: $1/page plus $1 FAX fee); copying, $.75/page. **HOLDINGS:** deeds, 1838 to present (indexed).

HANCOCK COUNTY

Court House
60 State Street
Ellsworth, ME 04605

I-95 to Ellsworth Exit; Rte 1A about 25
mi to Ellsworth; right at Dunkin'
Donuts; right at light on State.

Probate   [207] 667-8434   See above.
Mon-Fri 8:30am-4pm

Free and open to public; *limited* mail inquiries accepted; copying, $1/page in person, $1.50/page by mail.
HOLDINGS: probates, 1790 to present (indexed).

Deeds   [207] 667-8353   See above.
Mon-Fri 8:30am-4pm

Free and open to public; mail inquiries accepted (exact year required; no research); staff copying,
$1.50/page, self-service, $1/page. **HOLDINGS**: deeds, land records, and surveys, 1790 to present
(indexed).

KENNEBEC COUNTY

Probate Court   [207] 622-7558   Rte I-95N to Augusta/Winthrop Exit;
95 State Street   1st right (Western Av); to end; go entire-
Augusta, ME 04330   ly around rotary; take last Exit off rotary
                                                  before Western; bear left for State. Bldg
Mon-Fri 8am-4pm   just past Correctional Facility.

Free and open to public; mail inquiries accepted ($10 search fee); copying, $1/page. **HOLDINGS**:
probates, 1799 to present (indexed and filmed) – include petitions for probate of wills, intestacies,
guardianships, conservatorships, adoptions, changes of names, and petitions to establish parental rights
and responsibilities.

Registry of **Deeds**   [207] 622-0431   Across State St from Correctional
1 Weston Court   & -1598 (FAX)   Facility (County Jail); see above. Brick
Augusta, ME 04330   bldg on right.

Mail: P.O. Box 1053, Augusta, ME 04332

Mon-Fri 8am-4pm

Free and open to public; limited mail inquiries accepted; copying, $1/page; FAX, $2.50/page.
HOLDINGS: deeds, 1799 to present (indexed and filmed).

KNOX COUNTY

Court House
62 Union Street
Rockland, ME 04841

I-95N becomes Rte 1; follow to Rockland. Bldg on corner of Union &
Limerock.

Probate   [207] 594-0427   See above.
Mon-Fri 8am-4pm

Free and open to public; mail inquiries accepted; copying, $1/page. **HOLDINGS**: probates, 1860 to present (indexed and filmed).

| **Deeds** | [207] 594-0422 | See above. |

Mon-Fri 8am-4pm

Free and open to public; mail inquiries accepted (copies only; complete citation required); copying, $1/page. **HOLDINGS**: deeds, 1760 to present (indexed and filmed).

LINCOLN COUNTY

Court House
Route #1/P.O. Box 249
Wiscasset, ME 04578

I-95N becomes Rte 1; follow to Wiscasset; bldg on right of High St, just past jail/sheriff's.

Probate [207] 882-7392 See above.
Mon-Fri 8am-4pm

Free and open to public; mail inquiries accepted ($10 for research); copying, $1/page. **HOLDINGS**: probates, 1760 to present (indexed).

Deeds [207] 882-7431 See above.
Mon-Fri 8am-4pm

Free and open to public; reader/printer; mail inquiries accepted; staff copying, $1/first page, $.50/each consecutive page. **HOLDINGS**: deeds, 1760 to present (indexed). N.B.: also naturalization records, Revolutionary pension files, *etc.*

OXFORD COUNTY

Court House
26 Western Avenue *or*
P.O. Box 179
South Paris, ME 04281

I-95N to Exit 11 (at Gray); Rte 26N to So. Paris.

Probate [207] 743-6671 See above.
Mon-Fri 8am-4pm

Free and open to public; mail inquiries (copies only); copying, $1/page. **HOLDINGS**: probates, 1820 to present (some pre-1820). Indexed.

TWO OXFORD COUNTY DEED DISTRICTS

Eastern – all Oxford Co. towns *except* those listed below.

Western – Brownfield, Denmark, Fryeburg, Hiram, Lovell, Porter, Stoneham, Stow, and Sweden.

Eastern Registry of **Deeds** [207] 743-6211 See above.
Mon-Fri 8am-4pm

Free and open to public; mail inquiries (copies only); copying, $1/page. **HOLDINGS**: deeds, 1806 to present (indexed).

Western Registry of **Deeds** [207] 935-2565 I-95 to Exit 8 (Westbrook); Rte 302 into
12 Portland Street Fryeburg.
Fryeburg, ME 04037

Mon-Fri 9am-noon & 1-4pm

Free and open to public; mail inquiries (copies only); copying, $1/page. **HOLDINGS**: deeds, 1800 to present (indexed).

PENOBSCOT COUNTY

Court House I-95 to Hammond St Exit. From S, right;
97 Hammond Street from N, left. Toward downtown Bangor.
Bangor, ME 04401 Courthouse on left – 3-story brick bldg, corner of Court & Hammond Sts.

Probate [207] 942-8769 See above.
Mon-Fri 8am-4:30pm

Free and open to public; mail inquiries accepted ($10 fee for research, otherwise copies only); copying, $1/page. **HOLDINGS**: probates, 1816 to present. Computerized indexes, 1816-93, for wills, administrations, guardianships, and adoptions; 1893-1915, for wills and administrations; 1937 to present, for estates.

Deeds [207] 942-8797 See above.
Mon-Fri 8am-4:30pm

Free and open to public; mail inquiries accepted (names, dates, and places desired); copying, $1/page. **HOLDINGS**: deeds, 1814 to present (indexed by owner's name).

PISCATAQUIS COUNTY

Court House I-95 to Exit 37; Rtes 7 & 16 to Dexter,
51 East Main Street then 7 to Dover-Foxcroft.
Dover-Foxcroft, ME 04426

Probate [207] 564-2431 See above.
Mon-Fri 8:30am-4pm

Free and open to public; prepaid mail requests accepted; staff copying only, $1/page. **HOLDINGS**: probates, 1838 to present (indexed).

Deeds [207] 564-2411 See above.
Mon-Fri 8:30am-4pm

Free and open to public; mail inquiries accepted with SASE; copying, $1/page. **HOLDINGS**: deeds, 1838 to present (indexed).

SAGADAHOC COUNTY

Court House   Directions unavailable.
752 High Street *or*
P.O. Box 246
Bath, ME 04530

Register of **Probate**   [207] 443-8218   See above.
Mon-Fri 8:30am-4:30pm

Free and open to public; mail inquiries accepted ($5 plus copies); staff copying, $1/first page, $.50/each additional. **HOLDINGS**: probates, 1854 to present (indexed).

Registry of **Deeds**   [207] 443-8214   See above.
Mon-Fri 8:30am-4:30pm

Free and open to public; mail inquiries accepted; staff copying, $1/page; copies of plans, $5. **HOLDINGS**: deeds, 1826 to present (indexed).

SOMERSET COUNTY

Court House   At Skowhegan P.O. on Water St, turn
High and Court Streets   onto No. Av, then right on High.
Skowhegan, ME 04976

Probate   [207] 474-3322   See above.
Mon-Fri 8:30am-4:30pm

Free and open to public; mail inquiries accepted (staff will search indexes and advise as to contents); copying, $1/first page, $.50/each additional. **HOLDINGS**: probates, 1809 to present (indexed and filmed).

Deeds   [207] 474-3421   See above.
Mon-Fri 8:30am-4:30pm

Free and open to public; mail inquiries accepted; copying, $1/page. **HOLDINGS**: deeds, 1809 to present (indexed).

WALDO COUNTY

Probate Court   [207] 338-2780,   Downtown, at corner of High & Market
172 Church Street *or*   -2963, & -6360   Sts, in Superior Court bldg (which also
P.O. Box 323   (FAX)   has entry on Church St). Next to City
Belfast, ME 04915-0323   Hall & Police.

Mon-Fri 9am-4pm

Free and open to public; mail inquiries accepted ($5 per estate looked up, plus copies); copying, $1/page. **HOLDINGS**: probates, 1827 to present (indexed) – *e.g.*, probates of estates, testate and intestate;

guardianships/conservatorships for minors and adults; adoptions; name-changes; trusts; emergency protection for minors; *etc.*

Registry of **Deeds**	[207] 338-1710	Same *street* as probate (see above).
137 Church Street		
Belfast, ME 04915		

Mon-Fri 8am-4pm

Free and open to public; mail inquiries accepted (must include names, dates, and places); copying, $1/page. **HOLDINGS**: deeds, 1700 to present (indexed) – also, copies of all Hancock Co. deeds to what became Waldo County land, 1789-1827.

WASHINGTON COUNTY

Court House	After Machiasport Savings Bank on
47 Court Street *or*	Main St, left on Center St, then left on
P.O. Box 297	Court. Parking on right; 2nd brick bldg
Machias, ME 04654	on right from parking area.

Probate	[207] 255-6591	See above.
Mon-Fri 8am-4pm		

Free and open to public; handicapped accessible; mail inquiries accepted; copying, $1/page. **HOLDINGS**: probates, 1789 to present (indexed); 1850, '60, and '70 censuses (indexed).

Deeds	[207] 255-6512	See above.
Mon-Fri 8am-4pm		

Free and open to public; handicapped accessible; mail inquiries accepted; copying, $.50/page in person, $1/page by mail. **HOLDINGS**: deeds, 1784 to present (indexed).

YORK COUNTY

Court House	ME Tpk to Exit 4; right after toll. 12
Court Street *or*	mi to Alfred. Right at blinking yellow
P.O. Box 399	light. Courthouse on left, across from
Alfred, ME 04002	PO.

Probate	[207] 324-1577	See above.
Mon-Fri 8:30am-4:30pm		

Free and open to public; copying, $1/page; mail inquiries accepted (copies only). **HOLDINGS**: probates, 1687 to present. (See William M. Sargent, ed., *Maine Wills. 1640-1760.*; John E. Frost, *Maine Probate Abstracts* [to 1800]; and Joseph C. Anderson II, *York County, Maine Will Abstracts 1801-1858.*)

Deeds	[207] 324-1576	See above.
Mon-Fri 8:30am-4:30pm		

Free and open to public; copying, $1.25/page; mail inquiries accepted (no research). **HOLDINGS**: deeds, 1642 to present (filmed). (See various eds., *York Deeds* [1641-1737], 18 vols.)

CEMETERY RECORDS

While Maine has many designated graveyards, in early years the dear departed were often buried on private property – literally, the pasture or back yard. Before WWII, the DAR and others compiled many public and private cemetery transcripts. Among the major holders of such for Maine are the MAINE HISTORICAL SOCIETY, the MAINE STATE LIBRARY, and NEHGS. Some Maine public libraries have local transcripts not to be found elsewhere.

The MAINE STATE LIBRARY holds the records of the Surname Index Project (SIP) of the MAINE OLD CEMETERY ASSOCIATION (MOCA), covering the gravestones of hundreds of thousands of people who died in Maine from 1650 to 1900. The index is at NEHGS, the Lynnfield Public Library, and elsewhere. The MAINE STATE LIBRARY answers mail requests by searching these records for individual names, and assists in-house users. Copies, $.10/page; $1 minimum for out-of-state mail requests.

MAINE OLD CEMETERY ASSOCIATION (MOCA)

> P.O. Box 641
> Augusta, ME 04332-0641
> **Web**: http://www.rootsweb.com/~memoca/moca/htm

"Dedicated [since 1969] to the preservation of Maine's neglected cemeteries." Dues, $5/year, $100/life; limited mail inquiries accepted, $5/search. Coordinates the Bicentennial Project (BIP) (see under MILITARY RECORDS) and MOCA Index Project (MIP – a statewide compilation of Revolutionary-veteran gravestones; series 1 and 2 are on film at many libraries; the MAINE STATE LIBRARY has original bound copies). **HOLDINGS**: MOCA newsletters; MIP records; Marble Monumental Works records. Has published *York County Cemetery Inscriptions*, 4 vols. (Picton Press, limited number of copies available).

CHURCH RECORDS

Maine church records (baptism, marriage, and burial) are a major untapped genealogical resource. Most towns have some pre-1892 records (mostly baptisms and marriages). The MAINE HISTORICAL SOCIETY has transcripts, published and manuscript, of Congregational church registers; Quaker records are at the MAINE HISTORICAL SOCIETY. Few Episcopal, and almost no Methodist, registers have been transcribed – this is an open field for those eager to contribute.

MILITARY RECORDS

The major published work is *Soldiers, Sailors, and Patriots of the Revolutionary War, Maine* (1982), by Carleton E. and Sue G. Fisher.

Orono's FOGLER LIBRARY (University of Maine) is custodian of MOCA's BIP ("Bicentennial Project," see above), which has produced (in 1977 and 1981) a card index of Revolutionary veterans buried in Maine (to be updated at intervals). Fogler will mail copies for $2/card; include a long stamped envelope. Copies of the index are at the MAINE STATE LIBRARY, the MAINE HISTORICAL SOCIETY, and the CUTLER LIBRARY.

See also (under BOOKS AND ARTICLES) the list of printed military records in Frost's *Maine Genealogy: A Bibliographical Guide*. For pre-1820 military records, consult Mass. repositories as well.

(See also MAINE STATE ARCHIVES under VITAL RECORDS.)

IMMIGRATION AND NATURALIZATION

Records of immigration and naturalization are kept by the court in which the action occurred, and may be obtained directly from the court clerk. The Portland courthouse has a card index to all Maine naturalizations in any court, 1798-1906; there is a copy at the NATIONAL ARCHIVES in Waltham (see NEW ENGLAND chapter). After 1906, naturalization became a federal function, and records from that year onward may be got either from the local court house or the Immigration and Naturalization Service (INS; Department of Justice) in Washington, D.C. To request such a record from Washington, get the current form at the NATIONAL ARCHIVES (see NEW ENGLAND chapter); name, date, and court of naturalization must be known; fee is $10 for up to 20 pp.

See also this section in the CONNECTICUT chapter.

NEWSPAPERS

The best collection of Maine newspapers, by far, is at the FOGLER LIBRARY, on the University of Maine's Orono campus. Significant collections will also be found at the MAINE HISTORICAL SOCIETY LIBRARY in Portland; Colby College in Waterville; and the MAINE STATE LIBRARY in Augusta (which has Augusta, Bangor, Lewiston, and Portland papers only). Go also to the major towns themselves, which often keep archives of their own newspapers; the earlier years are typically kept at the town library.

See also Charles S. Candage and Ruth L. P. Candage, *Vital Records Published in Rockland, Maine Prior to 1892*, 2 vols. (1989: Camden, ME, Picton Press), a compilation of announcements of births, marriages, and deaths – spanning the entire mid-coastal region – which appeared in the *Lime Rock Gazette, Rockland Gazette*, and *Courier-Gazette* from 1846 to 1891.

CIVIL AND CRIMINAL COURT RECORDS

Maine's *own* early civil and criminal court records (as distinct from those for Mass. – of which it was a part until 1820) have been printed as *Province and Court Records of Maine* [1636-1727], 6 vols. (1928-75: Portland, Maine Historical Society). These are, in effect, records for York Co. – Maine's only county until 1760. The Mass. court structure was complex, and changed over time; see Catherine S. Menand, *A Research Guide to the Massachusetts Courts and Their Records*, 135 pp. and 1 fiche (1987: Boston, Massachusetts Supreme Judicial Court – Archives and Records Preservation).

For later years, York and Lincoln Cos. retain original records at their county courthouses; the rest of the counties have sent their original early records to the MAINE STATE ARCHIVES (which has also pre-1930 Superior and Supreme Judicial Court records). These records are all for *county* courts of common pleas, which handled all civil cases; records of legal processes occurring in Maine which passed through a *higher* (*i.e.*, statewide) court would now be in Mass. For example, before 1820, *appeals* from Maine courts went to Suffolk Co.; these records are now at the MASSACHUSETTS STATE ARCHIVES.

Past a certain point – which varies from county to county – later records are still at the county courthouses; call them for exact years.

LIBRARIES

Most Maine towns have public libraries – generally on the small side – which may contain items of genealogical interest. Many are open no more than 12 hours a week, and undertake no research. For a list, with hours, consult the *American Library Directory*.

AUBURN PUBLIC LIBRARY

49 Spring Street [207] 782-3191   ME Tpk to Exit 12; left off ramp; 5 mi
Auburn, ME 04210   into Auburn. At 3rd light (Court St &
Web: http://www.auburn.lib.me.us/genealogy.html   Minot Av), take right.
E-mail: sarah@auburn.lib.me.us   Library on left at next **X**.

winter: Mon, Thu 9am-8pm; Tue, Wed, Fri -6pm; Sat –5pm
summer: Mon 9am-8pm; Tue-Fri -6pm

Free and open to public; copying, $.20/page; mail and e-mail inquiries accepted (searches limited to library and Auburn City Clerk's office). **HOLDINGS**: genealogy and history collection (primarily local), housed in 'the cage' – *e.g.*: Auburn/Lewiston directories; local census on film (1800-1920, with indexes); Edward Little High School yearbooks; *Maine Register* (annual list of public officials); Maine and Mass. genealogies (over 250) and town histories; *NEHGR*; *Mayflower Descendant*. See website (above) for more complete description.

AUGUSTA – MAINE STATE ARCHIVES (see under VITAL RECORDS)

AUGUSTA – MAINE STATE LIBRARY

State House Station #64 [207] 287-5600   ME Tpk to Exit 15; Rte 202
Augusta, ME 04333   toward Augusta. Right at rotary
Web: http://www.state.me.us/msl   on Rte 27 (State St). 1st drive-
                                           way past Capitol. Archives and
Mon-Fri 9am-5pm (*all year*)   Library on left.
Sat noon-5pm (*Sep-Jun*)

Self-service copying, $.15/page; 9 microform readers, of which 5 are reader/printers ($.30/copy); out-of-state mail research-requests not accepted, but list of local researchers available; genealogical materials do not circulate. **HOLDINGS**: strongest for Maine, N.H., and Mass. (some on other New England states), as well as Maritime and French Canada; Maine censuses, 1800-50, on film (with indexes for most New England censuses, 1790-1850); vital and church records for many New England towns; 129 volumes of early cemetery transcripts from the 'Maine Index Project' by the MAINE OLD CEMETERY ASSOCIATION (MOCA); the *MOCA Surname Index* (200 reels of film); the *Bicentennial Index Project* for graves of Revolutionary veterans; DAR Bible records, town VRs, *etc.*; genealogical 'how-to' books; the Munsell supplement for works at State Library (locates 'buried' references — similar to NEHGS's Greenlaw Index); many periodicals, including *The American Genealogist*, *Mayflower Descendant*, *NEHGR*, *New York Genealogical and Biographical Record*, and *Maine Genealogist*; DAR and other lineage books; family histories; surname and heraldic references; "Burke's" publications; *American*

Genealogical and Biographical Index; New England regional, state, county, and town histories; and Maine Historical Society collections.

BANGOR PUBLIC LIBRARY

145 Harlow Street	[207] 947-8336	Rte I-95 to Bangor/Brewer Exit
Bangor, ME 04401		(Rte 1); to Main St; thru busi-
Web: http://www.bpl.lib.me.us		ness district. Right at X; left at
		lights, on Harlow, past City Hall
Mon-Thu 9am-9pm; Fri, -5pm		to library.
summer: Mon-Fri 9am-7pm		

Free and open to public; self-service copying; $.10/page, film/fiche copying, $.25/page. **HOLDINGS**: family histories; index to *Bangor Historical Magazine*; part of Charles E. Banks ms. collection (remainder at NEHGS and Library of Congress).

BATH HISTORICAL SOCIETY

Patten Free Library	[207] 443-5141	Rte 1 to Washington St Exit; if
33 Summer Street		from S, left; if from N, right;
Bath, ME 04530		take Washington to park – PFL
		only bldg (yellow brick); corner
Tue-Sat noon-4pm (*summers*: closed Sat)		of Washington & Summer.

Free admission for all to 'History Room;' donations welcome. One staffer, shared with PFL, volunteers from BHS; 1 (b&w/color) copier ($.25/each, b&w; $1-2/each, color), 1 film and 1 fiche reader/printer ($.25/each); no circulation. Annual dues: $10/student, $20/individual, $30/family, $50/organization (includes bi-monthly newsletter, and *Times of Bath* [3 issues/year]). **HOLDINGS**: focus on Sagadahoc County; general genealogical and historical references; town histories; VRs for all Sagadoc towns, beginning to 1892 – for Bath, to date (except births); some state military records (compiled lists, Revolution through WWI); journals; newsletters; photos; cemetery records; large set of Bath newspapers on film, 1824 to date.

BATH – MAINE MARITIME MUSEUM (ARCHIVES)

243 Washington Street	[207] 443-1316	Rte I-95 to Exit 22 to Rte 1
Bath, ME 04530		to Bath. Just before underpass,
		Historic Bath Exit. Right at
For research, *call for appointment*, Mon-Fri		light on Washington. Museum
		on left, past Bath Iron Works.

Free and open to public; staff copying. **HOLDINGS**: maritime photos and manuscripts; index of Maine ship captains; ship logs; family histories and pictures; newspapers.

BELFAST FREE LIBRARY

106 High Street	[207] 338-3884	From Rte 1, right into business
Belfast, ME 04915		district (High St).

Mon 9:30am-8pm; Tue, Thu, Fri -6pm; Wed noon-8pm; Sat 10am-2pm

Free and open to public; mail inquiries accepted (first ½ hour free; up to 2 hours extra, $10/hour [your authorization required]); most records copyable, $.10/page. **HOLDINGS**: Belfast and Waldo County history; genealogies; photos; newspapers.

BRUNSWICK – HAWTHORNE-LONGFELLOW LIBRARY

Bowdoin College   [207] 725-3280   Rte I-95 to Exit 22 to Brunswick;
Brunswick, ME 04011   straight to business district. Right on
Web: http://www.bowdoin.edu/dept/library   Maine St, past college. Library last bldg
on campus, on left.

Mon-Sat 8:30am-midnight; Sun 10am-midnight
summer & vacations: Mon-Fri 8:30am-5pm

No fees; mainly for students; copying service, $.05/page. **HOLDINGS**: Maine and New England genealogies.

MACHIASPORT HISTORICAL SOCIETY (GATES HOUSE)

P.O. Box 301   [207] 255-8461   Enter Machias on Rte 1 from W; at
Machiasport, ME 04665-0301   bottom of College Hill, Rte 92 3 mi to
Machiasport town hall. Gates Hse 200
Tue-Sat 12:30-4:30pm   yds past Hall, on left.

No fees, but donation welcomed; mail inquiries accepted with SASE; copying, $.20/page. **HOLDINGS**: records of early local families; Machiasport census records; Maritime Room with artifacts, some journals and logs.

MADAWASKA HISTORICAL SOCIETY LIBRARY

Main Street   [207] 728-3606   Downtown, on US Rte 1.
Madawaska, ME 04756

Mon-Fri 10am-8pm; Sat 1-3pm

Free and open to public; film reader/printer; no copier; no mail service. **HOLDINGS**: French-Canadian and Acadian genealogies; photos; maps; 40-volume St. John Valley genealogical collection; New Brunswick VRs, 1888-91; Aroostook County censuses; genealogies and family-reunion books; computer with some family lines.

ORONO – RAYMOND H. FOGLER LIBRARY – SPECIAL COLLECTIONS DEPT.

University of Maine   [207] 581-1686   Rte I-95 to Old Town Stillwater
Orono, ME 04469   Exit; straight to 3rd light. Right on
Web: http://www.libraries.maine.edu/marspecoll   College Av; 2 mi to campus.
/default.htm   Entrance on left, library at end
of mall.
Mon-Fri 9am-4pm; Sun 1-5pm

No fees; copying service; film readers. **HOLDINGS**: Maine newspapers on film; *Index of Revolutionary Veterans Buried in Maine* (see under MILITARY RECORDS).

PORTLAND – MAINE HISTORICAL SOCIETY LIBRARY

485 Congress Street   [207] 774-1822   ME Tpk to Exit 6A (I-295) to
Portland, ME 04101   Exit 5A (Congress); E thru busi-
Web: http://www.mainehistory.com   ness district. Library on left;
E-mail: postmaster@mainehistory.com   parking garage nearby.

Tue, Fri, 2nd & 4th Sat of month 10am-4pm
(*except holiday weekends*)

Free access to collections plus book-stack privileges for members; non-members pay $2/hour or $10/day for access to collections, but no stack privileges; $15 buys 3-day stack pass. Copying, $.25/page; 2 film readers, 1 reader/printer. Mail inquiries accepted ($20 fee plus copies). **HOLDINGS**: 75,000 monographs and serials published since 1497; world's premier collection of printed materials on Maine history. State, county, and local histories; family histories; early Maine newspapers; Maine censuses on film, 1790-1920; maps and atlases; Maine VRs; church and cemetery records; city and county directories; biographies; dictionaries and general references; magazines and journals of Maine interest; manuscripts and special collections; *etc*.

PORTLAND PUBLIC LIBRARY

5 Monument Square   [207] 871-1700   Sq downtown on Congress St;
Portland, ME 04101   parking garages, lots nearby.
Web: http://www.portlandlibrary.com

Mon, Wed, Fri 9am-5pm; Tue, Thu noon-9pm

Self-service copying, $.10/page; 1 film reader; 7 film and 2 fiche reader/printers, $.25/page; mail-order searches limited to specific dates. **HOLDINGS**: the 'Maine Collection,' relating to Maine by subject, author, or publisher. Town histories, Portland directories from 1823, newspapers from 1785. Library does not specialize in genealogy.

SACO – DYER LIBRARY

York Institute Museum   [207] 283-3861   Rte I-95 to Saco / Old Orchard Beach
371 Main Street   [207] 282-3031   Exit on Main (Rte 1); S .6 mi. Library
Saco, ME 04072   & Museum on left.

Mon, Wed, Fri 10am-5pm; Tue, Thu -8pm; Sat 9am-noon
Maine & Saco History Room: Tue 1-3pm; Thu 10am-noon

Copying. **HOLDINGS**: 6,000 documents and manuscripts of Saco and York County history; 360 volumes of 18th- and 19th-century newspapers; town histories; family histories and photos. References include *York Deeds*, *Essex Institute Historical Collections*, and *NEHGR*.

SEARSPORT – STEPHEN PHILLIPS MEMORIAL LIBRARY and **PENOBSCOT MARINE MUSEUM**

Church Street   Off Rte 1; last bldg in complex.
Searsport, ME 04974
Web: http://www.penobscotmarinemuseum.org/lib.htm

Mon-Fri 9am-4pm

Copying, $.25/page; film reader; donations welcome for mail service; no interlibrary loan. **HOLDINGS**: ship registers, logs; photos; customs records; local histories; Priscilla Jones genealogy collection (notes on 850 families); published genealogies; census and vital records.

SPRINGVALE PUBLIC LIBRARY

226 Main Street   [207] 324-4624   Main Street is Rte 109. On-street
Springvale, ME 04083   parking.
Web: http://www.springvale.lib.me.us

Mon-Thu 10am-8pm; Fri -5pm; Sat -4pm

Copying, $.20/page; film reader; fiche reader. Most materials do not circulate. No interlibrary loan of genealogical materials. Mail answered if accompanied by SASE. **HOLDINGS**: York County town histories; family histories; Sanford vital records, including cemetery; Sanford town reports and directories; York County census records on film; early Sanford/Springvale newspapers; Sanford/Springvale photos; *Sprague's Journal* and *Old Eliot*; works on Mayflower families and early American immigrants; IGI for U.S., Canada, England, Ireland, Scotland, and France. Library has begun adding French-Canadian and Acadian records.

HISTORICAL SOCIETY OF WELLS AND OGUNQUIT

Meetinghouse Museum   [207] 646-4775   ME Tpk to Exit 2, left on Rte 109; to
    and Library   end, then right on Rte 1S. Museum &
P.O. Box 801 / Post Road   library just past 1st light, on right,
Wells, ME 04090   opposite Wells Plaza.

All year: Thu 1-4pm; *May 15-Oct 15*: Wed 1-4pm; Sat 9am-1pm

Members get discount on copies. Mail queries: $5 for short search, $15/hour for extended. **HOLDINGS**: southern York County history and genealogy; 100 manuscripts on early Wells families; cemetery, census, church, military, pension, and vital records.

LDS FAMILY HISTORY CENTERS

Augusta *(see Farmingdale)*

Bangor – 639 Grandview Avenue (corner of Essex and Grandview); [207] 942-7310 x 816; Tue-Thu 10am-3pm & 6:30-8:30pm; Sat 10am-2pm (closed 3rd Sat of month)

Cape Elizabeth – 29 Ocean House Road; [207] 767-5000; Wed, Thu 1-9pm; Sat 1-5pm

Caribou – 67 Hardison Avenue; [207] 492-4381; Wed, Thu 6-9pm; Sat 9am-5pm

Farmingdale – 4 Hasson Street; [207] 582-1827; Tue, Thu 9am-8pm

Farmington – Perham Heights; [207] 778-4038; Tue 9am-9pm; Thu 9am-5pm; Sat 10am-2pm

Oxford – Skeetfield Road; [207] 743-8125; Wed 10am-4pm & 6:30-8:30pm; Sat 10am-2pm

Portland *(see Cape Elizabeth)*

Rockland – Old County Road; [207] 594-1018; Tue 9am-3pm; Wed eve by appointment; Thu 4-9pm

Topsham – Pinewood Drive; [207] 353-6070 (Harriett Anthony, librarian [her home, apparently]); by appointment only; currently has IGI, Ancestral File, and Social Security Death Index CDs only, and cannot order LDS films.

Waterville – 50 Washington Street; [207] 873-0054; Wed, Thu 10am-3pm & 6:30-8:30pm

(For FHC holdings, see NEW ENGLAND chapter.)

SOCIETIES

MAINE GENEALOGICAL SOCIETY (MGS)

> P.O. Box 221
> Farmington, ME 04938
> **Web**: http://www.rootsweb.com/~megs/MaineGS.htm

Founded in 1976 "to collect, preserve, and publish genealogical records, and to promote and encourage interest in genealogy in … Maine." Annual dues, $20 (includes third-class postage for mailings; first-class is optional – $7 more); life, $250 (includes first-class postage). 1,200 active members in 50 states, all Canadian provinces, and several foreign countries. Spring and fall meetings each year rotate around the state. Local chapters hold independent meetings in Greater Portland, Midcoast, Hancock County, Pejepscot, Sandy River, Taconnett Falls, and Boothbay region. Publications: *Maine Genealogist* (formerly *Maine Seine*; Feb, May, Aug, and Nov) and the *Maine Genealogical Society Newsletter* (Mar, Jun, Sep, and Dec) – both included in dues. MGS has also put out six volumes of *Maine Families in 1790*, several volumes of county marriage records to 1892, York County probate abstracts to 1800, and York County will abstracts, 1801-58.

MAINE HISTORICAL SOCIETY (MHS) (see also under LIBRARIES)

> 485 Congress Street
> Portland, ME 04101

Dues: $30/person, $40/family. Annual meeting; place rotates. Publications: *Maine History* (with membership) – no queries; articles must relate to Maine history; scattered back issues available. The MHS has also published six volumes of *Maine Province and Court Records*.

MAINE OLD CEMETERY ASSOCIATION (MOCA) (see under CEMETERY RECORDS)

YORK COUNTY GENEALOGICAL SOCIETY

Thelma L. Remick
P.O. Box 431
Eliot, ME 03903

Founded in 1985 "to share and mutually assist in the research of family genealogy, also to locate, compile and make available genealogical source data pertaining to York County." Dues: $12/individual; $10/institution (*e.g.*, library). Regular meetings on the fourth Wednesday of Mar, Apr, May, Aug, Sep, and Oct. Quarterly *Journal* (from 1985). N.B., all correspondence concerning queries, membership, *etc.* should be accompanied by SASE.

PERIODICALS

FOREBEARS IN YOUR MAINE FAMILY TREE
P.O. Box 2566
Kennebunkport, ME 04046

$20/year (4 issues). Published by Joanna W. Foust, Biddeford.

THE MAINE GENEALOGIST (formerly "The Maine Seine")
P.O. Box 221
Farmington, ME 04938

4 issues/year. Published by Penmor Lithographers; Joseph C. Anderson II, editor.

THE SECOND BOAT
P.O. Box 2782
Kennebunkport, ME 04046

$20/year (6 issues plus index). Published by Pentref Press; Rosemary E. Bachelor, editor.

BOOKS AND ARTICLES

Anderson, Joseph Crook II, *York County, Maine Will Abstracts 1801-1858* (1997: Camden, ME, Picton Press).

Attwood, Stanley Bearce, *The Length and Breadth of Maine* (repr. ed., 1977: Orono, ME, University of Maine at Orono Press).

Fisher, Carleton E. and **Sue G.**, *Soldiers, Sailors and Patriots of the Revolutionary War, Maine* (1982: Louisville, KY, National Society of the Sons of the American Revolution).

Frost, John E., *Maine Genealogy: A Bibliographical Guide* (rev. ed., 1985: ?Portland, Maine Historical Society).

_____, "Maine Genealogy: Some Distinctive Aspects," *NEHGR* 131[1974]:243-66; also in Ralph J. Crandall, ed., *Genealogical Research in New England* (1984: Baltimore, Genealogical Publishing Co.).

_____, *Maine Probate Abstracts, Volume 1, 1687-1775, Volume 2, 1775-1800* (1991: Camden, ME, Picton Press).

Gray, Ruth, *Maine Families in 1790,* vols. 1-6 (1988+: Camden, ME, Picton Press and Boston, NEHGS).

Haskell, John D., ed., *Maine: A Bibliography of Its History* (1977: Boston, G. K. Hall); review by John E. Frost in *NEHGR* 132[1978]:146-8.

Noyes, Sybil, **Charles Thornton Libby**, and **Walter Goodwin Davis**, *Genealogical Dictionary of Maine and New Hampshire* (repr. ed., 1972+: Baltimore, Genealogical Publishing Co.).

Varney, George J., *A Gazetteer of the State of Maine* (repr. ed., 1991: Bowie, MD, Heritage Books).

MASSACHUSETTS

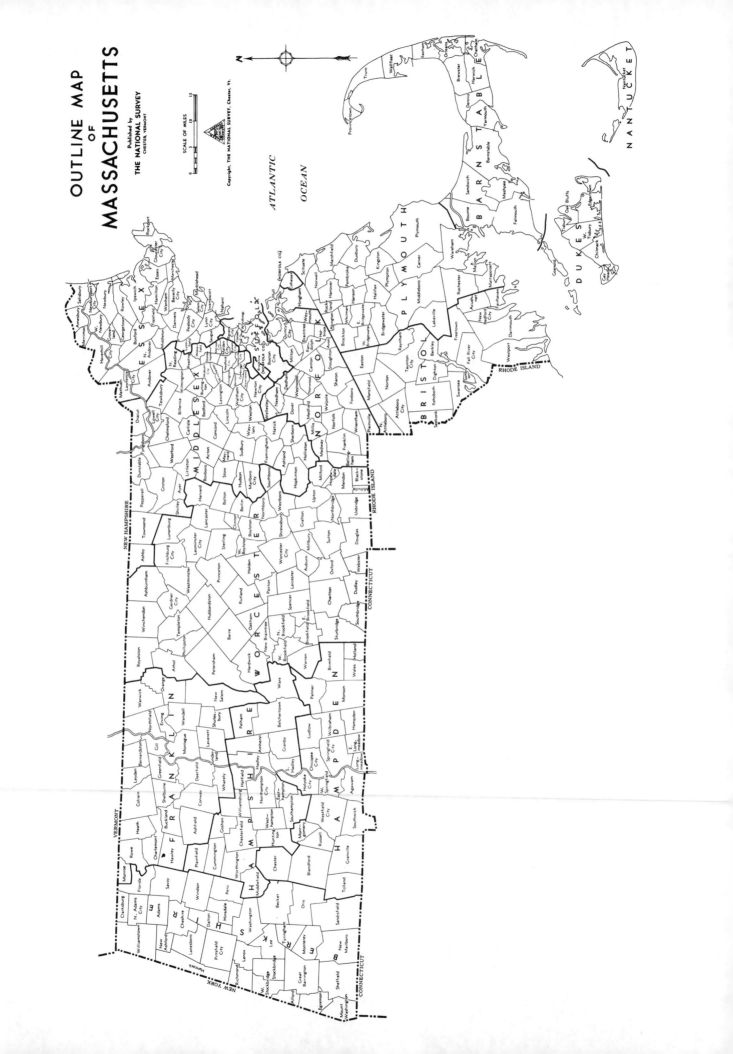

OUTLINE MAP OF MASSACHUSETTS

Published by
THE NATIONAL SURVEY
CHESTER, VERMONT

SCALE OF MILES

Copyright, THE NATIONAL SURVEY, Chester, Vt.

COUNTIES*

County	Estab'd	Parent(s)	Deed District(s)
Barnstable	1685	New Plymouth Colony	Barnstable
Berkshire	1761	Hampshire	Northern, Middle, Southern
Bristol	1685	New Plymouth Colony	Northern, Southern, Fall River
Dukes	1683 (*as a New York Cty*) 1695 (*as a Mass. Cty*)		Dukes
Essex	1643	-----	Northern, Southern
Franklin	1811	Hampshire	Franklin
Hampden	1812	Hampshire	Hampden
Hampshire	1662	Middlesex	Hampshire
Middlesex	1643	-----	Northern, Southern
Nantucket	1695	Dukes	Nantucket
Norfolk	1793	Suffolk	Norfolk
Old Norfolk**	1643	-----	(*see note, below*)
Plymouth	1685	New Plymouth Colony	Plymouth
Suffolk	1643	-----	Suffolk
Worcester	1731	Middlesex & Suffolk	Northern, Worcester

*County information from *Ancestry's Red Book* (1993) and *Historical Data Relating to Counties, Cities and Towns in Massachusetts* (1997).

**Old Norfolk Co., straddling what is now the border between Mass. and N.H., included Salisbury, Amesbury, and Haverhill (now in Mass.), and Hampton and Exeter (now in N.H.) Though technically abolished in 1679, and divided between Essex Co., Mass., and the Province of N.H. (loosely equal to Rockingham Co.), it continued to record deeds until 1714 (originals now at Essex Co. REGISTRY OF DEEDS in Salem, Mass.). For a complete discussion of this somewhat complicated topic, see David C. Dearborn, "The Old Norfolk County Records," *The Essex Genealogist*, 4[1984]:194-6.

TOWNS

Many Mass. towns had several names prior to the one currently in use. The towns listed below are taken from *Historical Data Relating to Counties, Cities and Towns in Massachusetts* (1997), which lists all archaic names, plus all subdivisions or villages within each town, and is cross-indexed. (It should be consulted also for any name *not* appearing on the following list.) For more information, see also Edward Hanson's town-by-town list of Mass. VRs, in *Genealogical Research in New England* (1984), 97-108, 113-14, and *NEXUS* 7[1990]:144-5, 218. N.B., Jay Mack Holbrook's fiche editions of original VRs for over 250 Mass. towns – including almost all with no 'official' printed books – are available; many extend past the official series' 1850 cutoff. For a complete list, with years covered and other sorts of records available, write to Archives Publishing at 4 Mayfair Circle, Oxford, MA 01540.

Codes for each town's VRs:

A	James Arnold, *Vital Record of Rhode Island, 1636-1850* (1st 7 volumes)
B	Rollin H. Cooke Collection (at BERKSHIRE ATHENAEUM)
C	Corbin Collection (at NEHGS)
D	Daughters of the American Revolution (DAR) Library, Washington, D.C.
H	Holbrook microfiche (Archives Publishing)
L	LDS (Family History Library of Church of Jesus Christ of Latter-day Saints, Salt Lake City)
M	*Mayflower Descendant*
N	Manuscript or typescript (at NEHGS)
P	Published volumes, miscellaneous – not part of 'official' series
R	*New England Historical and Genealogical Register*
S	'Official' series books
T	See parent town
U	No known published records – inquire at town hall

N.B., all records whose code letter is printed in **bold type** are available at or through NEHGS.

Town	Estab'd	Parent(s)	Alias(es)	Probate Dist(s)	Deed Dist(s)	Code
Abington	1712	Bridgewater		Plymouth	Plymouth	H,**S**
Acton	1735	Concord		Middlesex	Southern	**S**
Acushnet	1860	Fairhaven		Bristol	Southern	H,T
Acushena *(see Dartmouth)*						
Adams	1778	E. Hoosuck		Berkshire	Northern	H,**L**
Agawam	1855	W. Springfield	Feeding Hills	Hampden	Hampden	H,T
(see Ipswich)						
Alford	1773	Great Barrington		Berkshire	Southern	H,**S**
Amesbury	1668	Salisbury	Salisbury New Town	Essex	Southern	**S**
Amherst	1759	Hadley		Hampshire	Northampton	**C**
Andover	1646			Essex	Northern	**S**
Arlington	1807	Cambridge	W. Cambridge 'til 1867	Middlesex	Southern	**S**
Ashburnham	1765		Dorchester; Canada Pl	Worcester	Northern	H,**S**
Ashby	1767	Ashburnham, Fitchburg, & Townsend		Middlesex	Southern	H,**P**
Ashfield	1765		Huntstown Pl	Franklin	Franklin	H,**S**
Ashland	1846	Framingham, Holliston, & Hopkinton		Middlesex	Southern	H,T
Ashuelot Equivalent *(see Dalton)*						
Athol	1762		Payquage Pl	Worcester	Worcester	**S**
Attleboro	1694	Rehoboth		Bristol	Northern	H,**S**
Auburn	1778	Leicester & Worcester	Ward 'til 1837	Worcester	Worcester	H,**S**
Avon	1888	Stoughton		Norfolk	Norfolk	T
Ayer	1871	Groton		Middlesex	Southern	H,T
Barecove *(see Hingham)*						
Barnardstone's Grant *(see Florida)*						
Barnstable	1638			Barnstable	Barnstable	H,**M**,**P**
Barre	1753	Rutland	Rutland District 'til 1774	Worcester	Worcester	H,**S**

Town	Estab'd	Parent(s)	Alias(es)	Probate Dist(s)	Deed Dist(s)	Code
Becket	1765		No. 4 Pl	Berkshire	Middle	H,S
Bedford	1729	Billerica & Concord		Middlesex	Southern	S
Belchertown	1761		Cold Spring Pl	Hampshire	Northampton	C,H
Bellingham	1719	Dedham, Mendon, & Wrentham		Norfolk	Norfolk	S
Belmont	1859	Waltham, Watertown, & W. Cambridge		Middlesex	Southern	S
Berkley	1735	Dighton & Taunton		Bristol	Northern	H,N
Berlin	1784	Bolton & Marlborough		Worcester	Worcester	P
Bernardston	1762		Falltown Pl	Franklin	Greenfield	C,H
Beverly	1668	Salem		Essex	Southern	H,S
Billerica	1655			Middlesex	Northern	S
Blackstone	1845	Mendon		Worcester	Worcester	H,T
Blandford	1741		Glasgow	Hampden	Springfield	C,H
Bolton	1738	Lancaster		Worcester	Worcester	S
Boston	1630			Suffolk	Suffolk	H,P

(Boston VRs are in Reports of the Record Commissioners of Boston, *vols. 9, 24, 28, 30 – see VITAL RECORDS)*

Town	Estab'd	Parent(s)	Alias(es)	Probate Dist(s)	Deed Dist(s)	Code
Bourne	1884	Sandwich	Cataumet	Barnstable	Barnstable	T
Boxborough	1783	Harvard & Stow		Middlesex	Southern	H,S
Boxford	1694		Rowley Village	Essex	Southern	S
Boylston	1786	Shrewsbury		Worcester	Worcester	H,S
Bradford	1675			Essex	Southern	S

(annexed to Haverhill in 1897)

Town	Estab'd	Parent(s)	Alias(es)	Probate Dist(s)	Deed Dist(s)	Code
Braintree	1640	Boston	Mt. Wollaston	Norfolk	Norfolk	P
Brewster	1803	Harwich		Barnstable	Barnstable	H,S
Bridgewater	1656		Duxburrow Pl	Plymouth	Plymouth	H,S
Brighton	1817	Cambridge	Cambridge S. Parish	Suffolk	Suffolk	H,T
Brimfield	1714			Hampden	Springfield	H,S
Brockton	1821	Bridgewater	N. Bridgewater 'til 1874	Plymouth	Plymouth	S
Brookfield	1673			Worcester	Worcester	H,S
Brookline	1705	Boston	Muddy River	Norfolk	Norfolk	S
Buckland	1779	No-town Pl & Charlemont		Franklin	Greenfield	H,S

(VRs bound with Colrain & Montague)

Bullock's Grant *(see Florida)*

Town	Estab'd	Parent(s)	Alias(es)	Probate Dist(s)	Deed Dist(s)	Code
Burlington	1799	Woburn		Middlesex	Southern	S
Cambridge	1631		Newe Town 'til 1636	Middlesex	Southern	S

Cambridge S. Parish *(see Brighton)*
Cambridge Village *(see Newton)*

Town	Estab'd	Parent(s)	Alias(es)	Probate Dist(s)	Deed Dist(s)	Code
Canton	1797	Stoughton	Dorchester Village	Norfolk	Norfolk	S

Cape Ann *(see Gloucester)*

Town	Estab'd	Parent(s)	Alias(es)	Probate Dist(s)	Deed Dist(s)	Code
Carlisle	1780	Acton & Chelmsford		Middlesex	Northern	S
Carver	1790	Plympton		Plymouth	Plymouth	H,S
Charlemont	1765			Franklin	Greenfield	H,S
Charlestown	1630			Suffolk	Suffolk	H,P

Charlestown Village *(see Woburn)*

Town	Estab'd	Parent(s)	Alias(es)	Probate Dist(s)	Deed Dist(s)	Code
Charlton	1754	Oxford		Worcester	Worcester	H,S
Chatham	1712		Manamoit Village	Barnstable	Barnstable	H,P
Chebacco (see Essex)						
Chelmsford	1655		Pawtucket	Middlesex	Northern	H,S
Chelsea	1739	Boston	Pullin Point & Winnissimet	Suffolk	Suffolk	S
Cheshire	1793	Adams, Lanesborough, New Ashford District, & Windsor		Berkshire	Northern	H
Chester	1765		Murrayfield	Hampden	Northampton	H,S
Chesterfield	1762		New Hingham Pl	Hampshire	Northampton	C,H
Chicopee	1848	Springfield		Hampden	Hampden	H,T
Chilmark	1694			Dukes	Dukes	H,S
Clarksburg	1798		Bullock's Grant	Berkshire	Northern	H
Clinton	1850	Lancaster		Worcester	Worcester	H,T
Coaksett (see Dartmouth)						
Cohannett (see Taunton)						
Cohasset	1770	Hingham		Norfolk	Norfolk	H,S
Colechester (see Salisbury)						
Cold Spring Pl (see Belchertown)						
Colrain	1761			Franklin	Greenfield	H,S
(VRs bound with Buckland & Montague)						
Concord	1635		Musketquid	Middlesex	Southern	P
Conway	1767	Deerfield		Franklin	Greenfield	H,S
Cottage City (see Oak Bluffs)						
Cummington	1779	No. 5 Pl		Hampshire	Northampton	H,P
Dalton	1801		Ashuelot Equivalent	Berkshire	Middle	S
Dana (annexed to Petersham, 1850)	1801	Greenwich, Hardwick, & Petersham		Worcester	Worcester	H,S
Danvers	1752	Salem	Salem Village Middle Parishes	Essex	Southern	S
Dartmouth	1652			Bristol	Southern	H,S
Dedham	1636			Norfolk	Norfolk	S
Deerfield	1677			Franklin	Greenfield	H,S
Dennis	1793	Yarmouth		Barnstable	Barnstable	H,P
Dighton	1712	Taunton		Bristol	Northern	H
Dorchester	1630		Mattapan	Suffolk	Suffolk	H,P
(annexed to Boston in 1870; VRs in Reports of the Records Commissioner of Boston, vols. 21, 36)						
Dorchester-Canada (see Ashburnham)						
Dorchester Village (see Canton)						
Douglas	1746		New Sherburn	Worcester	Worcester	H,S
Dover	1784	Dedham		Norfolk	Norfolk	S
Dracut	1702			Middlesex	Northern	H,S
Dudley	1732	Oxford		Worcester	Worcester	H,S
Dunstable	1673		Litchfield	Middlesex	Northern	H,S
Duxburrow Pl (see Bridgewater)						
Duxbury	1637			Plymouth	Plymouth	S
E. Bridgewater	1823	Bridgewater		Plymouth	Plymouth	H,S
E. Brookfield	1920	Brookfield		Worcester	Worcester	T
E. Hoosuck Pl (see Adams)						
E. Longmeadow	1894	Longmeadow		Hampden	Hampden	T
E. Sudbury (see Wayland)						

Town	Estab'd	Parent(s)	Alias(es)	Probate Dist(s)	Deed Dist(s)	Code
Eastham	1646		Nawsett 'til 1651	Barnstable	Barnstable	**H,M,P**
Easthampton	1785	Northampton		Hampshire	Northampton	**C,H**
Easton	1725	Norton		Bristol	Northern	**H,N**
Edgartown	1671		Great Harbour	Dukes	Dukes	**H,S**
Egremont	1760			Berkshire	Southern	**H**
Elbows Pl *(see Palmer)*						
Enfield	1816	Belchertown &		Hampshire	Northampton	**C,H**
(annexed to Belcher-		Greenwich				
town, New Salem, Pelham,						
& Ware in 1938)						
Erving	1838			Franklin	Greenfield	**H**
Essex	1819	Ipswich	Chebacco	Essex	Esscx	**II,S**
Everett	1870	Malden		Middlesex	Southern	**T**
Fairhaven	1812	New Bedford		Bristol	Southern	**L**
Fall River	1803	Freetown	Troy, 1804-34	Bristol	Northern	**D,H**
		& Tiverton, RI				
Falltown Pl *(see Bernardston)*						
Falmouth	1694			Barnstable	Barnstable	**H,P**
(VRs in Genealogical Advertiser*)*						
Feeding Hills *(see Agawam)*						
Fitchburg	1764	Lunenburg		Worcester	Northern	**H,P**
Florida	1805	Barnardstone's		Berkshire	Northern	**H**
		Grant & Bullock's				
		Grant				
Foxborough	1778	Stoughton,		Norfolk	Norfolk	**H,S**
		Stoughtonham,				
		Walpole, & Wrentham				
Framingham	1675			Middlesex	Southern	**S**
Franklin	1778	Wrentham		Norfolk	Norfolk	**S**
Freetown	1683			Bristol	Northern	**H,P**
Gageborough *(see Windsor)*						
Gardner	1785	Ashburnham,		Worcester	Worcester	**H,S**
		Templeton,				
		Westminster, & Winchendon				
Gay Head	1855			Dukes	Dukes	**U**
(just became 'Aquinnah')						
Georgetown	1838	Rowley		Essex	Southern	**S**
Gerry *(see Phillipston)*						
Gill	1793	Greenfield		Franklin	Greenfield	**H,S**
Gloucester	1642		Cape Ann	Essex	Southern	**H,S**
Goshen	1781	Chesterfield		Hampshire	Northampton	**C,H**
Gosnold	1864	Chilmark		Dukes	Dukes	**T**
Grafton	1735		Hassanamisco Pl	Worcester	Worcester	**H,S**
Granby	1768	South Hadley		Hampshire	Northampton	**C,H**
Granville	1754			Hampden	Springfield	**H,S**
Great Barrington	1761	Sheffield		Berkshire	Berkshire	**H,S**
Great Harbour *(see Edgartown)*						
Greenfield	1753	Deerfield		Franklin	Greenfield	**H,S**
Greenwich	1754		Quabbin Pl	Hampshire	Northampton	**D,H,N**
(annexed to Hardwick, New Salem, Petersham , & Ware in 1938)						
Green's Harbour *(see Marshfield)*						
Groton	1655			Middlesex	Southern	**H,S**
Groveland	1850	Bradford		Essex	Southern	**T**
Hadley	1661		New Pl	Hampshire	Northampton	**C**

Town	Estab'd	Parent(s)	Alias(es)	Probate Dist(s)	Deed Dist(s)	Code
Halifax	1734	Middleborough, Pembroke, & Plympton		Plymouth	Plymouth	H,S
Hamilton	1793	Ipswich		Essex	Southern	H,S
Hampden	1878	Wilbraham		Hampden	Hampden	H,T
Hancock	1776		Jericho Pl	Berkshire	Northern	C,H
Hanover	1727	Abington & Scituate		Plymouth	Plymouth	H,S
Hanson	1820	Pembroke		Plymouth	Plymouth	H,S
Hardwick	1739		Lambstown Pl	Worcester	Worcester	H,S
Hartwood Pl (see Washington)						
Harvard	1732	Groton, Lancaster, & Stow		Worcester	Worcester	H,S
Harwich	1694		Satuckett	Barnstable	Barnstable	H,P
Hassanamisco Pl (see Grafton)						
Hatfield	1670	Hadley		Hampshire	Hampshire	C
Haverhill	1641		Bradford	Essex	Southern	S
Hawley	1792		No. 7 Pl	Franklin	Greenfield	H,C
Heath	1785	Charlemont		Franklin	Greenfield	H,S
Hingham	1635		Barecove 'til 1635	Plymouth	Plymouth (Norfolk, 1793-1803)	H
Hinsdale	1804	Dalton		Berkshire	Middle	H,S
Holbrook	1872	Randolph		Norfolk	Norfolk	H,T
Holden	1741	Worcester		Worcester	Worcester	S
Holland	1783	S. Brimfield		Hampden	Springfield	H
Holliston	1724	Sherborn		Middlesex	Southern	S
Holyoke	1850	W. Springfield		Hampden	Hampden	H,T
Hopedale	1886	Milford		Worcester	Worcester	T
Hopkinton	1715		Moguncoy	Middlesex	Southern	S
Hubbardston	1767	Rutland		Worcester	Worcester	H,S
Hudson	1866	Marlborough & Stow		Middlesex	Southern	H,S
Hull	1644			Plymouth	Plymouth (Norfolk, 1793-1803)	H,S
Huntington	1773	Murrayfield	Norwich 'til 1855	Hampshire	Northampton	L
Huntstown Pl (see Ashfield)						
Hutchinson (see Barre)						
Hyannis (see Barnstable)						
Hyde Park (annexed to Boston, 1911)	1868	Dedham, Dorchester, & Milton				H
Indian Town Pl (see Stockbridge)						
Ipswich	1634		Aggawam	Essex	Southern	H,S
Ipswich-Canada Pl (see Winchendon)						
Jamaica Plain (see Boston)						
Jericho Pl (see Hancock)						
Kingston	1726	Plymouth		Plymouth	Plymouth	H,S
Lakeville	1853	Middleborough		Plymouth	Plymouth	H,T
Lambstown Pl (see Hardwick)						
Lancaster	1653			Worcester	Worcester	H,P
Lanesborough	1765		New Framingham Pl	Berkshire	Northern	C,H,P
Lawrence	1847	Andover & Methuen		Essex	Northern	S
Lee	1777	Great Barrington		Berkshire	Middle	H,S

Town	Estab'd	Parent(s)	Alias(es)	Probate Dist(s)	Deed Dist(s)	Code
Leicester	1714			Worcester	Worcester	H,S
Lenox	1767	Richmont		Berkshire	Middle	B,H
Leominster	1740	Lancaster		Worcester	Northern	H,S
Leverett	1774	Sunderland		Franklin	Greenfield	C,H
Lexington	1713	Cambridge		Middlesex	Southern	S
Leyden	1784	Bernardston		Franklin	Greenfield	H
Lincoln	1754	Concord & Lexington		Middlesex	Southern	S
Litchfield *(see Dunstable)*						
Littleton	1715		Nashoba	Middlesex	Southern *(Northern, 1856-60)*	H,S
Longmeadow	1783	Springfield		Hampden	Springfield	H,R
Lowell	1826	Chelmsford		Middlesex	Northern	H,S
Loudon *(see Otis)*						
Ludlow	1774	Springfield		Hampden	Springfield	H
Lunenburg	1728	Dorchester, Boardman's Farm, Turkey Hills, & Woburn		Worcester	Northern	H,P
Lynn	1635		Saugus 'til 1637	Essex	Southern	S
Lynnfield	1782	Lynn		Essex	Southern	S
Malden	1649			Middlesex	Southern	S
Manamoit Village *(see Chatham)*						
Manchester	1645	Salem		Essex	Southern	H,S
(now called Manchester-by-the-Sea)						
Mansfield	1770	Norton		Bristol	Northern	H,S
Marblehead	1633			Essex	Southern	H,P,S
Marion	1852	Rochester		Plymouth	Plymouth	T
Marlborough	1660			Middlesex	Southern	S
Marshfield	1640		Green's Harbour	Plymouth	Plymouth	H,P
Mashpee	1763			Barnstable	Barnstable	H
Mattacheeset *(see Yarmouth)*						
Mattapan *(see Dorchester)*						
Mattapoisett	1857	Rochester		Plymouth	Plymouth	T
Maynard	1871	Stow & Sudbury		Middlesex	Southern	T
Medfield	1650	Dedham		Norfolk	Norfolk	S
Medford	1630			Middlesex	Southern	S
Medway	1713	Medfield		Norfolk	Norfolk	H,S
Melrose	1850	Malden		Middlesex	Southern	T
Mendon	1667			Worcester	Worcester	H,S
Merrimac	1876	Amesbury		Essex	Southern	T
Methuen	1725	Haverhill		Essex	Northern	S
Middleborough	1669		Namassackett	Plymouth	Plymouth	H,P
Middlefield	1783	Becket, Chester, Partridgefield (now Peru), Washington, Worthington, & 'Prescott's Grants'		Hampshire	Hampshire	H,S
Middle Parishes *(see Danvers)*						
Middleton	1728	Andover, Boxford, Salem, & Topsfield		Essex	Southern	S
Middletown *(see Tisbury)*						
Milford	1780	Mendon		Worcester	Worcester	H,S
Millbury	1813	Sutton		Worcester	Worcester	H,S

Town	Estab'd	Parent(s)	Alias(es)	Probate Dist(s)	Deed Dist(s)	Code
Millis	1885	Medway		Norfolk	Norfolk	T
Millville	1916	Blackstone		Worcester	Worcester	T
Milton	1662	Dorchester		Norfolk	Norfolk	**S**
Moguncoy *(see Hopkinton)*						
Monroe	1822	Rowe		Franklin	Greenfield	**H,L**
Monson	1760	Brimfield		Hampden	Springfield	**C,L**
Montague	1754	Sunderland		Franklin	Greenfield	**H,S**
(VRs bound with Buckland & Colrain)						
Monterey	1847	Tyringham		Berkshire	Southern	**H,T**
Montgomery	1780	Westfield, Norwich, & Southampton		Hampden	Springfield	**H,S**
Mt. Washington	1779		Tauconnuck Mt. Pl	Berkshire	Southern	**H**
Muddy River *(see Brookline)*						
Murrayfield *(see Chester)*						
Musketequid *(see Concord)*						
Myrifield *(see Rowe)*						
Nahant	1853	Lynn		Essex	Southern	T
Namassackett *(see Middleborough)*						
Nantucket	1687		Sherburn 'til 1713; Tuckannock 'til 1795	Nantucket	Nantucket	**H,S**
Naquag Tract *(see Rutland)*						
Narragansett No. 2 *(see Westminster)*						
Narragansett No. 6 Pl *(see Templeton)*						
Nashoba *(see Littleton)*						
Natick	1650			Middlesex	Southern	**S**
Nawsett *(see Eastham)*						
Needham	1711	Dedham		Norfolk	Norfolk	**H,N**
New Ashford	1781			Berkshire	Northern	**H,S**
New Bedford	1787	Dartmouth		Bristol	Southern	**S**
New Braintree	1751	Brookfield & Hardwick		Worcester	Worcester	**H,S**
New Cambridge *(see Newton)*						
New Framingham *(see Lanesborough)*						
New Hingham *(see Chesterfield)*						
New Lisburn Tract *(see Pelham)*						
New Marlbor-ough	1759			Berkshire	Southern	**B,H**
New Medfield *(see Sturbridge)*						
New Pl *(see Hadley)*						
New Salem	1753			Franklin	Greenfield	**H,S**
New Sherburn *(see Douglas)*						
Newbury	1635		Wessacucon	Essex	Southern	**S**
Newburyport	1764	Newbury		Essex	Southern	**S**
Newe Town *(see Cambridge)*						
Newton	1691		Cambridge Village & New Cambridge	Middlesex	Southern	**S**
Nichewoag Pl *(see Petersham)*						
Norfolk	1870	Franklin & Medway		Norfolk	Norfolk	T
N. Adams	1878	Adams		Berkshire	Berkshire	T
N. Andover	1855	Andover		Essex	Northern	T
N. Attleborough	1887	Attleborough		Bristol	Bristol	T
N. Bridgewater *(see Brockton)*						

Town	Estab'd	Parent(s)	Alias(es)	Probate Dist(s)	Deed Dist(s)	Code
N. Brookfield	1812	Brookfield		Worcester	Worcester	**H**
N. Chelsea *(see Revere & Winthrop)*						
N. Reading	1853	Reading		Middlesex	Southern	T
Northampton	1656			Hampshire	Hampshire	**C**,H
Northborough	1766	Westborough		Worcester	Worcester	H,S
Northbridge	1772	Uxbridge		Worcester	Worcester	H,S
Northfield	1714		Squakeag Pl	Franklin	Greenfield	**C**,H
Norton	1710	Taunton		Bristol	Northern	H,S
Norwell	1849	Scituate	S. Scituate 'til 1888	Plymouth	Plymouth	H,T
Norwich *(see Huntington)*						
Norwood	1872	Dedham & Walpole		Norfolk	Norfolk	T
No-town Pl *(see Buckland)*						
No. 1 Pl *(see Tyringham)*						
No. 3 Pl *(see Worthington & Sandisfield)*						
No. 4 Pl *(see Becket)*						
No. 7 Pl *(see Hawley)*						
Oak Bluffs	1880	Edgartown	Cottage City 'til 1907	Dukes	Dukes	T
Oakham	1762	Rutland		Worcester	Worcester	H,S
Orange	1783	Athol, Warwick, Royalston, & Ervingshire Tract		Franklin	Greenfield	**H**
Orleans	1797	Eastham		Barnstable	Barnstable	H,M,**P**
(VRs published with Eastham)						
Otis	1773	Tyringham Equivalent	Loudon 'til 1810	Berkshire	Middle	H,S
Oxford	1693			Worcester	Worcester	H,S
Palmer	1752		Elbows Pl	Hampden	Springfield	H,S
Parsons *(see W. Newbury)*						
Partridgefield *(see Peru)*						
Pawtucket *(see Chelmsford)*						
Paxton	1765	Leicester & Rutland		Worcester	Worcester	**C**,H
Pawmet Tract *(see Truro)*						
Payquage Pl *(see Athol)*						
Peabody	1855	Danvers	S. Danvers 'til 1868	Essex	Southern	H,T
Pelham	1743		New Lisburn Tract	Hampshire	Northampton	H,S
Pembroke	1712	Duxbury		Plymouth	Plymouth	H,S
Pepperell	1753	Groton		Middlesex	Southern	H,**P**
Peru	1771		Partridgefield 'til 1806	Berkshire	Middle	H,S
Petersham	1754		Nichewoag Pl	Worcester	Worcester	**H**,S
Phillipston	1786	Athol & Templeton	Gerry 'til 1814	Worcester	Worcester	H,S
Pittsfield	1761		Pontoosuck Pl	Berkshire	Middle	B,**H**
Plainfield	1785	Cummington		Hampshire	Northampton	B,**H**
Plainville	1905	Wrentham		Norfolk	Norfolk	T
Plymouth	1620			Plymouth	Plymouth	H,**P**
Plympton	1707	Plymouth		Plymouth	Plymouth	H,S
Pompositticut Pl *(see Stow)*						
Ponagansett *(see Dartmouth)*						
Pontoosuck Pl *(see Pittsfield)*						
Prescott	1822	Pelham & New Salem		Worcester	Worcester	H,**N**
(annexed by Pelham & New Salem, 1938)						
Princeton	1759	Rutland		Worcester	Worcester	H,S

Town	Estab'd Parent(s)	Alias(es)	Probate Dist(s)	Deed Dist(s)	Code
Provincetown	1727		Cape Cod Precinct	Barnstable	Barnstable	D,H
Pullin Point *(see Chelsea)*					
Quabbin Pl *(see Greenwich)*					
Quinsigamond *(see Worcester)*					
Quincy	1792	Braintree & Dorchester		Norfolk	Norfolk	H,N
Randolph	1793	Braintree		Norfolk	Norfolk	H,N
Raynham	1731	Taunton		Bristol	Northern	**H,R, P**
Reading	1644	Lynn		Middlesex	Southern	**S**
Rehoboth	1645		Seacunck	Bristol	Northern	**P**
Revere	1846	Chelsea	N. Chelsea 'til 1785	Suffolk	Suffolk	T
Rexhame *(see Marshfield)*					
Richmond	1765		Richmont 'til 1785	Berkshire	Middle	H,S
Richmont *(see Richmond)*					
Roadtown Pl *(see Shutesbury)*					
Rochester	1686		Scippican	Plymouth	Plymouth	H,S
Rockland	1874	Abington		Plymouth	Plymouth	T
Rockport	1840	Gloucester		Essex	Southern	H,S
Rowe	1785		Myrifield	Franklin	Greenfield	**C,H**
Rowley	1639			Essex	Southern	H,S
Rowley Village *(see Boxford)*					
Roxbury	1630			Suffolk	Suffolk	H,S
(annexed to Boston, 1868)					
Roxbury-Canada *(see Warwick)*					
Royalshire Tract *(see Royalston)*					
Royalston	1765		Royalshire Tract	Worcester	Worcester	H,S
Rumney Marsh *(see Chelsea)*					
Russell	1792	Montgomery & Westfield		Hampshire	Hampshire	**C,H**
Rutland	1714		Naquag Tract	Worcester	Worcester	H,S
Rutland District *(see Barre)*					
Salem	1630			Essex	Southern	**S**
Salem Village *(see Danvers)*					
Salisbury	1639		Colechester 'til 1640	Essex	Southern	**S**
Salisbury New Town *(see Amesbury)*					
Sandisfield	1762		No. 3 Pl	Berkshire	Southern	H,S
Sandwich	1638			Barnstable	Barnstable	**H,P**
Satuckett *(see Harwich)*					
Saugus	1815	Lynn		Essex	Southern	
(see also Lynn)					
Savoy	1797			Berkshire	Northern	**C,H**
Scippican *(see Rochester)*					
Scituate	1633			Plymouth	Plymouth	H,S
Seacunck *(see Rehoboth)*					
Seekonk	1812	Rehoboth		Bristol	Northern	**A,H**
Sharon	1765	Stoughton	Stoughtonham 'til 1783	Norfolk	Norfolk	H,S
Sheffield	1733			Berkshire	Southern	**B,H,N**
Shelburne	1768	Deerfield		Franklin	Greenfield	H,S
Sherborn	1674			Middlesex	Southern	**S**
Sherburn *(see Nantucket)*					
Shirley	1753	Groton		Middlesex	Southern	H,S
Shrewsbury	1720			Worcester	Worcester	H,S
Shutesbury	1761		Roadtown Pl	Franklin	Greenfield	**C,H**
Somerset	1790	Swansea		Bristol	Northern	**H**

Town	Estab'd	Parent(s)	Alias(es)	Probate Dist(s)	Deed Dist(s)	Code
Somerville	1842	Charlestown		Middlesex	Southern	T
S. Abington (see Whitman)						
S. Brimfield (see Wales)						
S. Danvers (see Peabody)						
S. Hadley	1753	Hadley		Hampshire	Northampton	**C**,**H**
S. Reading (see Wakefield)						
S. Scituate (see Norwell)						
Southampton	1753	Northampton		Hampshire	Northampton	**C**,**H**
Southborough	1727	Marlborough		Worcester	Worcester	**S**
Southbridge	1816	Charlton, Dudley, & Sturbridge		Worcester	Worcester	**H**,**P**
Southwick	1770	Westfield		Hampden	Springfield	**II**
Spencer	1753	Leicester		Worcester	Worcester	**H**,**S**
Springfield	1641			Hampden	Springfield	**C**,**H**,**R**
Squakeag (see Northfield)						
Sterling	1781	Lancaster		Worcester	Worcester	**H**,**P**
Stockbridge	1739		Indian Town Pl	Berkshire	Middle	**H**,**N**
Stoneham	1725	Charlestown		Middlesex	Southern	**S**
Stoughton	1726	Dorchester		Norfolk	Norfolk	**H**,**P**
Stoughtonham (see Sharon)						
Stow	1683		Pompositticut Pl	Middlesex	Southern	**H**,**S**
Sturbridge	1738		New Medfield	Worcester	Worcester	**H**,**S**
Sudbury	1639			Middlesex	Southern	**S**
Suffield Equivalent Lands (see Blandford)						
Sunderland	1714		Swampfield 'til 1718	Franklin	Greenfield	**C**,**H**
Sutton	1714			Worcester	Worcester	**H**,**S**
Swampfield (see Sunderland)						
Swampscott	1852	Lynn		Essex	Southern	T
Swansea	1667	Rehoboth	Wannamoisett 'til 1668	Bristol	Northern	**P**
Tauconnuck Mt. Pl (see Mt. Washington)						
Taunton	1639		Cohannett	Bristol	Northern	**S**
Templeton	1762		Narragansett No. 6 Pl	Worcester	Worcester	**H**,**S**
Tewksbury	1734	Billerica		Middlesex	Northern	**S**
Tisbury	1671		Middletowne	Dukes	Dukes	**H**,**S**
Tolland	1810	Granville		Hampden	Springfield	**H**,**U**
Topsfield	1648	Ipswich		Essex	Southern	**H**,**S**
Townsend	1732		Turkey Hills	Middlesex	Middlesex	**H**,**P**
Troy (see Fall River)						
Truro	1709		Pawmett Tract	Barnstable	Barnstable	**H**,**S**
Tuckannock (see Nantucket)						
Turkey Hills (see Townsend)						
Tyngsboro	1789	Dunstable		Middlesex	Northern	**S**
Tyringham	1762		No. 1 Pl	Berkshire	Middle	**H**,**S**
Upton	1735	Hopkinton, Mendon, Sutton, & Uxbridge		Worcester	Worcester	**S**
Uxbridge	1727	Mendon		Worcester	Worcester	**H**,**S**
Wakefield	1812	Reading	S. Reading 'til 1868	Middlesex	Southern	**S**
Wales	1762	Brimfield	S. Brimfield 'til 1828	Hampden	Springfield	**C**,**H**
Walpole	1724	Dedham		Norfolk	Norfolk	**S**
Waltham	1738	Watertown		Middlesex	Southern	**S**
Wannamoisett (see Swansea)						
Ward (see Auburn)						
Ware	1761		Ware River Parish	Hampshire	Northampton	**C**,**H**

Town	Estab'd	Parent(s)	Alias(es)	Probate Dist(s)	Deed Dist(s)	Code
Wareham	1739	Agawam Pl & Rochester		Plymouth	Plymouth	**H,M,P**
Warren	1742	Brimfield, Brookfield, & Kingsfield	Western 'til 1834	Worcester	Worcester	**S**
Warwick	1763		Roxbury Canada Pl	Franklin	Greenfield	**C,H**
Washington	1777		Hartwood Pl	Berkshire	Middle	**H,S**
Watertown	1630			Middlesex	Southern	**P**
Wayland	1780	Sudbury E.	Sudbury 'til 1835	Middlesex	Southern	**H,S**
Webster	1832	Dudley & Oxford		Worcester	Worcester	**H,P**
Wellesley	1881	Needham		Norfolk	Norfolk	**T**
Wellfleet	1763	Eastham		Barnstable	Barnstable	**H,N**
Wendell	1781	Ervingshire & Shutesbury		Franklin	Greenfield	**H**
Wenham	1643			Essex	Southern	**H,S**
Western *(see Warren)*						
Wessacucon *(see Newbury)*						
Wessaguscus *(see Weymouth)*						
W. Boylston	1808	Boylston, Holden, & Sterling		Worcester	Worcester	**H,S**
W. Bridgewater	1822	Bridgewater		Plymouth	Plymouth	**H,S**
W. Brookfield	1848	Brookfield		Worcester	Worcester	**H,T**
W. Cambridge *(see Arlington)*						
W. Hoosuck Pl *(see Williamstown)*						
W. Newbury	1819	Newbury	Parsons 'til 1820	Essex	Southern	**H,S**
W. Roxbury	1851	Roxbury				**H**
(annexed to Boston, 1874)						
W. Springfield	1774	Springfield		Hampden	Springfield	**S**
W. Stockbridge	1774	Stockbridge		Berkshire	Southern	**H,S**
W. Tisbury	1892	Tisbury		Dukes	Dukes	**T**
Westborough	1717	Marlborough		Worcester	Worcester	**H,S**
Westfield	1669	Springfield		Hampden	Springfield	**C,H**
Westford	1729	Chelmsford		Middlesex	Northern	**H,S**
Westhampton	1778	Northampton		Hampshire	Northampton	**C,H**
Westminster	1759		Narragansett No. 2	Worcester	Northern	**H,S**
Weston	1713	Watertown		Middlesex	Southern	**S**
Westport	1787	Dartmouth		Bristol	Southern	**H,S**
Westwood	1897	Dedham		Norfolk	Norfolk	**T**
Weymouth	1635		Wessaguscus	Norfolk	Norfolk	**H,S**
Weymouth Canada *(see Ashfield)*						
Whately	1771	Hatfield		Franklin	Greenfield	**H,P**
Whitman	1875	Abington & E. Bridgewater	S. Abington 'til 1886	Plymouth	Plymouth	**T**
Wilbraham	1763	Springfield		Hampden	Springfield	**C,D,H**
Williamsburg	1771	Hatfield		Hampshire	Northampton	**H**
Williamstown	1765		W. Hoosuck Pl	Berkshire	Northern	**H,S**
Wilmington	1730	Reading		Middlesex	Northern	**S**
Winchendon	1764		Ipswich Canada Pl	Worcester	Worcester	**H,S**
Winchester	1850	Medford, Woburn, & W. Cambridge		Middlesex	Southern	**T**
Windsor	1771		Gageborough 'til 1778	Berkshire	Northern	**H,S**
Winnissimet *(see Chelsea)*						

Town	Estab'd	Parent(s)	Alias(es)	Probate Dist(s)	Deed Dist(s)	Code
Winthrop	1846	Chelsea & Woburn	N. Chelsea 'til 1852	Suffolk	Suffolk	T
Woburn	1642		Charlestown Village	Middlesex	Southern	**P**
Wollonopaug (see Wrentham)						
Worcester	1684		Quansigamond Pl	Worcester	Worcester	H,S
Worthington	1768		No. 3 Pl	Hampshire	Hampshire	H,S
Wrentham	1673		Wollonopaug	Norfolk	Norfolk	S
Yarmouth	1639		Mattacheeset	Barnstable	Barnstable	H,**P**

MASSACHUSETTS

Mass. was the first New England state to be permanently settled and also the first to establish laws governing public record-keeping. However, no one agency has collected all kinds of records in one place; for the beginner, locating records can be a study in itself. One of the most complete collections of printed genealogies and manuscripts is at the NEHGS library (see NEW ENGLAND chapter). The BOSTON PUBLIC LIBRARY has many resources of genealogical interest, but they are scattered through several departments, which may discourage the novice. Likewise, the MASSACHUSETTS STATE LIBRARY has much of value, and the MASSACHUSETTS STATE ARCHIVES is a major repository for primary genealogical data – since moving to its new facility, the ARCHIVES has collected vital, probate, land, and (some) court records for many Mass. counties. In short, no single Mass. agency 'has it all,' but for those who know where to look, its records are the most complete of any state in the U.S.

STATE HOLIDAYS PECULIAR TO MASSACHUSETTS – REPOSITORIES MAY BE CLOSED – CALL

Patriots' Day [usually 3rd Mon in Apr]; Bunker Hill Day [Suffolk Co. only; usually Jun 17]; Evacuation Day [= St. Patrick's Day (Mar 17); Suffolk Co. only]

VITAL RECORDS

To 1850: … for 206 of Mass.'s 364 towns were printed under state auspices in the early 1900s, and copies deposited in libraries throughout the state. Most were carefully prepared and include not only civil VRs but cemetery, church, bible, and private records as well. (This inclusiveness can be a major help in determining what cemeteries and churches were in use before 1850.) Today, only major libraries have complete sets, but most have the books for their own area. Some volumes of VRs were compiled after the 'official series;' not all followed the same format. The *Mayflower Descendant* has published VRs for many towns in Plymouth, Barnstable, and Bristol counties; Leonard H. Smith reprinted most of these, with indexes. In recent years, the RHODE ISLAND SOCIETY OF MAYFLOWER DESCENDANTS has published, in book form, the VRs of Falmouth, Marshfield, and Yarmouth; the MASSACHUSETTS SOCIETY OF MAYFLOWER DESCENDANTS has published Middleborough; and the GENERAL SOCIETY, Dennis and Raynham. NEHGS has published Charlestown, Pepperell, Townsend, Swansea, and Sandwich. Manuscripts and typescripts of VRs for other towns are scattered across the state. In 1982, NEHGS published (on 55 reels of film) *The Corbin Collection: Genealogical and Historical Material Relating to Central and Western Massachusetts, 1650-1850*, which includes vital and other records for some 80 towns in Franklin, Hampshire, and Hampden counties, plus a few places elsewhere. NEHGS has manuscripts of VRs for many 'unpublished' towns; the BERKSHIRE ATHENAEUM holds the Rollin H. Cooke Collection of church, town, and cemetery records for all towns in Berkshire County, and some in surrounding counties. The SPRINGFIELD CITY LIBRARY has manuscript VRs for Springfield and

Wilbraham, and cemetery records for other towns. In 1979, the Microfilming Corporation of America fiched all published (*i.e.*, as books) Mass. VRs; University Microfilms International (Ann Arbor) now distributes this collection. The LDS's International Genealogical Index (IGI) abstracts all printed Mass. births, baptisms, intentions, and marriages; and Jay Mack Holbrook's Archive Publishing (Oxford, Mass.), offers fiche of original VRs for more than 200 Mass. towns. The originals themselves are at the town halls, and may be consulted with the clerk's permission.

Mass. births, marriages, and deaths are recorded first at the town clerk's office. Since 1841, copies have been sent to the State Registry of Vital Records. Thus, after that date, *either* town or state records may be consulted. (Boston, however, did not comply until 1848, so original records from 1841 to *ca.* 1849 are still in the BOSTON REGISTRY ARCHIVES, and available also on Holbrook microfiche (see address under intro to TOWNS, above) and at NEHGS and the BOSTON PUBLIC LIBRARY. Access policies and fees vary from town to town. At the REGISTRY OF VITAL RECORDS, statewide indexes to births, marriages, and deaths facilitate searches. In 1983, legislation opened the state VRs from 1841 to 1890; additional five-year periods have been opened (currently to 1905) as the most recent records contained in each period 'turn 90.' (*E.g.*, 1906-10 should be opened in 2000.) These state returns are at the STATE ARCHIVES and NEHGS.

CITY OF BOSTON REGISTRY ARCHIVES (Judy McCarthy, Registrar)

Room 201, City Hall	[617] 635-4175	<u>Subway</u>: Green line to Government Ctr
Boston, MA		stop.
Web: http://www.ci.boston.ma.us		

open *only* last Tue of month 10am-2pm (*and not always then; call to verify*)

Extremely limited and uncertain openings; always call ahead to verify. Admission, $10, payable at cashier's window next to birth registry. **HOLDINGS**: Boston VRs, 1630s to 1869 (compliance with state registration began in 1848); manuscript copies of most early Boston church records (all pre-1800 registers are indexed).

BOSTON CITY ARCHIVES (John McColgan, Deputy Archivist)

30 Millstone Road	[617] 364-8679	Rte 128 to Exit 2B; left on Neponset
Hyde Park, MA 02136		Valley Pkwy; left on Hyde Park Av;
		left on Millstone. <u>MBTA or Train</u>: Bus
Mon-Fri 9am-5pm *by appointment only*!		#32 from Forest Hills to Wolcott
		Sta or Commuter Rail from So.
		to Readville Sta; 3 blocks to bldg.

Free and open to public *by appointment only* (at least 24 hours ahead); mail inquiries accepted (no research – simple fact-checking only); staff copying, $.50/page. **HOLDINGS**: city censuses (1820, 1830, 1837, 1845 [summary only], 1850, and 1855); tax records, 1822-95 and 1945-73; voter registrations, 1857-1920; selected records series for Boston and annexed towns (1822-1990), including Mayor, City Council, City Clerk, Schools, Assessor, Building Inspection, Retirement, Treasurer, and Auditor. N.B., see also BOSTON PUBLIC LIBRARY – Rare Book and Manuscript Division, for records, 1630-1821; and Boston's REGISTRY OF VITAL RECORDS.

1841-1905:

MASSACHUSETTS STATE ARCHIVES

Columbia Point   [617] 727-2816   SE Expressway (Rte 93) to Columbia
220 Morrissey Boulevard   Rd Exit; signs to UMASS/JFK Library.
Boston, MA 02125   Ample free parking. Subway: Red line
    UMASS/JFK stop; shuttle to JFK
Mon-Fri 9am-5pm; Sat 9am-3pm (closed Sat before   Library & Archives.
Mon holiday; *no court records retrieved on Sat*)

Free and open to public; 20 film and fiche readers; 2 self-service reader/printers, $.25/page; limited staff copying (fees vary); briefcases, purses, and backpacks are checked in lockers. **HOLDINGS**: non-current Mass. records, including state returns of VRs (with indexes), 1841-1905; VR indexes only, 1906-71. (Certified copies of VRs, $3.) Lists of alien port arrivals, Boston, 1848-91, with index. Federal censuses of Mass., 1840-1900, including supplemental schedules, 1850-70, state copies of federal returns, 1850-80, and state census returns, 1855 and '65. 'Massachusetts Archives' collection (328 volumes of colonial and Revolutionary-era documents, including land grants by the General Court, military records (1643-1787), and tax valuations. Roughly one quarter of the collection has been indexed by surname and town; military records are indexed separately. First series of probate records for Suffolk, Middlesex, Plymouth, Worcester, Essex, and Dukes counties. (For Suffolk County, original papers to 1894; for Middlesex, to 1871; for Plymouth, 1881, plus copybooks on film to 1903; for Worcester, copybooks on film to 1881; for Essex, originals to 1840 and copybooks on film to 1881; and for Dukes, film only to 1938.) Archives also has court and naturalization records for several counties, and older records of a number of Mass. state institutions: especially hospitals (mental, cancer, *et al.*) and correctional facilities (prisons, reformatories, and the like) – some beginning as far back as the Civil War. (A shelf-list is available.) N.B., access to mental-hospital or correctional records is subject to privacy laws – call for details.

1906 to present:

REGISTRY OF VITAL RECORDS AND STATISTICS

150 Mt. Vernon Street, 1st floor [617] 740-2600   Next to Bayside Expo Center. SE
Boston, MA 02125-3105   x2649   Expressway (Rte 93) to Columbia Rd.
    Exit (exit 15); signs to UMASS/JFK
    Library. Subway: Red line to UMASS/JFK
    stop; 2 minute walk from there.

Mon, Tues, Fri 9am-4:30pm; Wed & Thurs 9am-7pm
New Research hours: Mon-Fri 9am-4:30pm (no longer
closed at lunchtime)

4 film readers. Researchers punch timeclock; 1st 20 minutes free, then $3/hour. Must also sign register on entry, and surrender driver's license, brief- and attaché cases, knapsacks, *etc.*; *PENCILS ONLY* in research room (available on request); clerk must inspect each birth or marriage record before user sees it; all death records open; staff copying only for certified copies, $6 each ($11 by mail, $14 by expedited mail [mail requests accepted only if accompanied by check]; $19 by phone order). **HOLDINGS**: births, marriages, and deaths from 1906 to present, with statewide indexes in 5-year increments; divorce index, 1952 to present.

FEDERAL CENSUS

Many Mass. libraries with sizable genealogical collections have census records for their own counties or the whole state. For *all* federal censuses, nationwide, 1790-1920, go to the NATIONAL ARCHIVES (see NEW ENGLAND chapter).

STATE CENSUS

Mass. state censuses for 1855 and '65 are at the STATE ARCHIVES. Ann S. Lainhart has published indexed transcriptions of these censuses for many towns in Essex, Middlesex, and Plymouth counties. (Copies at NEHGS.)

PROBATE AND LAND – MULTI-COUNTY REPOSITORIES

In Mass., all probate and land records are at the county level. There are 14 counties, 5 of which have more than one registry of deeds. It is important to know when the various counties and districts were set up (see COUNTIES and TOWNS).

Two facilities have records covering more than one Mass. county each. See also the entries, following, for individual counties.

TRIAL COURT RECORDS CENTER

188 State Street   [978] 463-9517   In basement of Newburyport District
Newburyport, MA 01950   Courthouse at Rte 1 rotary in Newburyport. Large granite bldg.

Wed 9am-3pm (*by appointment only; 1 week ahead*)

Mail: Michael Haire / Administrative Office of the Trial Court / Two Center Plaza / Boston, MA 02108

Free and open to public; mail inquiries accepted (must include court, docket number, name, and date); you must *provide your own copy paper*. **HOLDINGS**: records of Superior, Probate, and District Courts in Essex County; Land Court and Supreme Judicial Court for whole Commonwealth; Plymouth Probate Court; Boston Housing Court; Dorchester, Roxbury, Somerville, Lowell, and Woburn District Courts (*exact list in flux – call*).

WESTERN WORCESTER DISTRICT TRIAL COURT RECORDS CENTER

544 East Main Street   [508] 885-6033 or   MA Tpk (Rte 90) to Exit 9 (Sturbridge);
East Brookfield, MA 01515   [617] 742-8383 x 344   Rte 20E to Rte 49N; left (W) on Rte 9;
bldg ½ mi on right.

Fri 9am-3pm *by appointment – 2 weeks ahead*

All mail: Michael Haire (*address under TCRC, above*)

Free and open to public; mail inquiries accepted; copying. **HOLDINGS**: Berkshire, Franklin, Hampden, Hampshire, and Worcester County probates (1731-1881); State Judicial Court records.

PROBATE AND LAND – SINGLE-COUNTY REPOSITORIES

BARNSTABLE COUNTY

Courthouse Main Street / Route 6A Barnstable, MA 02630		Rte 6 to Rte 132; left; right on Rte 6A; 3 mi to village & courthouse. Deeds & Probate in same bldg.
Probate Court Mon-Fri 8:30am-4pm	[508] 362-2511	See above.

Free and open to public; mail inquiries accepted *if they take only a few minutes*; self-service copying, $.50/page. **HOLDINGS**: probates, 1686 to present (record books only; original papers were destroyed in fire – see below). Pre-1686 records at Plymouth.

Registry of **Deeds** 3195 Rte 6A *or* P.O. Box 368 Barnstable, MA 02630	[508] 362-7733 & -5065 (FAX)	See above.
Mon-Fri 8am-4pm		

Free and open to public; mail inquires accepted *if they take only a few minutes*; self-service copying, $.50/page; staff copying, $.75/page. **HOLDINGS**: deeds, 1703 to present. An 1827 fire destroyed 93 of the 94 volumes of prior records, but many deeds were re-recorded. Pre-1686 deeds at Plymouth.

BERKSHIRE COUNTY

Probate Court 44 Bank Row Pittsfield, MA 01201	[413] 442-6941	Rte 20 to Rte 7 / 20; 7.4 mi to rotary. 3rd on right, on Bank Row.
Mon-Fri 8:30am-4pm		

Free and open to public; pre-paid mail inquiries accepted; staff copying, $.50/page; certified copies, $10. **HOLDINGS**: all Berkshire probates, 1761 to present.

THREE BERKSHIRE COUNTY DEED DISTRICTS

Middle – Becket, Dalton, Hinsdale, Lee, Lenox, Otis, Peru, Pittsfield, Richmond, Stockbridge, Tyringham, and Washington.

Northern – Adams, Cheshire, Clarksburg, Florida, Hancock, Lanesborough, New Ashford, N. Adams, Savoy, Williamstown, and Windsor.

Southern – Alford, Egremont, Great Barrington, Monterey, Mt. Washington, New Marlborough, Sandisfield, Sheffield, and W. Stockbridge.

Registry of **Deeds** (Middle) [413] 443-7438 Same address & directions as probate
E-mail: mobdeeds@berkshire.net (see above).

Mon-Fri 8:30am-4:30pm

Free and open to public; copying, $.75/page. **HOLDINGS**: deeds, 1761 to present; pre-1761 records at Springfield.

Registry of **Deeds** (Northern) [413] 743-0035 Rte 9W to Rte 8A N to Rte **8 OR** Rte 7
65 Park Street & -1003 (FAX) to Rte 8; 2-story brick bldg.
Adams, MA 01220

Mon-Fri 8:30am-4:30pm

Free and open to public; mail inquiries accepted; will send indexing information and number of copies required; $.75/page. **HOLDINGS**: deeds, 1788 to present (1761-88 at Pittsfield, but copies available); pre-1761 deeds at Springfield.

Registry of **Deeds** (Southern) [413] 528-0146 Rte 102W becomes 7S; left at Red Lion
Great Barrington, MA 01230 Inn. 11.8 mi from end of Tpk to bldg –
  in town hall, 2-story brick.

Mon-Fri 8:30am-4:30pm

Free and open to public; mail inquiries accepted; records may be copied, $.75/page. **HOLDINGS**: deeds, 1788 to present (1761-88 at Pittsfield); pre-1761 deeds at Springfield.

BRISTOL COUNTY

Bristol County **Probate** Court [508] 824-4004 Rte 24S to Rte 44W; left at Taunton
11 Court Street, 2nd Floor *or* Green. Brick bldg.
P.O. Box 567
Taunton, MA 02780

Mon-Fri 8:30am-4:30pm

Free and open to public; mailed copy requests accepted (must prepay, $.50/page); on-site copying, $.25/page. **HOLDINGS**: probates, 1687 to present (earlier at Plymouth). N.B., probate records (to 1747) for *Rhode Island* towns of Tiverton, Little Compton, and Bristol are here.

THREE BRISTOL COUNTY DEED DISTRICTS

Northern – Attleborough, Berkley, Dighton, Easton, Mansfield, North Attleborough, Norton, Raynham, Rehoboth, Seekonk, and Taunton.

Southern – Acushnet, Dartmouth, Fairhaven, New Bedford, and Westport.

Fall River – Fall River, Freetown, Somerset, and Swansea.

Registry of **Deeds** (Northern) [508] 822-3081 Same address & directions as probate
Mon-Fri 8:30am-4:30pm (see above), but 1st floor.

Free and open to public; mail inquiries accepted for *copies only, no research*; copying, $.75/page. **HOLDINGS**: deeds, 1687 to present (earlier deeds at Plymouth, Mass., and Tiverton, Little Compton, and Bristol, Rhode Island).

Registry of **Deeds** (Southern)	[508] 993-2603	County St S to Williams St; left; 2
25 North 6th Street	& -2605	blocks to 6th. 1-story yellow brick bldg.
New Bedford, MA 02740	[508] 997-4250	
Mon-Fri 8:30am-5pm		

Free and open to public; staff copying, $.75/page; self-service, $.50/page; mailed copy requests accepted *if* volume and page cited. **HOLDINGS**: deeds, 1837 to present; earlier at Taunton and Plymouth.

Registry of **Deeds** (Fall River)	[508] 673-1651	Rte 195W to Exit 12 (Pleasant St); 2
441 North Main Street	& -2910	blocks; left on 8th St; 1 block; left on
Fall River, MA 02720		Bedford St; 4 blocks to No. Main; 7
		blocks to Walnut St; 2-story bldg at
Mon-Fri 8:30am-5pm (*counter closes, 4:30*)		corner of Walnut & Maple Sts (also
		faces No. Main). Bus: No. Main
		St line.

Free and open to public; mail inquiries accepted; staff copying, $.75/page; self-service, $.50/page. **HOLDINGS**: deeds, 1686 to 1891 (copies); original deeds, 1892 to present.

DUKES COUNTY

Probate Court and Registry of Deeds		Ferry: all year, from Woods Hole
81 Main Street		to Vineyard Haven in Tisbury, on
Edgartown, MA 02539		Martha's Vineyard.
Probate Court	[508] 627-4703	See above.
Mon-Fri 8:30am-4:30pm		

Free and open to public; mail inquiries accepted; copying, $.50/page; attested copies, $1.50/page. **HOLDINGS**: probates, 1696 to present.

Registry of **Deeds**	[508] 627-4025,	See above.
Mon-Fri 8:30am-4:30pm	-7821 (FAX),	
	& -9458 (Examiner)	

Free and open to public; mail requests accepted for *prepaid copies only* ($.75/page – call ahead to find out how many); onsite self-service copying, $.25/page. **HOLDINGS**: deeds, 1686 to present.

ESSEX COUNTY

Probate Court	[978] 741-0201	Rte 128 to Rte 114E to Rte 107 to
32 Federal Street		Washington St; right 1 block to Federal.
Salem, MA 01970		2-story granite bldg, 2 blocks on left.
		MBTA: No. Shore Commuter Train
Mon-Fri 8am-4:30pm		to Salem.

Free and open to public; self-service copying, $.35/page; certified, $.75/page. **HOLDINGS**: probates, 1896 to present (Essex probates, 1635-81, are in print). Probate files, 1882-96 (#s 58038-78954) and 1965-72 (divorce #s 32040-44219) are now at NEWBURYPORT RECORD CENTER (see under MULTIPLE COUNTY RECORDS). Probate files, 1638-1882 (#s 1-58037) are now at the MASSACHUSETTS STATE ARCHIVES (see under VITAL RECORDS – 1841-1905).

TWO ESSEX COUNTY DEED DISTRICTS

Southern – Amesbury, Beverly, Boxford, Danvers, Essex, Georgetown, Gloucester, Groveland, Hamilton, Haverhill, Ipswich, Lynn, Lynnfield, Manchester, Marblehead, Merrimac, Middleton, Nahant, Newbury, Newburyport, Peabody, Rockport, Rowley, Salem, Salisbury, Saugus, Swampscott, Topsfield, Wenham, and W. Newbury.

Northern – Andover, Lawrence, Methuen, and N. Andover.

Registry of **Deeds** (Southern)	[508] 741-0200	Same address & directions as probate
Mon-Fri 7am-4:30pm		(see above).

Free and open to public; mail inquiries *must* contain the following information: *name* of grantor or grantee; *town* of property; *year* of transaction; *volume* and *page*. Copying, $.35/page; certified, $.75/page. **HOLDINGS**: deeds – Salem series (primary Essex Co. registry), 1640 to present; Old Norfolk series (absorbed by Essex Co.; see under COUNTIES), 1637-1714; Ipswich series (also absorbed by Essex Co. registry), 1640-94.

Registry of **Deeds** (Northern)	[508] 683-2745	Rte 128 to Rte 93N to Rte 495N to Rte
381 Common Street	& -2746	114W; left on Canal St; right on Hamp-
Lawrence, MA 01840		shire St; right on Common. Metered
		on-street parking.
Mon-Fri 8am-4:30pm		

Free and open to public; see SOUTHERN DISTRICT for mail-request policy; copying, $.35/page. **HOLDINGS**: deeds, 1869 to present; earlier at Salem.

FRANKLIN COUNTY

Courthouse	2-story brick bldg at corner of Main &
425 Main Street	Hope Sts, opposite P.O.
Greenfield, MA 01301	

Probate Court	[413] 774-7011	See above.
Mail: P.O. Box 590		
Mon-Fri 9am-4pm		

Free and open to public; copying, $.50/page; attested copies, $1.50/page. **HOLDINGS**: probates, 1812 to present; earlier at Northampton.

Registry of **Deeds**   [413] 772-0239   See above.
P.O. Box 1495   [413] 774-7150 FAX
E-mail: fcrd@valinet.com

Mon-Fri 8:30am-4:30pm

Free and open to public; *limited* mail inquiries (copy requests, *etc.*) accepted; more detailed inquiries may be referred to professional researcher; copying, $.75/page; plans, $1/page (make checks payable to Commonwealth of Massachusetts). **HOLDINGS**: deeds, 1663-1786 (abstracts only); 1787 to present; earlier at Hampshire and Hampden County registries.

HAMPDEN COUNTY

Probate Court and Registry of Deeds   In new Hall of Justice.
50 State Street
Springfield, MA 01103

Probate Court   [413] 748-7759   See above.
Mon-Fri 8am-4:30pm

Free and open to public; mail inquiries accepted; copying, $.15/page. **HOLDINGS**: probates, 1812 to present (earlier at Northampton).

Registry of **Deeds**   [413] 748-8641   See above.
Mon-Fri 8:30am-4:30pm

Free and open to public; mail inquiries accepted; staff copying, $.75/page. **HOLDINGS**: deeds, 1636 to present (to 1812, 19th-century copies only).

HAMPSHIRE COUNTY

Probate Court and Registry of Deeds   Rtes 5 & 10 to Northampton Ctr. Hall
Hall of Records, 33 King Street   opposite Hotel Northampton.
Northampton, MA 01060

Probate Court   [413] 586-8500   See above.
Mon-Fri 9am-3pm

Free and open to public; mail inquiries accepted; self-service copying, $.25/page. **HOLDINGS**: probates, 1660 to present (earlier at Cambridge).

Registry of **Deeds**   [413] 584-3637   See above.
Mon-Fri 8:30am-4:30pm

Free and open to public; *no mail requests*; copying, $.75/page; plans, $1/page. **HOLDINGS**: record books and card indexes, 1787 to present (earlier at Springfield); plan books and indexes, 1900 to present; proprietors' books and maps for Northampton, Hadley, Hatfield, Granby, South Hadley, Pelham, and Narragansett Township #4; atlases; execution books from late 1700s; assessor's maps and indexes for all Hampshire County towns; flood maps.

MIDDLESEX COUNTY

Probate Court and Registry of Deeds
208 Cambridge Street
Cambridge, MA 02141

Storrow Dr thru Leverett Cir to O'Brien Hwy to Lechmere Sq; left under El to Cambridge St; 2 blocks. Brick bldg. Subway: Green line to Lechmere stop.

Probate Court   [617] 494-4530
Mon-Fri 8am-4pm

Free and open to public; self-service copying, $.25/page; certified, $10; *limited* mail inquiries accepted. **HOLDINGS**: probates, 1923 to present (1654-1871 are at MASSACHUSETTS STATE ARCHIVES; BOSTON PUBLIC LIBRARY has copies). N.B., probates, 1871-1923, are in storage – *must be ordered in advance.*

TWO MIDDLESEX COUNTY DEED DISTRICTS

Southern – Acton, Arlington, Ashby, Ashland, Ayer, Bedford, Belmont, Boxborough, Burlington, Cambridge, Concord, Everett, Framingham, Groton, Holliston, Hopkinton, Hudson, Lexington, Lincoln, Littleton, Malden, Marlborough, Maynard, Medford, Melrose, Natick, Newton, N. Reading, Pepperell, Reading, Sherborn, Shirley, Somerville, Stoneham, Stow, Sudbury, Townsend, Wakefield, Waltham, Watertown, Wayland, Weston, Winchester, and Woburn.

Northern – Billerica, Carlisle, Chelmsford, Dracut, Dunstable, Lowell, Tewksbury, Tyngsborough, Westford, and Wilmington.

Registry of **Deeds** (Southern)   [617] 494-4500
Mon-Fri 8am-4pm

Address & directions same as probate (see above).

Free and open to public; self-service copying, $.25/page; certified, $.75/page. **HOLDINGS**: deeds, 1649 to present; Hopkinton and Upton deeds, 1743-1833. Grantor/grantee indexes in 'basement;' follow signs to Courtroom 5. The old books are also there, but you are asked to use copies in microfilm room on 3rd floor; some are very poor. If original books seem to be missing, try the bindery room (4th floor).

Registry of **Deeds** (Northern)   [978] 458-8474
360 Gorham Street   & -8475
Lowell, MA 01852
Web: http://www.tiac.net/users/nmrd

Rte 3N to Lowell Connector to end of Gorham; left. 2-story sandstone bldg on right.

Mon-Fri 8:30am-4:30pm

Free and open to public; mail inquiries accepted (copies, $1.50/document, except mortgages, $5.25); copying, $.25/page. **HOLDINGS**: deeds, all real-estate records, and plans for 10 communities in district, 1649 to present (including copies of deeds pre-dating establishment of Northern Registry).

NANTUCKET COUNTY

Courthouse
16 Broad Street
Nantucket, MA 02554

2-story brick bldg on left of Broad, ½ mi from ferry.

Probate Court
P.O. Box 1116

[508] 228-2669
& -3662 (FAX)

See above.

Mon-Fri 8:30am-4pm

Free and open to public; limited mail inquiries accepted (no index searches); copying, $.50/page. **HOLDINGS**: probates, 1706 to present. (Probates, 1695-1705, in records of Nantucket Superior Court.)

Registry of **Deeds**
Mon-Fri 8am-4pm

[508] 228-7250

Same address & directions as probate (see above).

Free and open to public; limited mail inquiries accepted (no index searches); copying, $.50/page. **HOLDINGS**: deeds, 1659 (not a typo!) to present.

NORFOLK COUNTY (N.B., *OLD* Norfolk County – comprising Exeter, Salisbury, Hampton, Haverhill, Dover, and Strawbery Banke [later Portsmouth] – existed from 1643 to 1679. Its records are at Salem. Not to be confused with the present Norfolk County!)

Courthouse
649 High Street
Dedham, MA 02026

Rte 128 to Exit 15A; left at 3rd light on Eastern Av; at end, left on High; bldg at 2nd light, on right (parking in rear) **OR** Rte 1S to High; left. Bus: E. Walpole bus from Forest Hills; stops at Dedham Ctr; 2 blocks W.

Probate Court
Mon-Fri 8:30am-4:30pm

[781] 326-7200

See above.

Free and open to public; mail inquiries accepted (copies only, no research); copying, $.75/page. **HOLDINGS**: probates, 1793 to present (earlier at Boston).

Registry of **Deeds**
Mon-Fri 8:30am-4:30pm

[781] 461-6123

Address & directions same as probate (see above).

Free and open to public; mail inquiries accepted (copies only, no research); copying, $.75/page. **HOLDINGS**: deeds and plans, 1793 to present (earlier at Boston).

PLYMOUTH COUNTY

County Commissioners
11 South Russell Street
Plymouth, MA 02360

[508] 830-9100

Rte 44S to Rte 3A (Court St); 1 mi; right on Russell (which turns into South Russell). Bldg on left behind Third District courthouse; office on 2nd floor.

Mon-Fri 8am-5pm

Free and open to public; copying, $.50/page; mail inquiries accepted (copies only, $2 minimum). **HOLDINGS**: deeds, probates, and court orders, 1620-*ca.* 1692.

Plymouth **Probate** and Family Court Russell Street *or* P.O. Box 3640 Plymouth, MA 02360	[508] 747-6204	Rte 3 to Exit 6 (Rte 44E) to Rte 3A (Court St); then same as above.
Mon-Fri 8:30am-4pm		

Free and open to public; *limited* mail inquiries accepted *with SASE*; staff copying, $.50/page; self-service, $.25/page; *no personal checks*. **HOLDINGS**: probates, 1882 to present (-1935 as film and docket books only); pre-1881 records now at MASSACHUSETTS STATE ARCHIVES.

Registry of **Deeds** Mon-Fri 8:15am-4:30pm	[508] 830-9200	Address & directions same as Probate and Family Court (see above).

Free and open to public; mail inquiries accepted (copies [$1/page] of *specifically cited* book-and-page numbers only – staff *prohibited by law* from doing research or giving legal advice); self-service copying, $.50/page; staff, $.75/page. **HOLDINGS**: deeds, mortgages, and other real-estate-related Plymouth County documents, 1686 to present; atlases and maps, 1854+; assessors' maps for all 27 Plymouth County towns; plans, 1853 to present; certificates of title, 1899 to present; grantor/grantee indexes, 1686 to present. N.B., on-line "Titleview" service available. FAX ordering. Plan indexes, 1975+. Contact Registry for information and registration pamphlets (no fee to register).

SUFFOLK COUNTY

New Courthouse 24 New Chardon Street *or* P.O. Box 9660 Boston, MA 02114-9660	Rte 93S to Haymarket Sq Exit; bldg 1 block on right **OR** 93N to No. Sta Exit; left; left at light (Lancaster St); straight 1 block; bldg on right. Subway: Haymarket stop on Green or Orange line; 1 block on right.

Probate Court Mon-Fri 8am-5pm	[617] 788-8300	See above.

Free and open to public; limited mail inquiries accepted; self-service copying, $.25/page; by staff, $.50. **HOLDINGS**: probates, 1895 to present; pre-1894 records are at MASSACHUSETTS STATE ARCHIVES; records cover all estates over £50 for entire 'Dominion of New England,' 1686-9; *Suffolk County Wills* (1984) covers 1640-70. Indexes printed to 1979.

Registry of **Deeds** Mon-Fri 9am-4:45pm	[617] 788-8575	See above.

Free and open to public; limited mail inquiries accepted; self-service copying, $.25/page. **HOLDINGS**: deeds, 1639 to present (*but see note*); Block Island records to 1663; maps of early Boston estates; first 14 volumes of Suffolk deeds in print; records of towns annexed by Boston – Brighton, Charlestown, Dorchester, Hyde Park, Roxbury, and West Roxbury – are at City Hall.

N.B., Suffolk County has sent its older original deed books to the STATE ARCHIVES, and has *film only* of deeds pre-dating *ca.* 1920. Unfortunately, the Archives will not currently (Apr 1999) allow the old originals to be viewed; it also lacks indexes. While it *will* copy deeds ($.75/page) if given exact book-and-page citations, these can be obtained only from indexes at the Registry; furthermore, the Archives' current practice is to photoreduce the original folios to 8½ x 11 pages; as these are then FAXed to the researcher, legibility may be less than optimal, so the Registry's films (though old) may be your best bet. *However, the above policies are in rapid flux; call for up-to-date information.*

WORCESTER COUNTY

Probate Court 2 Main Street Worcester, MA 01608 Mon-Fri 8am-4:30pm	[508] 770-0825	MA Tpk (I-90) to Exit 10 (I-290); E towards Worcester to Exit 17. At end of ramp, left on Rte 9W (Belmont St); ¼ mi to Lincoln Sq. Bldg on corner of Highland & Main Sts.

Free and open to public; limited mail inquiries accepted; staff copying, $.50/page; certified, $1.50. **HOLDINGS**: probates, 1881 to present; copybooks, 1731-1881, on film at MASSACHUSETTS STATE ARCHIVES; originals at WESTERN WORCESTER DISTRICT TRIAL COURT RECORDS CENTER (see under MULTIPLE COUNTY RECORDS, above).

TWO WORCESTER COUNTY DEED DISTRICTS

Worcester – Athol, Auburn, Barre, Berlin, Blackstone, Bolton, Brookfield, Charlton, Clinton, Douglas, Dudley, E. Brookfield, Gardner, Grafton, Hardwick, Holden, Hopedale, Hubbardston, Lancaster, Leicester, Mendon, Milford, Millville, New Braintree, N. Brookfield, Northborough, Northbridge, Oakham, Paxton, Petersham, Phillipstown, Princeton, Royalston, Rutland, Shrewsbury, Southborough, Southbridge, Spencer, Sterling, Sturbridge, Sutton, Templeton, Upton, Uxbridge, Warren, Webster, Westborough, W. Boylston, W. Brookfield, Winchendon, and Worcester.

Northern – Ashburnham, Fitchburg, Leominster, Lunenburg, and Westminster.

Registry of **Deeds** (Worcester) Mon-Fri 8:15am-4:30pm	[508] 798-7713	Same address & directions as probate (see above); Deeds on 1st floor.

Free and open to public; self-service copying, $.50/page; limited mail inquiries accepted ($1.25/page). **HOLDINGS**: deeds, 1731 to present. Upton deeds, 1743-1833, at Cambridge (see note above).

Registry of **Deeds** (Northern) 84 Elm Street Fitchburg, MA 01420 Mon-Fri 8:30am-4:30pm	[978] 342-2132 & -2637	Rte 2 to Rte 12N to Rte 2A to Pritchard St; right on Elm; left. 3-story brick bldg, 2 blocks on right.

Free and open to public; limited mail inquiries (copies [$.50, pre-paid] only; request must state volume and page number[s]); self-service copying, $.25/page. **HOLDINGS**: deeds, 1884 to present (earlier at Worcester).

N.B., pre-1731 deeds for Worcester, Lancaster, Westborough, Shrewsbury, Southborough, Leicester, Rutland, and Lunenburg are at Cambridge; for Mendon, Woodstock, Oxford, Sutton, and Uxbridge, at Boston; for the Brookfields and parts of Southbridge, Sturbridge, and Woodstock, at Springfield.

CEMETERY RECORDS

There is no central repository of Mass. cemetery records. Printed, typed, and manuscript transcripts for individual towns, however, are plentiful. Most volumes of the 'official series' of *Massachusetts Vital Records to 1850* include gravestone data. Inscriptions from many 'old burying grounds' have been published in the *Register, Essex Institute Historical Collections*, and *Mayflower Descendant*; the DAR has transcribed many graveyards; and public libraries and historical societies often have transcripts from local cemeteries. The Corbin, Cooke, and Hale collections at NEHGS and the BERKSHIRE ATHENAEUM contain transcripts of cemeteries in many western Mass. and Conn. towns. Larger cemeteries often maintain on-site or nearby record offices. These offices keep card files which may have much more information than appears on the gravestones, especially for more recent years. They will usually assist – some for a fee – in the search for a particular surname; many, however, only by mail. It is always helpful to *visit* a cemetery, since the *arrangement* of stones may provide clues to relationships not otherwise apparent.

The ASSOCIATION FOR GRAVESTONE STUDIES has information on cemeteries in New England and elsewhere (see NEW ENGLAND chapter).

See also David Allen Lambert's forthcoming book, under BOOKS AND ARTICLES.

CHURCH RECORDS

Church records vary considerably from one denomination to the next, but most include baptisms (for Baptist sects, of adults only!) and marriages; some, burials and/or admissions and dismissals (the latter can be crucial for tracking a family's migration); a few – essentially, Catholic, high Episcopal, and Lutheran – confirmations. Church records are highly reliable – Quaker and Lutheran being the most detailed. The local pastor is custodian of church records, and the first person to consult. If early records are not at the church, he may know where they are. The records of *defunct* churches should be sought first at the nearest historical society or library; some denominations archive such records at regional or national headquarters. The following denominations have Mass. repositories.

CATHOLIC

Catholic records are under parish jurisdiction. Recently, however, a move has begun to centralize early records by diocese. Mass. has four: Boston, Fall River, Springfield, and Worcester. Only the Boston diocese, serving eastern Mass., has established an archive; a project to microfilm the collection is underway. (See Virginia Humling, *U.S. Catholic Sources* [under BOOKS AND PERIODICALS], for the other three diocesan addresses.)

Archives of the Archdiocese   [617] 746-5797
  of Boston
2121 Commonwealth Avenue
Brighton, MA 02135

From W: Rte 30 becomes Commonwealth Av. Archives in Creagh Library on seminary campus. Ample parking. Subway: Green line to Boston College stop.

Mon-Fri 10am-4:30pm (*appointments preferred; closed holy days*)

Free and open to public; donations welcome; copying, $.25/page; brief mail requests answered (no extensive research). **HOLDINGS**: records arranged chronologically by parish; pre-1920 baptismal and marriage records for about 150 eastern-Mass. parishes. (NEHGS has a guide to the Archives' holdings at its 4th-floor desk.)

CONGREGATIONAL

The Congregational Library [617] 523-0470 Diagonally across from State House,
14 Beacon Street & -0491 (FAX) near corner of Park St. Subway: Green
Boston, MA 02108 or Red line to Park St stop.
E-mail: blwhfw@aol.com

Mon-Fri 8:30am-4:30pm (*by appointment only, at least 1 day ahead*)

The Library was established in 1853. Free and open to ministers and laymen of all denominations. 4-week free book loan, by mail. Copying, $.25/page. Limited mail queries accepted. N.B., focus on individuals rather than families. **HOLDINGS**: 225,000 books and pamphlets, including local church and town histories, theological works of five centuries, sermons, Bibles, *etc*. (See Harold Worthley, *An Inventory of the Records of the Particular* [Congregational] *Churches of Massachusetts Gathered 1620-1805*, under BOOKS AND ARTICLES.)

EPISCOPAL

Diocesan Library and [617] 482-5800 x 504 Facing Common near Tourist Informa-
  Archives tion Booth. Garages at Government Ctr
Episcopal Diocese of Massachusetts or Common. Subway: Green or Red
138 Tremont Street line to Park St stop.
Boston, MA 02111

Labor Day-Jul 4: Mon-Fri 8:30am-4:30pm (*by appointment*)
Jul 4-Labor Day: Mon-Fri 8:30am-3:30pm (*ditto*)

Free and open to public; mail inquiries accepted (1st ½ hour free; $20/hour thereafter, with $20 minimum); records cannot be photocopied. **HOLDINGS**: pre-1905 registers (on film) of 104 active and closed parishes in the Diocese of Massachusetts; including baptisms, marriages, burials, and communicants. Copies of registers of 11 of diocese's 13 colonial parishes also here.

JEWISH (see LIBRARIES – WALTHAM – AMERICAN-JEWISH HISTORICAL SOCIETY LIBRARY)

METHODIST

Boston University School of [617] 353-1323 Subway: Green line to Boston
  Theology Library University stop. On-street parking.
745 Commonwealth Avenue
Boston, MA 02215

Mon-Fri 9am-4pm (*by appointment only, 2 days ahead*)

Free and open to public; mail inquiries accepted. **HOLDINGS**: records of closed Methodist (Episcopal) churches, or older records of current United Methodist churches in New England Conference; Commission on Archives and History Collection (mostly Mass., but some eastern Conn., Rhode Island, and N.H.). Records may be copied at staff's discretion, $.10/page.

QUAKER (SOCIETY OF FRIENDS)

Records for most of New England are at the RHODE ISLAND HISTORICAL SOCIETY LIBRARY (see under LIBRARIES – PROVIDENCE). NEHGS has records of the Dartmouth, New Bedford, and Westport, Mass., and Vermont Meetings; Salem's ESSEX INSTITUTE and the LYNNFIELD PUBLIC LIBRARY have the Salem Meeting records (all on film).

UNITARIAN-UNIVERSALIST

Andover-Harvard   [617] 496-5153   Off Kirkland St. Parking permit $5/day
   Theological Library   at Divinity School Office (same
45 Francis Avenue   address). Subway: Red line to Harvard
Cambridge, MA 02138   Sq stop.

Mon-Fri 9am-5pm (*by appointment only, 2 days ahead*)

Open to public; copying (at curator's discretion), $.10/page; limited mail inquiries accepted (no research). **HOLDINGS**: Unitarian-Universalist records and archives, including Library of Universalist Historical Society (world's major repository of Universalism), given to Harvard in 1976, and archives of Unitarian-Universalist Association, American Unitarian Association, and Unitarian-Universalist Service Committee. Records are of closed Unitarian and Universalist churches, with a few (on film) still active, including minute books, financial records, membership lists, births and deaths, records of women's and youth groups, Sunday schools, some ministers' VRs, *etc*. Contact the Curator of Manuscripts at Harvard Divinity School (same as above).

MILITARY RECORDS

Mass. military matters are well recorded. Two major sets of books are important first references: *Massachusetts Soldiers and Sailors of the Revolutionary War* (17 volumes, plus microfilm supplement) and *Massachusetts Soldiers, Sailors and Marines in the Civil War* (9 volumes). There are also single published volumes for King Philip's War and other colonial wars, and for the War of 1812. The *D.A.R. Patriot Index* should be checked as well. Original military records of colonial Mass. (including Maine) are at the MASSACHUSETTS STATE ARCHIVES (see under VITAL RECORDS). The "General Index to Compiled Military Service Records of Revolutionary War Soldiers" is at the NATIONAL ARCHIVES (see NEW ENGLAND chapter).

Mass. military records from 1781 (militia) to the Vietnam War are at the state Adjutant General's Office. Pre-1681 records cover men who served in the state militia, and may have been called to active duty during emergencies. However, this office was closed to the public in March 1998 and all records transferred to:

COMMONWEALTH OF MASSACHUSETTS – MILITARY DIVISION – HISTORY RESEARCH AND MUSEUM

44 Salisbury Street [508] 797-0334 From E: Rte 290W to Exit 13; right on
Worcester, MA 02169 Salisbury St. From W: Rte 290E to Rte
E-mail: MRARCHIVES@aol.com 9 Exit; left; right on Central Blvd; left
on Salisbury.

Tue-Fri (*by appointment only, 3-7 days ahead*)

Free and open to public; copying with archivist's permission. **HOLDINGS**: early militia (1776-1819); Mass. militia (1820-39); pre-Civil War (1840-60); Civil War (1861-5); Reconstruction (1866-97): Spanish American War / Philippines Insurrection (1898-1916); World War I (1917-19), including State Guard records; National Guard (1920-40). Originals pertaining to Mass. militia, beginning with the Revolution, and to veterans of all conflicts from the Civil War through the Spanish-American War / Philippines Insurrection. N.B., for a more complete list, see James C. Neagles, *U.S. Military Records* (NEW ENGLAND – BOOKS AND ARTICLES).

IMMIGRATION AND NATURALIZATION

Records are kept by the court in which the petitioner was naturalized, and may be obtained directly from the clerk. Naturalization records from 1906 onward may also be obtained from the U.S. Department of Justice in Washington, D.C., or from each state's federal office. Indexes of naturalizations from late 18th or early 19th century to third quarter of 20th (varies by state) are at the NATIONAL ARCHIVES (see NEW ENGLAND chapter); NEHGS has indexes of the pre-1906 records.

Immigration and Naturalization [617] 565-3879 Subway: Green or Blue line to Govern-
US Department of Justice ment Ctr stop. Parking garages nearby.
JFK Federal Building, Government Center
Boston, MA 02203

Mon-Fri 7am-3pm

Naturalization records are provided free – *via* Freedom of Information Act requests – *only* if name, date, and location of naturalization are stated. Use form G-639, available at JFK Building or by mail. The office of the Clerk of Courts, Suffolk County Courthouse (old building), has an index to pre-1906 Suffolk County naturalizations. The NATIONAL ARCHIVES has an index to all pre-1906 Mass. naturalizations, as well as indexes of some post-1906 records. See also VITAL RECORDS – MASSACHUSETTS STATE ARCHIVES.

See also this section in the CONNECTICUT chapter.

NEWSPAPERS

Two major repositories for early Mass. newspapers (starting in 1704 with the *Boston News-Letter*) stand in a class of their own. The best collection of such *on film* is to be found in the BOSTON PUBLIC LIBRARY's microtext department, whose holdings also include many early newspapers from other New England states. In addition, the AMERICAN ANTIQUARIAN SOCIETY (Worcester) has the "finest collection of 18th- and 19th-century American newspapers anywhere," almost entirely as *original* copies, including not only all the Commonwealth's oldest newspapers, but holdings, as well, for the rest of the Colonies, Canada, England, and the West Indies.

The AMERICAN ANTIQUARIAN SOCIETY also published, as bound photocopies of an original WPA typescript, an 8-volume *Index of Marriages in Massachusetts Centinel and Columbian Centinel 1784-1840* (n.d., The Society); it likewise compiled and, in 1952, released – in like format – a 12-volume *Index of Deaths*, from the same newspapers and covering the same range of years.

In 1968, the BOSTON ATHENAEUM published, as bound photocopies of two card-files, its *Index of Obituaries in Boston Newspapers 1704-1800*; volume 1 is *Deaths Within Boston*; volumes 2 and 3, *Deaths Outside Boston* (all, 1968: Boston, G. K. Hall).

At press, NEHGS is preparing to issue *Notices of Boston Deaths, 1700-1799* [tentative title], by Robert J. Dunkle and Ann S. Lainhart; this will incorporate all death notices from all 18th-century Boston newspapers accessible to the compilers.

CIVIL AND CRIMINAL COURT RECORDS

The organization of Mass.'s complex civil and criminal court system has changed many times over its 369-year history; a 1-paragraph précis not being feasible, the reader is urged to consult Catherine S. Menand, *A Research Guide to the Massachusetts Courts and Their Records*, 135 pp. and 1 fiche (1987: Boston, Massachusetts Supreme Judicial Court – Archives and Records Preservation).

As for location, the records themselves fall, *roughly*, into three groups. Much of the earliest (17th-century) material has been published; for the Mass. Bay Colony, see Nathaniel B. Shurtleff, ed., *Records of ... Massachusetts ...* [1628-86], 6 vols. (1853-4: Boston, William White Press) and John Noble, ed., *Records of the Court of Assistants ... Massachusetts ... 1630-1692*, 2 vols. (1901-4: Boston, Suffolk Co.); for the Plymouth Colony, see Nathaniel B. Shurtleff, ed., *Records of the Colony of New Plymouth ...*, 9 vols. (1855-61: Boston, William White Press); for Plymouth County to a much later date, see David T. Konig, ed., *Plymouth Court Records 1686-1859*, 16 vols. (1978-81: Wilmington, DE, Michael Glazier Inc.); for Essex Co., see George F. Dow, ed., *Records and Files of the Quarterly Courts of Essex County ...* [1636-86], 9 vols. (1911-21: Salem, Essex Institute). Some – but not all – 18th- and early 19th-century Mass. Supreme Judicial Court, county, and (a host of) other court records are available on film at the MASSACHUSETTS STATE ARCHIVES (see under VITAL RECORDS; unfortunately, it appears that no *simple* list of the Archives' court holdings exists). Finally, past a cutoff-year that varies from county to county, the records should be found at the county courthouse. (However, exceptions exist.)

LIBRARIES

Mass. has 351 public libraries, whose holdings vary greatly. Most have small collections, which may or may not include items of genealogical interest; many are open less than 12 hours a week and undertake no research. For a list of all libraries, with hours, consult the *American Library Directory* in most large libraries. The facilities listed below have significant genealogical collections. N.B., the website for any library in Mass. can be reached *via* the homepage of the Mass. Library Information Network – http://www.mlin.lib.ma.us.

AMHERST – JONES LIBRARY

43 Amity Street	[413] 256-4090	From corner of Rtes 9 & 16 in Amherst
Amherst, MA 01002	& -4096 (FAX)	center, N, to NW corner of Common.
		Library on left, just past bank.

Mon, Wed, Fri 9am-5:30pm
Tue, Thu 9am-9:30pm; Sun 1-5pm (*some sections close ½ hour earlier all week*)

Staff copying, $.10/page ($.25/page by mail, plus $.50 handling; $5 minimum); 3 film readers; genealogical materials are in Special Collections department – curator's permission required for access; materials do not circulate. **HOLDINGS**: 950 published genealogies, 400 reference works, 6,500 books and documents of local history – mostly Mass., especially the Conn. River valley; Lucius Boltwood papers; local newspapers; all federal censuses for Hampshire County through 1920; some local church records (curator's permission required for use); subscribes to 3 genealogical and 2 historical journals.

AMHERST – UNIVERSITY OF MASSACHUSETTS – W.E.B. DUBOIS LIBRARY

Amherst, MA 01003	[413] 545-0150	On campus. Parking at Campus Center
Web: http://www.library.umass.edu		Garage.

hours vary with academic year

Free admission, open stacks; copying, $.10/page; 18 film, 9 fiche, and 2 micro-opaque readers; 7 film/fiche reader/printers ($.20/print); Mass. adults may borrow. **HOLDINGS**: in microform – federal censuses for all states, 1790-1830; for all New England states, most of New York, some Ohio and Virginia, 1840-80; for Mass., 1900-20; extensive set of U.S. city directories to 1860; selected cities, 1861-1935; newspapers; early Suffolk County deed, probate, and court records; part of early MASSACHUSETTS STATE ARCHIVES collection; Boston passenger arrivals, 1820-1943 (indexes: 1848-91, 1889-1940, 1902-20); New Bedford passenger arrivals, 1902-42 (index: 1902-54); crew lists for New Bedford arrivals, 1917-43; crew lists for port of Gloucester, 1918-43; some Mass. VRs to 1850; Hampshire County probates to 1820; inventory of Franklin County probates; some Middlesex County town records to 1830 (also Amherst, Greenwich, Hadley, Sunderland, and Whately); Howes Brothers' photo collection, *ca.* 1882-1907; all Massachusetts Harbor and Land Commission town-boundary atlases, 1898-1916. Printed: New England local histories, some genealogies. In Special Collections: land-ownership maps; atlases of New England, New York, and New Jersey, *ca.* 1865-*ca.* 1920; and a regional names index for account books and other local manuscript materials.

ATHOL PUBLIC LIBRARY

568 Main Street	[978] 249-2544	Rte 2 (E or W) to Athol Exit; signs to
Athol, MA 01331	& -7636 (FAX)	town. Library next to town hall. On-
E-mail: rgagliar@cwmarsmail.cwmars.org		street parking.

Mon, Wed, Thu 9:30am-7pm; Tue 2-7pm; Fri 9:30am-5pm; Sat 9am-1pm
(*summer*: closed Tue, Sat)

Free and open to public; mail inquiries accepted (copies, $.15 each, plus postage); 1 film and 1 fiche reader/printer ($.10/page). **HOLDINGS**: some genealogies and local histories (Archives Room); most published Mass. VRs to 1850; local newspaper (1870s+; on film); town reports and directories (late 1800s+). Please contact before traveling any distance.

BARNSTABLE – STURGIS LIBRARY (see also WEST BARNSTABLE)

3090 Main Street	[508] 362-6636	Rte 6 (Mid-Cape Hwy) to Exit 6 (Barnstable); left on Rte 132N; at end, right on Rte 6A. Library 2.5 mi E, on left, just past St. Mary's Church **OR** if going W on 6A toward Barnstable, library on right, 300 yds past Village ctr.
Barnstable, MA 02630		
E-mail: sturgis@capecod.net		
Mon, Thu 10am-2pm; Tue, Wed 1-9pm		
Fri 1-5pm; Sat 10am-4pm		

Non-residents of Barnstable, $5/day; members, $25/year; mail and e-mail inquiries accepted (up to 20 minutes' research free; call for overtime fees); most records copyable, $.20/page; 1 film/fiche reader/printer; 1 Web browser; 1 CD workstation with Family Tree Maker (call ahead to reserve film, Web, or CD facilities); handicapped accessible. **HOLDINGS**: all published Mass. VRs to 1850; Mayflower Society and Colonial Dames records; federal censuses for Maine, Mass., Vermont, and N.H.; heraldry references; town histories (Boston, southeast Mass., Rhode Island, New Jersey, and Conn.); Plymouth Colony records; gravestone transcripts, including Barnstable and Dennis; Essex County records; Barnstable VRs, 1643-1840 (handwritten) and 1643-1890 (fiche); histories of Barnstable County and the Islands, and their towns; Amos Otis's "Genealogical Notes of Cape Cod Families;" "Cape Cod Library of History and Genealogy;" East Parish (Unitarian) records, 1715-1950s; Barnstable *Patriot*, 1830 to present, and *The Register*, 1836 to present (newspapers on film); Sandwich and Bourne historical papers; 300 published genealogies of Barnstable families; 500 manuscripts or pamphlets on Barnstable history and genealogy; and 1500 Barnstable County deeds, 1726-1859.

BOSTON ATHENAEUM

10½ Beacon Street	[617] 227-0270	Near State House. <u>Subway</u>: Red or Green lines to Park St stop.
Boston, MA 02108	& -5266 (FAX)	
Mon-Fri 9am-5:30pm; Sat 9am-4pm (*Oct-May only*)		

Open to members and *qualified researchers* (by appointment only); no fees; copier and film reader/printer, $.25/page; ask for photo-services price sheet; on-line search and access to specialized databases, members only. **HOLDINGS**: special collections – Wirth's *Boston Evening Transcript* Obituary Index, 1830-74; Codman's genealogies of Boston, New York, and Newport families; Boston deaths, 1704-1825; marriages and deaths from *New York Commercial Advertiser,* 1800-25, and *New York Evening Post,* 1801-47; 19th-century Boston newspapers; family papers (letters, diaries, *etc.*).

BOSTON – GRAND [MASONIC] LODGE OF MASSACHUSETTS, A.F. & A.M.

186 Tremont Street	Green line to Boylston stop; across street.
Boston, MA 02111	
E-mail: kaulback@glmasons-mass.org	

Despite its convenient placement here, the Lodge is *NOT* a library, but headquarters for the Masons of Mass.; the building is open *only* to Masons. (Which is why no hours are listed.) **HOLDINGS**: a massive cardfile of nearly half a million Mass. (including pre-1820 Maine) Masons, ranging from 1733 to modern times. The cards include details of membership, and sometimes other facts, such as birth and/or death years, removals to other lodges, *etc.* While one must be a Mason to consult the cardfile itself, the Lodge will reply to snail- or e-mail inquiries by copying and sending cards, free of charge. Inquiries must state the exact name of the Mason in question, and – at least approximately – when he lived. (Enclosing a SASE is always a good idea, too.)

Each of the five other New England states has its own Grand Lodge, and a similar cardfile; their addresses are: *Conn.* – Masonic Ave., P.O. Box 250, Wallingford, CT 06492 (E-mail: maw.m.mccrv@masonic.chime.org); *Maine* – Masonic Temple, P.O. Box 15058, Portland, ME 04112-5058; *N.H.* – 813 Beech St., Manchester, NH 03104-3136; *Rhode Island* – Freemasons' Hall, 222 Taunton Ave., E. Providence, RI 02914-4556; *Vermont* – E. Rd., R.R. #3, Box 6742B, Barre, VT 05641-8611.

BOSTON – MASSACHUSETTS HISTORICAL SOCIETY LIBRARY

1154 Boylston Street	[617] 536-1608	Storrow Dr to Kenmore Sq/Park St Exit;
Boston, MA 02215	& -1609	up ramp; left at lights on Boylston. 1st
E-mail: library@masshist.org		bldg on right. Subway: Hynes Convention Center stop on Green line.
Mon-Fri 9am-4:45pm		
Sat 9am-1pm (*by appointment only*)		

Free; staff copying; 2 self-service film printers. **HOLDINGS**: personal and family papers; manuscripts and rare printed material; books and periodicals relating to history of Mass., New England, and U.S.; Thwing Index of early Boston residents (1630-1800); historic photos; maps; portraits. *Does not attempt to duplicate sources at NEHGS.*

BOSTON – MASSACHUSETTS STATE ARCHIVES (see under VITAL RECORDS)

BOSTON – NEW ENGLAND HISTORIC GENEALOGICAL SOCIETY (NEHGS) (see NEW ENGLAND chapter – LIBRARIES AND RESEARCH FACILITIES)

BOSTON PUBLIC LIBRARY

Copley Square	[617] 536-5400	From N: Rte 93S or Rte 1S to Storrow Dr to Beacon St; left on Exeter St; 4
Boston, MA 02117		blocks. From S: Rte 93N to East Berkeley St; left on St. James Av. From W:
Web: http://www.bpl.org		MA Tpk to Copley Exit; left on Dartmouth St. Subway: Copley stop on
Mon-Thu 9am-9pm; Fri, Sat 9am-5pm		Green line or Back Bay on Orange.
Sun 1pm-5pm (*Oct-May only*)		

State residents entitled to free library card; out-of-staters with ID may have free courtesy card; 19 film and 3 microprint-or-card readers; 1 micro-opaque and 4 film/fiche printers ($.25/page). Staff cannot answer genealogical or heraldic queries by mail; copying from genealogies or armorials may be arranged *only* if author, title, and specific page number(s) are stated; shipping and passenger lists and city directories will be searched *only* for specific year. **HOLDINGS**: many genealogies and local histories, supplemented by *Local History and Genealogy Collection* (160,000 fiche). Separate catalog for genealogies, with analytics and vertical file material not in main catalog. 2000-entry index to coats of arms (chiefly British). *Family Search* (LDS CD database). 300 city directories for 700 towns. Colonial and Mass. newspapers, 1704+; indexes to obits in Boston and New England newspapers (1704-1840; 1875+); index to *Boston Evening Transcript* genealogical column (1901-35); *Hartford Times* genealogical column (1940-67, with index). Immigration: passenger arrival lists, with indexes, for New England, New York, and some Atlantic and Gulf ports; indexes to New England naturalization petitions. Census: federal schedules for all New England states, 1790-1920, with printed indexes and Soundexes; 1890 veterans census for New England. VRs: for many Mass. towns, generally to 1850; index for whole state,

1841-95; for many other New England localities. Also, records of Boston and its annexed communities, and of many Middlesex County towns; Boston voter lists, 1861-1959; Essex County probates to 1681, Hampshire to 1820, Middlesex to 1871, Suffolk to 1852, with Middlesex and Suffolk probate indexes to 1909. Military: indexes to Revolutionary service records, and to New England Civil War volunteer records; records of Union and Confederate forces; and Loyalist claims against British Crown. *The above list is a representative sample only of the BPL's genealogically useful holdings.*

BOSTON – STATE LIBRARY OF MASSACHUSETTS

State House, Room 341 [617] 727-2590 (Ref) Storrow Dr to Beacon. Parking under
Beacon Street   Boston Common. Subway: Park St
Boston, MA 02133   stop on Red or Green line.

Mon-Fri 9am-5pm

Free; copying, $.20/page; film reader/printer, $.25/page. No extensive genealogical research possible *via* phone or mail, but researchers welcome to visit. **HOLDINGS:** Mass. town and county histories; publications by state agencies (official repository); Mass. maps, atlases, and city directories (for latter, see Special Collections, below); index to Mass. newspapers, *ca.* 1878-1937; legislators' biographies, 1780 to present. Some federal records (no censuses).

Special Collections [617] 727-2595 See above.
State House, Room 55

Mon-Fri 9am-5pm

Staff copying, $.25/page. **HOLDINGS:** city directories; some Mass. 'reverse' or 'criss-cross' directories (listings ordered by street or telephone number), chiefly late 1960s and early '70s; eligible-voter lists (by ward and precinct); maps.

BOSTON – UNIVERSITY OF MASSACHUSETTS – HEALEY LIBRARY

Archives and Special [617] 287-5944
   Collections – 10th Floor
100 Morrissey Boulevard
Boston, MA 02125

Mon-Fri 9am-5pm (*appointment required*!)

Free and open to public; access to some collections may require prior permission from donor; no research undertaken; staff copying only, $.10/page, up to 10 pp., $.20/page thereafter. **HOLDINGS:** 19th- and early 20th-century records of Boston-area charitable and benevolent organizations, chiefly child-related; including Boston Children's Aid Society, Boston Female Asylum (orphanage), Boston Children's Friends Society, Massachusetts Society for Prevention of Cruelty to Children, Boston Asylum and Farm School (on Thompson's Island), Gwynne Temporary Home, *et al.*

BOXFORD HISTORIC DOCUMENT CENTER (BHDC)

173A Washington Street   [978] 887-9413   I-95 to Exit 54 (Rte 133W), thru
West Boxford, MA 01885   Georgetown. At X of 133 & Main St,
                                          next to church.

Wed 9am-4pm & 7:30-9:30pm
1st & 2nd Sat 10am-3pm

Free and open to public; mail inquiries accepted; film reader/printer; copying, $.10/page. **HOLDINGS**: genealogical and historical materials relating to Boxford and surrounding Essex County towns; family papers; photos; maps and plans; records of local businesses and organizations; collections of Boxford Historical Society and Second Church; town and First Church records on film; and local weekly newspaper.

BROCKTON PUBLIC LIBRARY

304 Main Street   [508] 580-7890   Rte 24 to Rte 123E (Belmont St) to
Brockton, MA 02401-5390   Brockton ctr; right on Main; 1 block;
                                       bldg on left, corner of White Av &
Mon, Tue noon-8pm; Wed, Thu, Sat 9am-5pm   Main, beside YMCA. <u>Train</u>: Old Colo-
Fri 1-5pm (*summer*: closed Sat)   ny RR, Middleboro line, stops 2 blocks
                                       from bldg; Plymouth/Boston or BAT
                                       bus to BAT terminal, 1 block from bldg.

Free, but modest donation/SASE appreciated with *brief* requests for information or obits; patrons must sign at desk to use locked Crosby Historical Room; copying, $.15/page; 2 film readers; 1 reader/printer, $.25/page; copies from Brockton directories and poll-tax and street lists, $2 each; Brockton newspaper obits on film, $3/copy; no interlibrary loan of Historical-Room materials, *except* newspaper films (form must be filed from researcher's local library). **HOLDINGS**: 3,000 New England genealogies and Mass. and Brockton town histories; Brockton poll-tax books, 1896+; directories, 1869+; *The Mayflower Descendant*, volumes 1-34; NEHGS *Register*; and the 'official series' of published Mass. VRs to 1850; Brockton and North Bridgewater newspapers, 1850+ (film; ask at circulation desk).

CAMBRIDGE PUBLIC LIBRARY

449 Broadway   [617] 349-4044   Near Harvard Sq. Adjacent parking lot,
Cambridge, MA 02138   also off-street. <u>Subway</u>: 10-min walk
                                         from Harvard stop on Red line.
Genealogy room: Mon-Fri 9am-5pm

Free; must register at Reference desk, leave ID; copying with librarian's permission, $.15/page; film and fiche readers and reader/printer; after 5pm and on weekends, staff retrieves specific titles for use in Reference Room – service may be limited when busy; staff will answer *limited* mail queries as time/staffing allow; substantial research, $25/hour plus copies. No interlibrary loan. **HOLDINGS**: New England local history and genealogy.

CHATHAM – ELDREDGE PUBLIC LIBRARY

564 Main Street	[508] 945-0274	Mid-Cape Hwy to Exit 11; left; straight
Chatham, MA 02633		to Rte 28; left; to Chatham Center. Bldg
		on left, opposite Puritan Clothing store.
Genealogy collection: Tue, Thu 1-5pm		Parking at rear or in town lot.

Excellent and underused; free and open to public; 2 rooms (hold 10 people); mail inquiries (minimal research as time allows; copies and postage charged); copying, $.10/page; outlets for laptops; lockers for large bags and briefcases. **HOLDINGS**: most Mass. VRs to 1850; records and histories from Maritime Provinces, down eastern seaboard; *Massachusetts Soldiers and Sailors of the Revolutionary War*; many published genealogies; Cape Cod materials; New York, Conn., Penn., N.J., Maryland, and Virginia resources; census indexes on CD; Social Security Death Index; *Mayflower Descendant*; NEHGS *Register*; Periodical Source Index (PERSI).

CLINTON – BIGELOW FREE PUBLIC LIBRARY

54 Walnut Street	[978] 365-4160	I-495 to Berlin/Clinton Exit; left on Rte
Clinton, MA 01510		62; all the way to Clinton.

Tue, Thu 9am-6pm; Wed -8pm; Fri -5pm; Sat -1pm (*summer*: -noon)

Free and open to public; self-service copying, $.10/page; film/fiche copying, $.25/page. **HOLDINGS**: Civil and Revolutionary War lists; filmed local newspapers – *Courant* (weekly, 1868+) and *Daily Item* (1890s+).

CONCORD FREE PUBLIC LIBRARY

Special Collections Dept.	[978] 371-6242	Rte 2W to Rte 62E (Main) to X of
129 Main Street		Main & Sudbury Rd (near Concord Ctr).
Concord, MA 01742		Parking lot on Sudbury Rd side of bldg.
		Train: Fitchburg line to Concord Ctr;
Mon-Thu 9am-5pm; Fri, Sat -1pm (*call ahead*)		from front of sta, right to X & lights;
Jul, Aug: Mon-Fri 9am-5pm		left at Friendly's on Sudbury; ¼ mi
		toward town ctr; bldg on left.

Free and open to public; copying at staff discretion, $.15/page; mail inquiries accepted (brief only, as time allows; copies sent). Appointment advisable for Special Collections (1-2 days ahead). **HOLDINGS**: genealogical – primarily Concord families, but some for Mass. and New England generally. Printed Mass. VRs to 1850; Concord VRs, 1850-*ca.* 1935; genealogical references; NEHGS *Register* (with indexes); *Massachusetts Historical Society Collections* and *Proceedings*; New England town histories; Concord directories; poll-tax rolls; census film; obituary scrapbooks (indexed); biographical sources; photos; maps; and building files. Special Collections also includes manuscripts, pamphlets, ephemera, broadsides, town records and reports, works of art, and artifacts. The holdings have not been filmed by LDS.

DANVERS – PEABODY INSTITUTE LIBRARY – DANVERS ARCHIVAL CENTER

15 Sylvan Street	[978] 774-0554	Rte 128 to Rte 35W (High St) to Dan-
Danvers, MA 01923		vers Ctr; left on Sylvan; 1 mi. Large
		white bldg on right.

Archival Center: Mon 1-7:30pm
Wed, Thu, 1st Sat 9am-noon & 1-5pm; 2nd & 4th Fri 1-5pm

Free and open to public; film reader; reader/printer; all copying at archivist's discretion, $.15/page; mail inquiries accepted. **HOLDINGS**: Danvers collection; local history collection of Danvers Historical Society; records of churches and town organizations; printed sources for history of Danvers (previously Salem Village), including *Danvers Historical Society Collections* (1913+), *Records and Files of the Quarterly Courts of Essex County* ... [1636-86], and *Essex Institute Historical Collections* (1859+); Danvers genealogies; Mass. VRs to 1850; *Massachusetts Soldiers and Sailors in the Revolutionary War*, in the *War of 1812*, and in the *Civil War*; Danvers VRs (ms.; to 1917); the Ellerton J. Brehaut Witchcraft Collection (1,000+ items), including all early imprints concerning the witchcraft hysteria, as well as 17th-century English treatments; manuscripts: 500 volumes and 75,000 town records, including *Salem Village Records of Transactions* (1672-1715), daybooks, journals, diaries, wills, and inventories.

N.B., staff is limited; if coming from any distance, call ahead to be sure DAC will be open.

DEERFIELD MEMORIAL LIBRARIES

P.O. Box 53
Memorial Street
Deerfield, MA 01342

[413] 774-5581 x 125

Rte 5 to Old Deerfield; W on Memorial. Large brick bldg on right. Limited parking, adjacent to bldg.

Mon-Fri 9am-5pm

Franklin County's only free, full-time historical collection; film and fiche readers; copying, $.15/page; stacks largely closed; small staff undertakes no research, but tries to answer all inquiries. Two distinct libraries: Pocumtuck Valley Memorial Association (PVMA) Library and Henry N. Flynt Library of Historic Deerfield (latter supports activities of Historic Deerfield [runs a museum, inn, and store]). **HOLDINGS**: the PVMA library, focusing on Franklin County, has several hundred published and manuscript genealogies; 200+ collections of family papers, diaries, and account books; VRs; Hampshire County probates, town records, and censuses; cemetery transcripts, local history materials and indexes.

HARVARD PUBLIC LIBRARY

Harvard Common
P.O. Box 666
Harvard, MA 01451

[978] 456-4114
& -4115 (FAX)

Rte 2 to Exit 38A (Rte 110); 2 mi to town ctr **OR** Rte 495 to Exit 28 (Rte 111); 2 mi to town Ctr.

Mon, Wed, Fri 10am-5pm; Tue, Thu 1-9pm
Sat 10am-4pm (*summer*: -2pm)

Sears Genealogy Room; free, but donations to book fund welcome; no interlibrary loan; copying, $.10/page; film/fiche reader/printer, $.25/page; *brief* mail inquiries accepted. **HOLDINGS**: Sears Collection (Harvard history and genealogies; Shakers); most Mass. VRs; Harvard town reports; some Worcester and Middlesex County town histories; several genealogies. Patrons encouraged to donate copies of their family research.

HAVERHILL PUBLIC LIBRARY – SPECIAL COLLECTIONS

99 Main Street   [978] 373-1586   Rte 495 to Rte 97 to Rte 125 (Main);
Haverhill, MA 01830   uphill; bldg at corner of Main &
                                                Summer Sts. Free parking lot. Train:
Mon, Tue 10am-1pm & 2-5pm & 6-8:30pm   Boston to Haverhill; about 1 hr.
Wed, Thu, Sat 10am-1pm & 2-5pm

Climate-controlled; ample seating; several professional staffers; prompt staff copying, $.25/page; materials do not circulate. **HOLDINGS**: Haverhill History Collection (4,000 volumes); Pecker Genealogy Collection (3,000 volumes; emphasis on lower Merrimack Valley, Essex County); Pecker Local History Collection (5,000 volumes; New England and other town histories; Revolutionary and Civil War histories); Mass. VRs to 1850 (books), 1841-1900 (film); *American Genealogical and Biographical Index*; NEHGS *Register*; *Essex Institute Historical Collections*; federal censuses for Essex and (1860-1920) Rockingham Counties; state censuses, 1855 and '65 (film), with transcript for Haverhill; all Haverhill newspapers, 1794 to present (originals and film); typescripts of Haverhill proprietors' and selectmen's records (600 pages) and town records (1,400 pages); *Mayflower Descendant*; *The American Genealogist*; *Bangor Historical Magazine*; *Putnam's Genealogical Quarterly Magazine*; *New Hampshire Genealogical Record*; *Essex Genealogist*; *Connecticut Nutmegger*; *Our French Canadian Ancestors*; *Search for the Passengers on the Mary and John*; and *Quaker History*. N.B., the DAR collection, formerly housed at NEHGS, is now here.

LANCASTER TOWN LIBRARY

717 Main Street *or* P.O. Box 5   [978] 368-8928   Rte 2 to Exit 35 (Rte 70S); left at 'T' jct
Lancaster, MA 01523 (*but see below!*)   with Rte 117; right at flashing light; 2
                                               mi on Main; left on Thayer Memorial
Mon, Wed 1-8pm; Tue, Thu 9:30am-8pm   Dr.
Sat 9:30am-1:30pm (*Sep-May only*)

Renovating and expanding (as of May 1999) – *temporarily located at 40 Maple Street in South Lancaster, on the Atlantic Union College campus* – some materials may be unavailable during construction. Mail inquiries accepted; copies ($.10/page) and postage charged for extensive research. **HOLDINGS**: Lancaster Collection – town reports, diaries, scrapbooks, early newspapers, *etc.* New England History Collection – state and town histories, vital records, historical society publications, *etc.* Civil War Collection – regimental histories, Union and Confederate biographies, period pamphlets, *etc.* Broader American History Collection – American Indian and Colonial histories, 19th-century American histories. Some records filmed by LDS.

LAWRENCE – IMMIGRANT CITY ARCHIVES (ICA)

6 Essex Street   [978] 686-9230   I-495 to Exit 45 (Marston St) – *Exit 1 mi*
Lawrence, MA 01840   [978] 975-2154 FAX   *long.* After "Welcome to Lawrence"
                                                 sign, left on Canal St; at 1st light, right
Sat 9am-1pm (*except holiday weekends; or*   on Union St; at next light – bldg will be
by appointment)   on left – left on Essex. On-street park-
                                                 ing; few spaces in bldg courtyard.

Free for members, otherwise $15 day-fee; professional historical and genealogical research by appointment; mail or phone requests also accepted. Evening genealogy group meets monthly (except summer) in ICA offices. Yearly dues: seniors, $10; individual, $25; family, $35. **HOLDINGS**: Lawrence directories, 1847+; voters lists, 1886+; death registers, 1890-1947 (plus some war deaths, 1942-5); annual reports, 1872-1913; city atlases, 1875-1926; Essex Company land and sales maps and original deeds, pre-1845 (limited access); VRs to 1850; "Central File" – index to resident biographies, photos, obits, and business histories, 1847 to present; Mele Genealogical Index to Lawrence family histories at ICA (updated regularly); all published Lawrence histories; Bellevue Cemetery transcript, 1847-99; St. Mary and Immaculate Conception [Irish] Cemetery transcripts; 1880 contributors (male and female mill workers) to Lawrence Soldiers and Sailors Memorial Fund; Lawrence chattel mortgages, 1847-1958; records of Lawrence's ethnic settlers; federal censuses of Lawrence, 1850-1920 (film; no index); *Morton Allen Directory of European Steamship Arrivals 1890-1930 (NY) & 1904-1926 (NY, Philadelphia, Boston & Baltimore)*; *Anuta's Ships of Our Ancestors* (photos of passenger vessels).

LEOMINSTER PUBLIC LIBRARY

30 West Street
Leominster, MA 01453

[978] 534-7522

Rte 2 to Leominster Exit (Rte 12); S to 5th light; right; 1 block. Bldg on left; free parking at rear.

Mon-Thu 9am-9pm; Fri, Sat 9am-5pm
summer: same, except Sat -1pm

Free and open to public; mail inquiries answered (as staffing permits); 2 copiers, $.15/page; 2 film readers, 1 fiche; 1 film printer; materials do not circulate; no interlibrary loan; handicapped accessible, except for Historical Collection and restrooms. **HOLDINGS**: most published Mass. VRs to 1850; NEHGS *Register*; Leominster directories, 1899-1987; genealogies, mostly local; *Leominster Enterprise*, 1873 to date, and some short-run Leominster newspapers; Leominster VRs, 1700-1840 (fiche); Sanborn Insurance Maps for Leominster and Fitchburg (film); John "Johnny Appleseed" Chapman collection.

LYNN PUBLIC LIBRARY

North Common Street
Lynn, MA 01902
E-mail: lynnlib@shore.net

[781] 595-0567

Rte 129 to Rte 107 (Western Av) to Franklin St to North Common. Limited metered parking in front; ample side-street parking; small lot at rear. Train: to Central Sq. Bus: MBTA Rte 426 stops in front.

Mon, Wed 1-9pm; Tue 9am-9pm; Fri, Sat 9am-5pm
(*summer hours vary – call ahead*)

Free; reference collection does not circulate; staff retrieval only from closed stacks; 3 film readers, 1 fiche; 2 reader/printers, $.20/page; on-site, phone, e-mail, or mail research requests accepted (detailed requests *via* e-mail or mail preferred; postage and copies – $.15 each – billed). On-line catalog *via* telnet at public.noblenet.org. **HOLDINGS**: genealogies and town histories; all early Lynn newspapers (film); most published Mass. VRs to 1850; *Boston Transcript* genealogy column and card index; Lynn collection (including newspaper clippings); Civil War regimental histories; city clerk's VRs, 1629-1900.

LYNNFIELD PUBLIC LIBRARY

18 Summer Street
Lynnfield, MA 01940

[781] 334-5411

Rte 128 to Exit 41W; 3 mi to town ctr. Large white wooden bldg with portico faces village green. Free parking.

Mon-Thu 10am-9pm; Fri, Sat 10am-5pm
(*summer*: closed Sat)

Free; open stacks; 3 film and 2 fiche readers; 1 film and 1 fiche reader/printer; self-service copying – subject to U.S. copyright limitations – $.10/page; mail inquiries accepted (in-Library research only). HQ for Essex Society of Genealogists (ESOG) – maintains Special Genealogy Collection on 1st floor at rear. 'On-your-own' research – ESOG cannot assist, library staff limited. Taped genealogy lectures circulate. **HOLDINGS**: 3,000 genealogies and town histories for New England and eastern Canada; subscribes to 20 genealogical journals; full runs of all such journals for all six New England states; *New York Genealogical and Biographical Record*; federal censuses of Essex County, 1850-1920 (with everyname cardfile for 1850); Essex County deeds and probate copybooks to 1800; Mass. VRs to 1850; and Essex County city directories.

NEW BEDFORD PUBLIC LIBRARY

613 Pleasant Street	[508] 991-6275	On-street parking difficult; 2 municipal
New Bedford, MA 02740	[508] 961-3077 FAX	garages in walking distance.
Genealogy Room:	[508] 991-6276	
Mon, Wed, Fri 1-5pm		
Tue, Thu 1-9pm; Sat 9am-5pm		

Free, but donations welcome; materials do not circulate; 3 copiers, $.10/page; 2 reader/printers, $.25/page; coin-operated typewriter; interlibrary loan of post-1850 newspaper film; limited research by mail. **HOLDINGS**: focus on southeast Mass. – Bristol, Plymouth, Barnstable, Dukes, and Nantucket Counties, as well as Tiverton and Little Compton, Rhode Island; Acadian and French-Canadian material from Québec, Maritime Provinces, and New England; immigration records from Portugal, Azores, Madeira, and Cape Verde Islands; local Afro-American material, including Cuffe-family papers; most published Mass. VRs to 1850; Mass. state VRs, 1841-1900 (film), and death indexes, 1901-70; New Bedford births and marriages, 1787-1900, and deaths, 1787-1969; indexes to obits in *New Bedford Standard Times* (1969 to present) and to marriages and obits in *New Bedford Mercury* (1807-74); New Bedford newspapers (1792 to present); federal censuses of Mass., 1790-1920, with indexes to New Bedford, 1850-80, 1900-20; 1855 and '65 state censuses of southeast Mass.; New Bedford immigrant arrivals, 1826-1942, with index, 1826-1954 (some years missing); immigrant arrivals for some other New England ports; New Bedford Customs House records, including 7,000 crew lists (with 250,000-card index), shipping articles, and seamen's protection papers (1807-1925); LDS FHL catalog, IGI, and Social Security Death Index (see also in NEW ENGLAND chapter); Pardon Gray Seabury Collection relating to Freetown, Fall River, and Tiverton and Little Compton, Rhode Island; Elisha Leonard's and Emma Pierce's notes on southeast Mass. families.

NEWBURYPORT PUBLIC LIBRARY

Hamilton Room	[978] 465-4428	Rte 95N to Exit 57; right **OR** 95S to
94 State Street		Exit 57; left – Rte 113 (Storey Av),
Newburyport, MA 01950		merges with High St; 2.7 mi to **X** of
		High & State (2nd light); straight thru;
Mon-Thu 9am-8pm; Fri, Sat 9am-5pm		1st left on Fruit St; 2nd left (Temple St);
(*summer*: closed Sat)		cross State to Prince Pl; bldg on corner.
		2-hour on-street parking – *enforced*.
N.B., moving 9/99 & Spring 2000; *call ahead*		

Free; Genealogy and Local History Collection in climate-controlled Hamilton Room – seats 8; volunteer staff only, so *call ahead*; self-service copying, $.10/page; 1 film/fiche reader/printer. **HOLDINGS**: most published Mass. VRs to 1850; genealogies; Newburyport town and tax records; Corbin Collection (Mass.

VRs, church records, cemeteries, *etc.* – chiefly central and western towns); NEHGS *Register*; Newburyport directories, federal censuses of Essex County, 1870-1920; Newburyport history collection – 4,000 books, pamphlets, photos, maps, and broadsides.

NORTHAMPTON – FORBES LIBRARY

20 West Street   [413] 584-8399   From Northampton Ctr, Rte 9W ½ mi to
Northampton, MA 01060   Rte 66 (West St).

Mon-Thu 9am-9pm; Fri, Sat -5pm

Free; 2 film readers, 1 fiche; 1 reader/printer, $.15/page. **HOLDINGS**: small collection of genealogies and local histories; originals and film of Judd manuscripts, mainly on Hampshire County families; Hampshire County probate and town records (film); Coolidge Collection on Coolidge family.

PEPPERELL – LAWRENCE LIBRARY

15 Main Street *or*   [978] 433-0330   Rte 3N to Exit 35 (Rte 113); at end of
P.O. Box 1440   & -0317 (FAX)   ramp, right; 9 mi to bldg.
Pepperell, MA 01740

Genealogy Room: Wed 1-4pm & 6-8pm; most Sats 9am-noon (*call ahead for appointment*)

Free and open to public; volunteer staff, so call ahead (non-standard hours possible with director's permission); copying, $.10/page. **HOLDINGS**: all published Mass. VRs to 1850; NEHGS *Register* (with indexes to volumes 1-148); military records; Pepperell directories, 1907-26 (5 years only); Savage's *Genealogical Dictionary of ... New England*; histories of Quabbin Reservoir and the towns it submerged; *Mayflower Ancestral Index*; Butler's VRs of Groton, Shirley, and Pepperell; genealogies (some mss. by locals) and town histories; old maps of Pepperell, naming residents, and its cemeteries; CD workstation with Family Tree Maker.

PETERSHAM MEMORIAL LIBRARY

23 Common Street   [978] 724-3405   Rte 2 to Rte 32S **OR** MA Tpk to Rte
Petersham, MA 01366   32A **OR** Rte 202 to Rte 122; bldg on
                                                  town common.
Mon-Sat 2:30-5:30pm; Sat 10:30am-noon

Free and open to public; appointment preferred (1 week in advance); mail inquiries accepted (postage charged); copying, $.10/page. **HOLDINGS**: local and family histories; published Mass. VRs to 1850; Quabbin-area information; town reports; Shays' Rebellion information. N.B., Petersham Historical Society is across common (historian has key). PHS has more genealogical records, photos, some school records, crafts, newspaper clippings, and church records.

PITTSFIELD – BERKSHIRE ATHENAEUM

Local History, Genealogy,   [413] 499-9486   MA Tpk to Lee Exit (Rte 90); Rte 7A
  and Literature Department   towards Williamstown. Bldg just off
20 Wendall Avenue   Park Sq; parking garage across Sq;
Pittsfield, MA 01060   metered lots nearby.
E-mail: pittslhg@cwmars.org

Mon-Thu 9am-9pm; Fri -5pm; Sat 10am-5pm
summer: Mon, Wed, Fri 9am-5pm; Tue, Thu -9pm; Sat 10am-5pm

Free; 5 film and 4 fiche readers; 2 film reader/printers, $.25/page, 1 fiche reader/printer, $.10/page; *limited* mail inquiries (no extensive historical, or *any* genealogical, research; will refer to professionals); phone, e-mail, and mail queries, $2 (includes up to 5 copies; $.25 each for 6 and up); *call ahead to verify hours*. **HOLDINGS**: focus on Berkshire County history and genealogy, but covers all New England states and eastern New York, plus some French-Canadian; local genealogies and town histories; published sermons; town annual reports; *American Genealogical and Biographical Index*; Vermont VRs to 1908; Barbour Collection of Conn. VRs to *ca.* 1850; LDS's Family Search program on CD (see NEW ENGLAND chapter); indexes to Mass. state VRs, 1841-95; Soundexes to 1880 and 1900 federal censuses of Mass.; 1855 and '65 state censuses; Arthur Kelley's New York records (70+ volumes); Loiselle Index (French-Canadian marriages); and Corbin and Hale Collections. Special collections: the Rollin H. Cooke Collection of 18th- and 19th-century church and cemetery records for all Berkshire County towns, plus surrounding towns in western Mass., New York, Vermont, and Conn.; the William Bradford Browne Collection of notes and data on northern Berkshire County towns and families; and the Elmer Shepard Collection of notes and VRs for western Mass. families.

N.B., please contribute your own family research to the Athenaeum's collection.

PLYMOUTH PUBLIC LIBRARY

Plymouth Collection: Local [508] 830-4250
   History and Genealogy
132 South Street
Plymouth, MA 02360
Web: http://www.idt.net/~ppl1

Rte 3 to Exit 5. From N: E thru 2 lights, to bottom of hill; bldg on left. From S: E thru 1 light, then same.

Mon-Wed 10am-9pm; Thu -6pm; Fri, Sat -5:30pm
Sun (*Labor Day to Memorial Day*) 12:30-5pm

Free and open to public; call ahead for appointment if research help desired; volunteers monitor and assist; mail inquiries answered (4- to 6-week turnaround), postage billed; copying, $.10/page. **HOLDINGS**: 1,200 books on descendants of *Mayflower* Pilgrims and other 17th- to 20th-century immigrants to Plymouth; family and collective (*i.e.*, town) genealogies; journals; military records; VRs. N.B., the Collection has free flyers and bibliographies on Plymouth's cemeteries, houses, and genealogies, and has published a 26-page handbook, *Genealogical & Local History Resources Available in Plymouth, Massachusetts,* which may be bought at the library.

PRINCETON PUBLIC LIBRARY

2 Town Hall Drive [978] 464-2115
Princeton, MA 01541
E-mail: wpape@cwmarsmail.cwmars.org

Rte 2 to Exit 28 (Rte 31) to Princeton Ctr; at flashing light atop hill – Catholic church on left – take right. Stone bldg at head of common, next to Congregational Church.

Tue-Thu 10am-8pm; Fri 3-5pm; Sat 10am-3pm
(*summer hours vary – call ahead*)

Free and open to public; *minimal* mail inquiries accepted; copying, $.10/page. **HOLDINGS**: focus on Princeton history; some Worcester County material.

READING PUBLIC LIBRARY

64 Middlesex Avenue   [781] 944-0840
Reading, MA 01867
Web: http://www.readingpl.org

Mon-Thu 10am-9pm; Fri, Sat -5:30pm
Sun 1-5pm (*Oct-May only*)

Rte 128N to Exit 38B (Rte 28N); thru Reading Ctr, past town green; at X of Rtes 28 & 129 (large white church at light), left on 129 toward Wilmington; 2 blocks; 3rd left. Large yellow brick bldg on right **OR** Rte 128S to Exit 40B (Rte 129) thru same X; 3rd left; bldg on left.

Free and open to public; self-service copying, $.10/page; film copying, $.25/page; mail inquiries accepted (no extensive research). **HOLDINGS**: Reading VRs, 1644-1975; town reports, 1847 to present; street lists, 1907 to present; maps; Reading, Wakefield, and Stoneham directories, 'teens and '20s; index to *Reading Chronicle*, 1974 to present; list of persons buried in Reading cemeteries; list of pre-1890 burials in Reading Old Burial Ground (now in Wakefield); vertical file of Reading families; local and county histories.

ROWLEY PUBLIC LIBRARY

17 Wethersfield Street   [978] 948-2850
Rowley, MA 01969
E-mail: mro@mvlc.lib.ma.us

Mon, Tue, Thu 2-5pm & 7-9pm
Wed 9am-noon & 7-9pm; Sat 9am-noon

Rte 1 **OR** I-95 to Rte 133E toward Rowley/Ipswich; left on Rte 1A N; past town hall; left at light on Central St; 1st left on Wethersfield. Bldg on right.

Free and open to public; mail inquiries accepted; copying, $.10/page. **HOLDINGS**: Mass. VRs to 1850; *Massachusetts Soldiers and Sailors of the Revolutionary War*; some genealogies; index to Revolutionary service records; 1855 and '65 Mass. censuses; Rowley town reports; Rowley town records, 1639-72, 1846 to present.

SALEM – JAMES DUNCAN PHILLIPS LIBRARY

Peabody Essex Museum   [978] 745-9500 x 3053
132 Essex Street
Salem, MA 10970
E-mail: pem@pem.org

Tue, Wed, Fri 10am-5pm; Thu 1-8pm
(*summer*: Mon as well, 10am-5pm)

Rte 128 to Exit 25A (Rte 114E) toward Salem. Limited metered on-street parking; garage & lot, 1 block. <u>Train</u>: North Sta to Salem (Rockport/Ipswich Line).

$8.50/day, adult non-members; $7.50, seniors or students; $5, children (6 to 16). Annual membership, $40/individual, $60/family. Staff copying, $.25/printed page, $.35/manuscript page; 1 film reader, 1 reader/printer. **HOLDINGS**: focus on pre-1860 history of Essex County and region – maritime affairs; domestic life; religion; arts, crafts, and architecture; literature; business and labor. One million photos (including Civil War, Asia, Pacific); 19th- and 20th-century images of ships, other maritime subjects. Largest collection of Essex County history and genealogy, including extensive manuscript collection (5,000 linear feet); 400,000 books; newspapers (on film); original Essex County court records (1636-

1820); most Mass. town histories and published VRs to 1850. (N.B., see also SOCIETIES – PEABODY ESSEX MUSEUM.)

SALEM PUBLIC LIBRARY

370 Essex Street Salem, MA 01970 **E-mail**: sal@noblenet.org	[978] 744-0860	Rte 128 to Rte 114 toward Salem; at **X** of 114 and Essex ("Witch House"), right; bldg on right **OR** 128 to Lowell St Exit (toward Salem) to end – becomes Main St, then Boston St; when Boston ends on Essex, left; bldg on left.
Mon-Thu 9am-9pm; Fri, Sat -5pm Sun (*Labor Day-Apr*) 1-5pm		

Free and open to public; climate-controlled room on 2nd floor; self-service copying, $.10/page; film copies, $.25/page; mail inquiries accepted. **HOLDINGS**: published Mass. VRs to 1850; many Mass. Civil War regimental histories; vertical file on Salem people and history; Salem directories, 1838+; newspapers (mostly on film) include *Salem Evening News* (1880 to present), *Salem Gazette*, and other early papers (with gaps).

SHIRLEY – HAZEN MEMORIAL LIBRARY

3 Perimeter Road Shirley, MA 01464 **E-mail**: hazenlib@bicnet.net	[978] 425-2620	Rte 2 to Exit 36 (Shirley). <u>From W</u>: right at end of ramp, then 1st left on Shirley/Lancaster Rd. <u>From E</u>: exit directly on Shirley/Lancaster; 1.5 mi to stop sign. Right; .8 mi to library (on right).
Mon, Wed noon-5pm; Tue, Thu 1-8pm Sat (*except summer*) 9am-1pm		

Free and open to public; copying, $.10/page; mail inquiries accepted. **HOLDINGS**: small local history collection; most published Mass. VRs to 1850.

SPRINGFIELD – CONNECTICUT VALLEY HISTORICAL MUSEUM LIBRARY AND ARCHIVES

220 State Street Springfield, MA 01103	[413] 263-6800 x 230	I-91 to State St Exit; follow signs 1 mi to bldg (on public library grounds). Parking across St or on Edwards St.
Wed-Sun noon-4pm (*extended hours during school vacations, except summer*)		

$4 admission (includes all 4 museums on quad); 3 film and 3 fiche readers; 2 computers; copying, $.20/page; no interlibrary loan; research by mail, $15/hour. **HOLDINGS**: Springfield collection (1636 to present) includes 40,000 photos; maps and atlases; 300 feet of vertical files; 3,000 linear feet of local history and manuscripts; directories (1845 to present); Warren's *Springfield Families 1636-1850*; VRs, 1636-1894; newspapers, 1788-1900; early (1638-96) Pioneer Valley VRs; Pynchon record book; published Mass. VRs to 1850; Mass. VRs on Holbrook fiche; Corbin Collection on film; cemetery records for most Hampden County towns, as well as many others in western Mass.; large French-Canadian genealogy collection, including Drouin, Tanguay, Charbonneau, Talbot, Langlois, and Bergeron; printed indexes to federal censuses of New England, New York, and Pennsylvania, 1800-50; federal censuses of Mass., 1790-1920; 1855 and '65 Mass. censuses; Mass. state VRs, 1841-1905; index to New England naturalizations, 1791-1906; Irish collection, including O'Casey set for Counties Cork and Kerry; large collection of New England and eastern Canada family histories; ethnic materials; 140

genealogy journals; LDS Family Search program on CD (see NEW ENGLAND chapter). Beginners are given individual guidance; genealogical classes are offered.

TAUNTON – OLD COLONY HISTORICAL SOCIETY LIBRARY

66 Church Green   [508] 822-1622   From Boston: Rte 24S to Rte 44W; left
Taunton, MA 02780   at Church Green. Parking garage behind
                                            courthouse.

Tue-Sat 10am-4pm (*closed Sat before Mon holiday*)

$5/day, non-members; appointment desired, 2-3 days ahead; staff copying, $.25/page (non-members) or $.15/page (members and students); 1 film and 1 fiche reader; 1 film printer; mail inquiries accepted (research, $10/hour – 1-hour minimum); materials do not circulate. **HOLDINGS**: focus on southeast Mass.; published VRs, genealogies, and town and military histories; manuscripts. (See also under SOCIETIES.)

WALTHAM – AMERICAN-JEWISH HISTORICAL SOCIETY LIBRARY

2 Thornton Road   [781] 891-8110   On Brandeis campus. Train: commuter
Waltham, MA 02154   [781] 899-9208 FAX   rail to Brandeis/Roberts stop.
E-mail: ajhs@ajhs.org
Web: http://www.ajhs.org

Mon-Fri 9am-4:30pm

Free; appointment (2-3 weeks ahead) strongly recommended; staff copying, $.25/page (plus $15/hour for more than 50 copies); film reader/printer; mail queries answered promptly (call for research rates). **HOLDINGS**: several hundred family histories, many unavailable elsewhere; 500 manuscripts on individuals or families; histories of Jewish communities and synagogues; Boston's Hebrew Immigration Aid Society papers – indexed records of Jewish immigrants arriving at Boston and Providence, 1882-1929; incomplete list of ship and passenger arrivals, 1904-53; New York Mayor's court, naturalization, insolvency, and incorporation papers – copies (film and bound xerox) of papers now in New York City Hall of Records (first 3 items cover pre-1860 period; last covers incorporation in New York City of all Jewish and related organizations, 1848-1920).

WALTHAM PUBLIC LIBRARY – WALTHAM ROOM

735 Main Street   [781] 893-1750 x 207   Rte 128 to Exit 26 (Rte 20/Main) to
Waltham, MA 02154   Waltham. Train: Fitchburg line.
E-mail: walmail12@mln.lib.ma.us   MBTA bus.

Mon-Thu 9am-9pm; Fri, Sat -5pm; Sun (*except summer*) 1-5pm
(regular hours for *book-use only*; *original* records by *appointment only*, weekdays)

Open-shelf genealogy collection; archival holdings retrieved from closed stack by appointment only; copying at librarian's discretion, $.15/page; mail inquiries accepted (brief look-ups only, ½-hour maximum – copies [$.25 each] and postage billed). **HOLDINGS**: genealogical journals, including NEHGS *Register;* published inventories of genealogy collections at other libraries; family and town histories; genealogical 'how to' and computer books; Waltham-related manuscripts; most published Mass. VRs to 1850; Waltham VRs to early 20th century (film); Waltham newspapers; "Waltham

Rediscovered" collection – oral family histories, working papers (for drafts of book with same title), and other primary Waltham-related documents; directories; voting lists.

WAREHAM FREE LIBRARY

59 Marion Road	[508] 295-2343	I-95 to Exit 21 (Wareham); right at top
Wareham, MA 02571		of ramp on Rte 28S; right at fork; right
E-mail: warelibr@ultranet.ma.com		on Gibbs Av; left on Main St; right at
		1st light on Marion (Rte 6). Bldg on
Mon, Fri 9:30am-5pm; Tue-Thu -8pm; Sat -2pm		right, opposite town hall.

Free and open to public; copying, $.15/page (some items too fragile); Genealogy Room volunteers assist every Wed, 1-4pm; WAREHAM GENEALOGY CLUB meets 1st Thu of month, 6:30pm; some members willing to research mail queries. **HOLDINGS**: Wareham town reports; old town records (film); Wareham VRs; church records; *Wareham Courier*, 1905 to present (newspaper; on film).

WATERTOWN PUBLIC LIBRARY

123 Main Street	[617] 972-6436	Rte 128 to Rte 20E; 5 mi; bldg on left
Watertown, MA 02472		**OR** MA Tpk (Rte 90) to Newton Corner
		Exit; Galen St to Watertown Sq; left on
Mon-Wed 9am-9pm; Thu 1-9pm; Fri, Sat 9am-5pm		Rte 20; bldg on right.
Sun 2-5pm (*summer*: closed Sat & Sun)		

Free and open to public, but donations welcome; mail inquiries accepted (3 questions per letter); copying, $.15/page; film, $.25/page. **HOLDINGS**: Watertown VRs (film; births to 1900, marriages to '68, deaths to '80); federal censuses of Middlesex County (film); Watertown directories (film; incomplete); all local newspapers, 1879+ (film; some years had none); published Watertown records; Bond's *Genealogies of Families and Descendants of the Early Settlers of Watertown* (including Waltham and Weston). Publications: Henry Bond, *Map of the Original Allotments of Land* ($3.00 includes s & h); Maud Hodges, *Crossroads on the Charles* ($16.10 includes s & h).

WEST BARNSTABLE – CAPE COD COMMUNITY COLLEGE – NICKERSON ROOM

2240 Route 132	[508] 362-2131	Rte 6 to Exit 6 (Rte 132/Iyanough Rd).
West Barnstable, MA	x 4445	1st floor of CCCC Library Resource Ctr.
02668-1599		
Mon, Wed, Fri 8:30am-4pm; Tue 9am-3pm		

Free and open to public; appointment desirable; mail inquiries accepted; copying, $.10/page. **HOLDINGS**: 5,000 items – Cape Cod-related books, manuscripts, and video/audio materials; small genealogical collection; outstanding finding aid – "Name File" of 15,000 Cape Codders; Burke's 10-volume *Cape Cod Bibliography*; maritime document collection; vertical file.

WINCHENDON – BEALS MEMORIAL LIBRARY

50 Pleasant Street	[978] 297-0300	On Rte 12/202, N of town hall & police
Winchendon, MA 01475		sta, at end of War Memorial Park.
		On-street parking. Bus: Vermont Tran-
Mon-Fri 1-8pm		sit (from Boston) stops 3 blocks away.

Free and open to public; not handicapped accessible (but staff will accommodate – please call ahead); mail inquiries accepted (as staffing allows; copies [$.15/page] and postage billed). **HOLDINGS**: *Winchendon Courier* (newspaper; on film), 1880-1988; some VRs to 1850; some Civil War regimental histories; a few genealogies of local families; local tax records and annual reports, 1850+.

WOBURN PUBLIC LIBRARY

45 Pleasant Street Woburn, MA 01801	[781] 933-0148	Rte 93, to Montvale Av Exit to Woburn Ctr; right at 1ˢᵗ Congregational Church; around common; bldg on right **OR** Rte 128 to Winn St Exit; to end; right; bldg on right.
summer: Mon, Wed, Fri 9am-5:30pm Tue, Thu -9pm *winter*: Mon-Thu 9am-9pm; Fri, Sat -5:30pm		

Free and open to public; self-service copying, $.10/page; film, $.25/page; mail inquiries accepted (no extensive research). **HOLDINGS**: Woburn VRs, 1640-1913; genealogies of Woburn families; town and county histories; some published Mass. VRs to 1850; Woburn directories and poll lists; annual reports, 1845+; newspapers (partially indexed) include *Woburn Daily Times* (1901 to present) and other local papers.

WORCESTER – AMERICAN ANTIQUARIAN SOCIETY LIBRARY

185 Salisbury Street Worcester, MA 01609-1634 **E-mail**: mel@MWA.org	[508] 755-5221	Rte 290 to Exit 17 to Belmont St, Lincoln Sq, & Salisbury. Bldg at corner of Park Av and Salisbury. Parking at rear.
Mon-Fri 9am-5pm		

Free and open to all qualified adults (determined by interview); staff copying, $.20/page (approved materials only; limited number of pages; write for complete policies and prices); mail-order copy-requests limited to 20 pages ($5 minimum plus copies and postage); coat rack and lockers; phone; may bring lunch and eat at Society's Goddard-Daniels House, across street; closed stacks; materials do not circulate; no interlibrary loan. **HOLDINGS**: 3 million books, pamphlets, broadsides, manuscripts, prints, maps, directories, and newspapers – largest single collection of printed works on history, literature, and culture of first 250 years of what is now U.S. – focus on "the printed record of the American experience prior to 1877." Finest set of 18ᵗʰ- and 19ᵗʰ-century American newspapers anywhere. Extensive collection of family and local histories.

LDS FAMILY HISTORY CENTERS

Belmont – 15 Ledgewood Place; [617] 484-9744; Tue, Wed 7-9pm; 1ˢᵗ & 3ʳᵈ Sat 9am-1pm

Boston – NEHGS, 101 Newbury Street; [617] 536-5740; Tue, Fri, Sat 9am-5pm; Wed, Thu -9pm

Brewster – 94 Freeman's Way; [508] 896-9863; Tue 10am-2pm & 6-9pm; Wed, Fri 10am-2pm; Thu 9am-1pm; 2ⁿᵈ Sat 9am-noon

Cambridge – 2 Longfellow Place; [617] 491-4749; Wed 6pm-9pm; Sat 9am-1pm

Foxboro – 76 Main Street (Route 140); [508] 543-0298; Tue-Thu, Sat 10am-3pm; Wed, Thu 7-10pm

Hingham – 379 Garner Street; [781] 749-4815; Wed 6-9pm; Thu, Sat 9am-2pm

Lynnfield – 400 Essex Street; [781] 334-5586; Wed 10am-9pm; Thu 9am-4pm; 2nd & 4th Sat 10am-4pm

N. Dartmouth – 400 Cross Road; [508] 994-8215; Wed, Sat 10am-2pm; Fri 6:30-9:30pm

Weston – 150 Brown St. (X of Brown/Route 30); [781] 235-2164; Wed, Thu 7-9pm; Fri, Sat 9am-3pm

Worcester – 67 Chester Place; [508] 852-7000; Wed, Thu, Sat 10am-2pm; Tue-Thu 6-9pm

(For FHC holdings see NEW ENGLAND chapter.)

SOCIETIES

ACADIAN CULTURAL SOCIETY (see NEW ENGLAND chapter)

BERKSHIRE FAMILY HISTORY ASSOCIATION

P.O. Box 1437   [413] 499-9486 (Local History Department of BERKSHIRE
Pittsfield, MA 01202-1437   ATHENAEUM – call for info on BFHA)

Founded in 1975 "to research, promote and encourage ... family history and genealogy." Dues: individual, $12; student, $5; family, $14. Mail inquiries accepted from *members only* (copies [$.25/page] plus postage). Meets monthly (Sep-May) at BERKSHIRE ATHENAEUM auditorium. Publishes *The Berkshire Genealogist* (1978+; with membership; all back issues available). Volunteers index old books; for a list of their publications, send a SASE to the above address.

CAPE COD GENEALOGICAL SOCIETY

P.O. Box 1394
East Harwich, MA 02645

"To encourage and assist in the location, acquisition, indexing, and preservation of genealogical records, with emphasis on Cape Cod ... to make the records available to members and to the general public; to encourage and instruct members in ... genealogical research and compilation; to elevate and maintain genealogical standards of excellence." Annual membership ($15) includes Society's *BULLETIN* (published winter, spring/summer, and fall). Meets at 1pm, 2nd Thu of month (Jul-May), at S. Yarmouth Library, 312 Main Street (X of Rte 28 and Station Av); annual meeting and luncheon in June (place to be announced). N.B., CCGS-sponsored subgroups include: "C3 G2 Computer Users' Group;" "PAF Users' Group;" "Canadian Interest Group;" "German Interest Group;" and "Irish Interest Group." Society also organizes day trips to genealogical repositories on Cape.

CENTRAL MASSACHUSETTS GENEALOGICAL SOCIETY

P.O. Box 811   Rte 2 to Exit 25; right at light on Rte 2A
Westminster, MA 01473-0811   to Westminster Ctr (Main St); Forbush
                                 Memorial Library – current CMGS
                                 meeting place – on Bacon St.

Founded in 1993 "to promote interest in genealogy and family history; teach research procedures [and encourage high] standards; exchange data; publish information; ... preserve public and private records and artifacts and ... ensure their accessibility." Annual dues: organizations, $20; families, $17; individuals, $12; students, $10 (includes *The Searcher* – bimonthly newsletter). Meets 4th Tue of month (except Dec) at Forbush Library; 8 guest speakers, 2 general workshops, and 1 dinner meeting per year. CMGS also publishes *A Guide to Genealogical and Historical Holdings of Massachusetts Libraries – Vol. 1 – North Central* ($18, includes s & h).

ESSEX SOCIETY OF GENEALOGISTS (ESOG)

P.O. Box 313   [781] 334-5411
Lynnfield, MA 01940-0313
E-mail: ESSEXSOC@aol.com

"To encourage research in family history ... instruct beginners ... provide speakers at monthly meetings ... maintain a genealogical collection at the Lynnfield Public Library ... maintain files and indexes ... plan projects of lasting value to genealogists [and exchange] information in an atmosphere of camaraderie." Annual dues: $18 (includes *The Essex Genealogist* [TEG] and *ESOG Newsletter* [quarterly]). Meets 3rd Sat of month (Sep-Dec & Feb-May) at Centre Congregational Church, Lynnfield. See LIBRARIES – LYNNFIELD for details of collection. ESOG also publishes *A Guide to Cemeteries in Essex County* ($15 postpaid + 5% sales tax for Mass. residents) and *Surname Search* ($17 postpaid + 5% sales tax for Mass. residents). Current projects: everyname card index to 1850 census of Essex County (completed); "Early Lynn Families" (in progress; published serially in *TEG*).

GENEALOGICAL ROUND TABLE

P.O. Box 654
Concord, MA 01742-0654

Membership open to all, $10/year; research undertaken for hire. Write for further information. Meets at 1pm on 4th Mon of month (except Jun-Aug, Nov, Dec), usually at CONCORD FREE PUBLIC LIBRARY. Newsletter (6 issues per year). Occasional field trips to facilities of interest.

GENERAL SOCIETY OF MAYFLOWER DESCENDANTS (see NEW ENGLAND chapter)

THE IRISH ANCESTRAL RESEARCH ASSOCIATION (TIARA) (see NEW ENGLAND chapter)

MASSACHUSETTS GENEALOGICAL COUNCIL

P.O. Box 5393
Cochituate, MA 01778

"To ... promote growth, study, and ... exchange of ideas among persons and organizations interested in ... genealogy." Programs designed to complement those of other genealogical and hereditary societies in state, and provide a statewide genealogical forum; to represent genealogists' concerns to state government, and monitor activities and policies of genealogically relevant state agencies. Promotes preservation and publication of, and disseminates information about, state and local records. Guards right of access to public records and educates genealogists as to their proper use and preservation. Sponsors annual conference on topics of genealogical interest. Annual dues: individuals, $7.50; organizations, $10 (includes newsletter). Also publishes pamphlets on Mass. records, $1-$1.50 each – send SASE for list.

MASSACHUSETTS SOCIETY OF GENEALOGISTS (MSOG)

Mail: P.O. Box 215   [508] 792-5066
Ashland, MA 01721-0215
Library: 705 Southbridge Street, Worcester, MA 01610

Wed 11am-3pm; Sat 10am-4pm (*or by appointment with Peggy Amberson, [508] 799-5897*)

A non-profit, educational society "to promote and encourage genealogical research for all ... interested in Massachusetts ancestry ... beginner, amateur, or professional." Annual dues: individuals, $21; families, $26. Members may, if they wish, affiliate with semi-autonomous county chapters, which meet both annually and once a month (except in summer); program usually includes speaker. Chapters are: Bristol (meets at various locations); Hampden (Church in the Acres, Springfield); Middlesex (various locations); and Worcester (Auburn Public Library). Meetings are free and open to public. MSOG's annual meeting is sponsored by the chapters in rotation. Publications: *MASSOG* (quarterly) and *Past Times* (newsletter; monthly, except Jul, Aug). Mail queries: send to Research Committee at library address, with business-sized SASE; reasonable fees. Library's collection comprises 1800 books, journals, and microforms.

MASSACHUSETTS SOCIETY OF MAYFLOWER DESCENDANTS

New location: [617] 338-1991   Subway: Green line to Boylston stop.
100 Boylston Street, Suite 750   Limited on-street parking; Boston
Boston, MA 02116-3812   Common garage nearby.

Mon-Fri 9am-4pm (*by appointment only*)

Founded in 1896 "to perpetuate to a remote posterity the memory of our Pilgrim fathers and mothers. To maintain and defend the principle of civil and religious liberty as set forth in the Compact of the Mayflower." Library open to public; donations welcome. Membership (includes semiannual *Mayflower Descendant*; otherwise $18/year) limited to those who can document descent from one of 26 Mayflower-passenger heads of family. (Write for application.) Three meetings per year.

OLD COLONY HISTORICAL SOCIETY

66 Church Green   [508] 822-1622   (For directions, see LIBRARIES –
Taunton, MA 02780   TAUNTON.)

Tue-Sat 10am-4pm

Founded in 1853. Museum housed in 1852 Bristol Academy building; extensive collection covers history of Mass.'s Old (*i.e.*, Plymouth) Colony region. Special collections include portraits, silver, military artifacts, fire-fighting equipment, Rogers Groups (19th-century statuary), stoves, toys, dolls, furniture, and Indian artifacts. $15/year, student; $25, regular; $35, family of two at same address.

PEABODY ESSEX MUSEUM

132 Essex Street   [978] 744-3390   (For directions, see LIBRARIES –
Salem, MA 01970   SALEM.)
mail: East India Square

Founded in 1821 as "Essex Institute;" merged with Peabody Museum. One of the oldest and largest privately endowed historical societies in U.S. Annual dues: household, $60; individuals, $40; seniors and students, $30. Annual spring meeting, lectures, exhibits, and public programs. Museum contains over 40,000 artifacts. Publishes *Essex Institute Historical Collections*, yearly since 1859, and pamphlets and books, including nine volumes of *Records and Files of the Quarterly Courts of Essex County* ... [1636-86].

PILGRIM SOCIETY

75 Court Street   [508] 746-1620   Rte 3S to Plymouth; Exit 6 on Rte 44E
Plymouth, MA 02360   to 1st light; right on Court; 2 blocks.
                                                    Pilgrim Hall is granite bldg on left.

daily: 9:30am-4:30pm
(library *by appointment ONLY*; closed Christmas, Jan)

Founded in 1820 "to perpetuate the memory of the virtues, ... enterprise, and ... unparalleled sufferings of the first settlers of New England who landed ... December 21st 1620." Research for fee for members only. Dues: annual, $20/individual, $25/family; life, $300/individual, $400/couple (includes free admission to Pilgrim Hall Museum; use of Society's library of 12,000 books, rare books, and manuscripts; 10% discount on gift-shop purchases over $10; invitation to many lectures; and annual dinner on Forefathers' Day [held since 1769]). Publishes *Pilgrim Society Newsletter*, *Pilgrim Society Note* series.

SOUTH SHORE GENEALOGICAL SOCIETY

64 South Street   [781] 837-8364
or P.O. Box 396
Norwell, MA 02061

"To bring together those on the South Shore who share [an] interest in ... family history." Beginners and professionals work together to maintain high ethical standards and *educate, assist,* and *disseminate techniques and sources to* members. Outreach Programs bring 'Getting Started' classes to libraries and other societies in 27 South Shore towns. Meetings feature speakers and workships on specific ethnic groups. Annual dues: $10 (includes bimonthly newsletter). SSGS maintains a private library of family histories, cassette and video tapes of past speakers, and genealogical forms. Meets at 1:30pm on 2nd Sat of month (Sep-Jun) at Norwell Public Library; visitors welcome. Publications: a compilation of newsletters, 1983-97; Norwell and Scituate cemetery inscriptions – including Revolutionary and Civil War soldiers.

WESTERN MASSACHUSETTS GENEALOGICAL SOCIETY

P.O. Box 80206
Forest Park Station
Springfield, MA 01138-0206

"To provide programs of interest and help to genealogists and [to] exchange ... information and materials." Dues: annual, $10/individual, $12.50/family; life, $100 and $250 (includes *American Elm*). Meets 1st Wed of month (Sep-May, plus Jun banquet) at Connecticut Valley Historical Museum (see LIBRARIES – SPRINGFIELD); visitors welcome and encouraged to join. WMGS has no holdings of its own – uses Springfield Library's genealogy section for meetings and research, 5-9pm on meeting nights (library not open to public those nights). Queries accepted at above address.

PERIODICALS

Guides include Donald L. Jacobus, *Index to Genealogical Periodicals*; *Genealogical Periodical Annual Index (GPSI)*; and *Periodical Source Index (PERSI)*. The two major 'Mass.' (and national) journals are *THE NEW ENGLAND HISTORICAL AND GENEALOGICAL REGISTER* (see under NEHGS) and *THE AMERICAN GENEALOGIST* (quarterly; David L. Greene, ed.; P.O. Box 398, Demorest, GA 30535-0398).

The *NEW YORK GENEALOGICAL AND BIOGRAPHICAL RECORD* (quarterly; Harry Macy Jr., ed.; New York Genealogical and Biographical Society, 122 East 58th Street, New York, NY 10022-1939) also publishes much material on Mass. families.

For Essex County, see *THE ESSEX GENEALOGIST* (under ESSEX SOCIETY OF GENEALOGISTS), *THE ESSEX ANTIQUARIAN* (quarterly; ran 1897-1909 only; widely available in reprint), and *ESSEX INSTITUTE HISTORICAL COLLECTIONS* (under SOCIETIES – PEABODY ESSEX MUSEUM), plus the several 'Essex' magazines published early this century by Eben Putnam.

For Plymouth County and Cape Cod, see *THE MAYFLOWER DESCENDANT* (under MASSACHUSETTS SOCIETY OF MAYFLOWER DESCENDANTS) and *MAYFLOWER QUARTERLY* (under NEW ENGLAND chapter – GENERAL SOCIETY OF MAYFLOWER DESCENDANTS).

BOOKS AND ARTICLES

Barlow, Claude W., *New England Genealogy: A Research Guide with Special Emphasis on Massachusetts and Connecticut* (1976).

Blatt, Warren S., *Resources for Jewish Genealogy in the Boston Area* (1996: Boston, Jewish Genealogical Society of Greater Boston).

Bowen, Richard LeBaron, *Massachusetts Records: A Handbook for Genealogists, Historians, Lawyers, and other Researchers* (1957: Rehoboth, MA, the author).

Davis, Charlotte Pease, *Directory of Massachusetts Place Names* (1987: Lexington, MA, Bay State News).

Dodge, Winifred Lovering Holman, "Massachusetts," in Milton Rubincam and Kenn Stryker-Rodda, eds., *Genealogical Research: Methods and Sources* (1960: Washington, DC, American Society of Genealogists).

Flagg, Charles A., *A Guide to Massachusetts Local History* (1907: Salem, MA, Salem Press).

Galvin, William Francis, *Historical Data Relating to Counties, Cities, and Towns in Massachusetts* (1997: Boston, NEHGS).

Gardner-Westcott, Katherine A., *Massachusetts Sources*, 1st ed. (1988: Ashland, MA, Massachusetts Society of Genealogists).

Hanson, Edward W. and **Homer Vincent Rutherford**, "Genealogical Research in Massachusetts: A Survey and Bibliographical Guide," in *NEHGR*, 135[1981]:163-98; also in Ralph J. Crandall, ed., *Genealogical Research in New England* (1984: Baltimore, Genealogical Publishing Co.).

Haskell, John D., ed., *Massachusetts: A Bibliography of Its History* (1976: Boston, G. K. Hall).

Hindus, Michael S., *et al.*, *The Records of the Massachusetts Superior Court and Its Predecessors: An Inventory and Guide* (1977: Boston, Archives Division, Office of the Secretary of the Commonwealth).

Lainhart, Ann Smith, *Digging for Genealogical Treasure in New England Town Records* (1996: Boston, NEHGS).

Lambert, David Allen, *A Guide to Cemeteries Located in the Commonwealth of Massachusetts* (to appear in 2000, from NEHGS).

Longver, Phyllis O. and **Pauline J. Oesterlin**, *A Surname Guide to Massachusetts Town Histories* (1993: Bowie, MD, Heritage Books).

Massachusetts State Archives, *Subject Guide to Records in the Massachusetts State Archives* (1996).

Schweitzer, George K., *Massachusetts Genealogical Research* (1990).

Worthley, Harold Field, "An Inventory of the Records of the Particular (Congregational) Churches of Massachusetts Gathered 1620-1805," *Harvard Theological Studies*, 26[1970].

Wright, Carroll D., *Report on the Custody and Condition of the Public Records of Parishes, Towns, and Counties* (1889: Boston, Wright and Potter Printing Co.).

NEW HAMPSHIRE

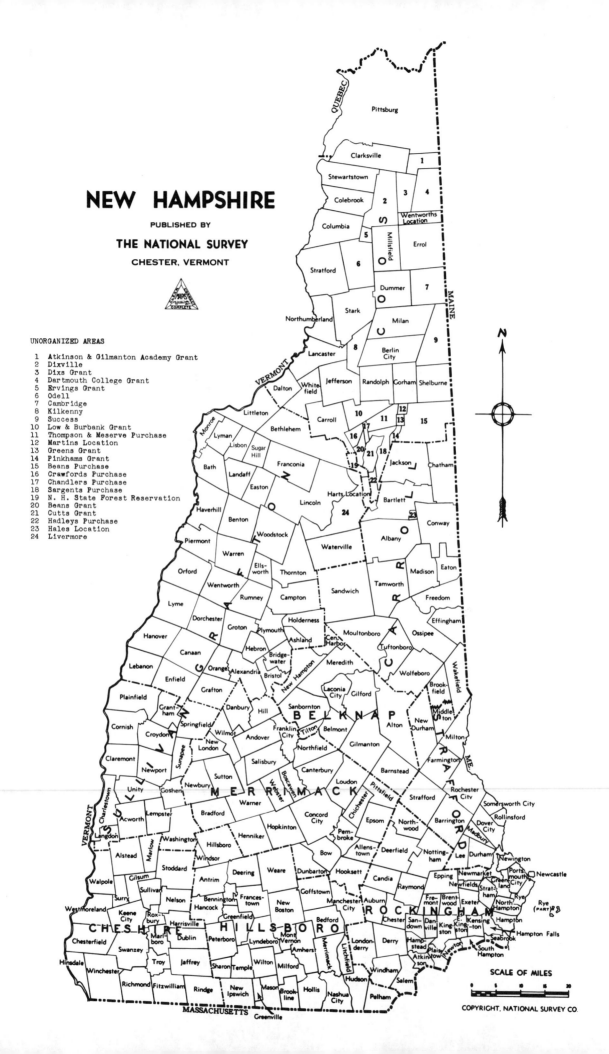

NEW HAMPSHIRE

PUBLISHED BY

THE NATIONAL SURVEY

CHESTER, VERMONT

UNORGANIZED AREAS

1 Atkinson & Gilmanton Academy Grant
2 Dixville
3 Dixs Grant
4 Dartmouth College Grant
5 Ervings Grant
6 Odell
7 Cambridge
8 Kilkenny
9 Success
10 Low & Burbank Grant
11 Thompson & Meserve Purchase
12 Martins Location
13 Greens Grant
14 Pinkhams Grant
15 Beans Purchase
16 Crawfords Purchase
17 Chandlers Purchase
18 Sargents Purchase
19 N. H. State Forest Reservation
20 Beans Grant
21 Cutts Grant
22 Hadleys Purchase
23 Hales Location
24 Livermore

SCALE OF MILES

COPYRIGHT, NATIONAL SURVEY CO.

COUNTIES

County	Formed	Parents	Seat
Belknap	1840	Strafford	Laconia
Carroll	1840	Grafton & Strafford	Ossipee
Cheshire	1769/71	-----	Keene
Coos	1803	Grafton	Lancaster
Grafton	1769/71	-----	Haverhill
Hillsborough	1769/71	-----	Nashua
Merrimack	1823	Grafton, Hillsborough, & Rockingham	Concord
Old Norfolk	1643*	-----	
Rockingham	1769/71	-----	Exeter
Strafford	1769/73	-----	Dover
Sullivan	1827	Cheshire	Newport

*For a discussion of this historical oddity, see MASSACHUSETTS – COUNTIES, second footnote to table.

TOWNS

Town	Estab'd	Named	Parent	County/Probate	Aliases
Acworth	1735/6	1766		Sullivan	Barnet
Adams (see Jackson)					
Addison (see Marlow)					
Albany	1833	1833		Carroll	Burton
Alexandria	1753	1753		Grafton	
Alexandria Addition (see New London)					
Allenstown	1722	1721		Merrimack	
Alstead	1735/6	1763		Cheshire	No. 4 & Newton
Alton	1796	1796		Belknap	New Durham Gore
Amherst	1728	1760		Hillsborough	Narragansett No. 3
Andover	1751	1779		Merrimack	New Breton, Emerystown

Town	Estab'd	Named	Parent	County/Probate	Aliases
Antrim	1777	1777		Hillsborough	Cumberland
Ashland	1868	1868	Holderness	Grafton	
Atkinson	1767	1767	Plaistow	Rockingham	
Atkinson Grant *(unincorporated)*				Coos	Gilmanton Grant
Auburn	1845	1845	Chester	Rockingham	
Baker's Town *(see Salisbury)*					
Barnet *(see Acworth)*					
Barnstead	1727	1727		Belknap	
Barrington	1722	1722		Strafford	
Bartlett	1790	1790		Carroll	
Bath	1761	1761		Grafton	
Bean's Grant *(unincorporated)*				Coos	
Bean's Purchase *(unincorporated)*				Coos	
Bedford	1733/4	1730		Hillsborough	Narragansett No. 5
Bellowstown *(see Walpole)*					
Belmont	1859	1869	Upper Gilmanton	Belknap	
Bennington	1842	1842	Hancock, Deering, & Greenfield	Hillsborough	
Benton	1764	1839		Grafton	Coventry
Berlin	1771	1829		Coos	Maynesborough
Bethlehem	1774	1799		Grafton	
Beverly Canada *(see Weare)*					
Boscawen	1732	1760		Merrimack	Contoocook
Bow	1727	1727		Merrimack	
Boyle *(see Gilsum)*					
Bradford	1735/6	1787		Merrimack	New Bradford & Bradfordton
(see also Orange)					
Bradfordton *(see Bradford)*					
Brentwood	1744	1741	Exeter	Rockingham	
Bretton Woods *(see Carroll)*					
Bridgewater	1788	1788	New Chester	Grafton	
Bristol	1819	1819	Hill & Bridgewater	Grafton	
Brookfield	1794	1794	Middleton	Carroll	
Brookline	1769	1798		Hillsborough	
Buckingham *(see Unity)*					
Buckstreet *(see Pembroke)*					
Burton *(see Albany)*					
Cambridge *(unincorporated)*				Coos	
Camden *(see Washington)*					
Campbell's Gore *(see Windsor)*					
Campton	1761	1761		Grafton	
Canaan	1761	1761		Grafton	
Candia	1763	1763	Chester	Rockingham	
Canterbury	1727	1727		Merrimack	
Cardigan *(see Orange)*					
Carroll	1772	1832		Coos	Bretton Woods

Town	Estab'd	Named	Parent	County/Probate	Aliases
Center Harbor	1797	1797	New Hampton	Belknap	
(formerly part of Moultonborough Addition)					
Chandler's Purchase	1835			Coos	
Charlestown	1735	1753		Sullivan	No. 4
Chatham	1767	1767		Carroll	
Chester	1720	1722		Rockingham	
Chesterfield	1735	1752		Cheshire	No. 1
Chester Woods *(see Hooksett)*					
Chichester	1727	1727		Merrimack	
Chiswick *(see Lincoln)*					
Claremont	1764	1764		Sullivan	
Clarksville	1792	1853		Coos	Dartmouth College Grant
Cocheco Township *(see New Durham)*					
Cockburntown *(see Columbia)*					
Cockermouth *(see Groton)*					
Colebrook	1762	1770		Coos	Dryden
Columbia	1762	1811		Coos	Preston & Cockburntown
Concord	1659	1765		Merrimack	Penacook & Rumford
(see also Lisbon)					
Contoocook *(see Boscawen)*					
Conway	1765	1765		Carroll	
Cornish	1763	1763		Sullivan	
Coventry *(see Benton)*					
Crawford's Purchase		1834		Coos	
Crawford's Notch		1834		Coos	
Croyden	1763	1763		Sullivan	
Cumberland *(see Antrim)*					
Cutt's Grant *(unincorporated)*				Coos	
Dalton	1784	1784		Coos	
Danbury	1795	1795	Alexandria	Merrimack	
Dantzig *(see Newbury)*					
Danville	1760	1760	Kingston	Rockingham	Hawke
Dartmouth College Grant *(see Clarksville)*					
Deerfield	1766	1766	Nottingham	Rockingham	
Deering	1774	1774		Hillsborough	
Derry	1827	1827	Londonderry	Rockingham	
Derryfield *(see Manchester*					
Dist. of So. Hampton *(see Seabrook)*					
Dixville *(unincorporated)*				Coos	
Dorchester	1761	1761		Grafton	
Dover	1623	1623		Strafford	
Dover Parish *(see Durham)*					
Dryden *(see Colebrook)*					
Dublin	1749	1749		Cheshire	Monadnock

Town	Estab'd	Named	Parent	County/Probate	Aliases
Dummer	1773	1773		Coos	
Dunbarton	1735	1735		Merrimack	Gorhamstown & Starkstown
Dunstable (see Nashua)					
Dupplin (see Lempster)					
Durand (see Randolph)					
Durham	1732	1732		Strafford	Dover Parish
East Kingston	1738	1738	Kingston	Rockingham	
Easton	1876	1867	Landaff	Grafton	
East-town (see Wakefield)					
Eaton	1766	1760		Carroll	
Effingham	1749	1749		Carroll	Leavitt's Town
Ellsworth	1769	1802		Grafton	Trecothick
Emerystown (see Andover)					
Enfield	1761	1761		Grafton	
Epping	1741/2	1741	Exeter	Rockingham	
Epsom	1727	1727		Merrimack	
Errol	1774	1774		Coos	
Erving's Grant (unincorporated)				Coos	
Exeter		1638		Rockingham	
Fairfield (see Woodstock					
Fall Side or Fall Parish (see Hampton Falls)					
Farmington	1798	1798	Rochester	Strafford	
Fisherfield (see Newbury)					
Fitzwilliam	1752	1773		Cheshire	Monadnock No. 4
Francestown	1772	1772		Hillsborough	
Franconia	1764	1782		Grafton	Indian Head & Morristown
Franklin	1828	1828		Merrimack	Pemigewasset
Freedom	1831	1831		Carroll	North Effingham
Freetown (see Raymond)					
Fremont	1764	1854	Exeter	Rockingham	Poplin
Gerrishtown (see Salisbury)					
Gilford	1812	1812		Belknap	Gunstock Parish of Gilmanton
Gilmanton (see also Gifford)	1727	1727		Belknap	
Gilmanton Grant (see Atkinson Grant)					
Gilsum	1752	1763		Cheshire	Boyle
Goffstown	1733/4	1748		Hillsborough	Narragansett No. 4
Gorham	1770	1836	Shelburne	Coos	
Goshen	1791	1791	Sunapee	Sullivan	
Grafton	1761	1761		Grafton	
Grantham	1761	1761		Sullivan	
Great Meadow (see Westmoreland)					
Greenfield	1872	1791		Hillsborough	Lyndefield Addition
Greenland	1721	1704	Portsmouth	Rockingham	
Green's Grant (unincorporated)				Coos	

Town	Estab'd	Named	Parent	County/Probate	Aliases
Greenville	1872	1872		Hillsborough	
Grenville *(see Newport)*					
Groton	1761	1792		Grafton	Cockermouth
Gunstock Parish *(see Gifford)*					
Gunthwaite *(see Lisbon)*					
Hadley's *(unincorporated)* Purchase				Coos	
Hale's Location *(unincorporated)*				Carroll	
Halestown *(see Weare)*					
Hampstead	1749	1749		Rockingham	Timberlane Parish of Haverhill, MA
Hampton	1635	1635		Rockingham	
Hampton Falls	1726	1726	Hampton	Rockingham	Falls Side or Parish
Ham's-town *(see Wakefield)*					
Hancock	1779	1779		Hillsborough	
Hanover	1761	1761		Grafton	
Harrisville	1870	1870		Cheshire	Twitcheville
Harrytown *(see Manchester)*					
Hart's Location *(unincorporated)*				Carroll	
Haverhill	1763	1763		Grafton	Lower Coos
Hawke *(see Danville)*					
Hebron	1792	1792	Cockermouth	Grafton	
Heidelberg *(see New London)*					
Henniker	1735/6	1768		Merrimack	No. 6
Hereford *(see Newbury)*					
Hill	1753	1837		Merrimack	New Chester
Hillsborough	1735/6	1748		Hillsborough	No. 7
Hinsdale	1753	1753		Cheshire	
Holderness	1751	1751		Grafton	
Hollis	1746	1746		Hillsborough	
Hooksett	1822	1822		Merrimack	Chester Woods, Rowe's Corner, Isle a Hooksett
Hopkinton	1735/6	1735		Merrimack	No. 5
Hudson	1746	1741		Hillsborough	Nottingham West
Indian Head *(see Franconia)*					
Indian Stream *(see Pittsburg)*					
Isle a Hooksett *(see Hooksett)*					
Jackson	1800	1829		Carroll	New Madbury & Adams
Jaffrey	1749	1773	Rowley, Canada	Cheshire	
Jefferson	1765	1796		Coos	
Jennestown *(see Warner)*					
Keene	1733	1753		Cheshire	Upper Ashuelot
Kensington	1737	1730		Rockingham	
Kilkenny *(unincorporated)*				Coos	

Town	Estab'd	Named	Parent	County/Probate	Aliases
Kingston	1694	1694		Rockingham	
Laconia	1855	1855	Meredith, Gilford, & Gilmanton	Belknap	
Lancaster	1763	1763		Coos	
Landaff	1764	1774		Grafton	
Langdon	1787	1787	Charlestown & Walpole	Sullivan	
Leavitt's Town (see Effingham)					
Lebanon	1761	1761		Grafton	
Lee	1766	1766		Strafford	
Lempster	1735/6	1761		Sullivan	No. 9 & Dupplin
Limerick (see Stoddard)					
Lincoln (unincorporated)				Grafton	
Lisbon	1763	1824		Grafton	Concord, Chiswick, & Gunthwaite
Liscomb (see Orange)					
Litchfield	1729	1729		Hillsborough	Naticook
Littleton	1764	1784	Lisbon	Grafton	
Livermore (unincorporated)				Grafton	
Londonderry	1722	1722		Rockingham	
Loudon	1773	1773	Canterbury	Merrimack	
Lovewell's Town (see Pembroke)					
Lowe/Burbank (unincorporated) Grant				Coos	
Lower Coos (see Haverhill)					
Lyman	1761	1761		Grafton	
Lyme	1761	1761		Grafton	
Lyndeborough	1735	1735		Hillsborough	
Lyndefield Addition (see Greenfield)					
Madbury	1755	1755	Durham	Strafford	
Madison	1852	1852	Eaton & Albany	Carroll	
Manchester	1735	1800s		Hillsborough	Harrytown & Derryfield
Marlborough	1752	1776		Cheshire	Monadnock # 5, New Marlborough, & Oxford
Marlow	1753	1761		Cheshire	Addison
Martin's (unincorporated) Location				Coos	
Mason	1749	1768		Hillsborough	No. 1
Maynesborough (see Berlin)					
Meredith	1748	1768		Belknap	Palmer's Town & New Salem
Merrimack	1746	1746	Nashua	Hillsborough	

Town	Estab'd	Named	Parent	County/Probate	Aliases
Middleton	1749	1749		Strafford	
Middletown *(see Orange)*					
Milan	1771	1824		Coos	Paulsborough
Milford	1794	1746	Monson	Hillsborough	
Millsfield	1774	1774		Coos	
Milton	1802	1802	Rochester	Strafford	
Monadnock *(see Dublin)*					
Monadnock No. 4 *(see Fitzwilliam)*					
Monadnock No. 5 *(see Marlborough*					
Monadnock No. 6 *(see Nelson)*					
Monadnock No. 7 *(see Stoddard*					
Monadnock No. 8 *(see Washington)*					
Monroe	1854	1854	Lyman	Grafton	
Mont Vernon	1803	1803	Amherst	Hillsborough	
Morristown *(see Franconia)*					
Moulton-borough	1763	1763		Carroll	
Narragansett No. 3 *(see Amherst)*					
Narragansett No. 4 *(see Goffstown)*					
Narragansett No. 5 *(see Bedford)*					
Nashua	1746	1836		Hillsborough	Dunstable
Naticook *(see Litchfield)*					
Nelson	1746	1836		Cheshire	Monadnock No.6 & Packersfield
New Amesbury *(see Warner)*					
New Boston	1735/6	1763		Hillsborough	
New Bradford *(see Bradford)*					
New Chester *(see Hill)*					
New Concord *(see Washington)*					
New Durham	1749	1762		Strafford	Cocheco Twp.
New Durham Gore *(see Alton)*					
Newcastle	1693	1693	Portsmouth	Rockingham	
New Garden *(see Ossipee)*					
New Hampton	1765	1777	Moultonbor-ough Addition	Belknap	
New Ipswich	1735/6	1735		Hillsborough	
New London	1753	1779		Merrimack	Heidelberg & Alexandria
New Madbury *(see Jackson)*					
New Marlborough *(see Marlborough)*					
New Plymouth *(see Plymouth)*					
New Salem *(see Meredith)*					
Newbury	1753	1837		Merrimack	Dantzig, Hereford, & Fisherfield
Newfields	1849	1895	Newmarket	Rockingham	
Newington	1764	1714		Rockingham	
Newmarket	1727	1727	Exeter	Rockingham	
Newport	1753	1761		Sullivan	Grenville

Town	Estab'd	Named	Parent	County/Probate	Aliases
Newton	1749	1749	South Hampton	Rockingham	
(see also Alstead)					
North Effingham *(see Freedom)*					
North Hampton	1738	1742		Rockingham	No. Hill & No. Parish
Northfield	1780	1780	Canterbury	Merrimack	
North Hill *(see North Hampton)*					
North Parish *(see North Hampton)*					
North Parish of Methuen, MA *(see Salem)*					
Northumber-land	1761	1771		Coos	Stonington
Northwood	1773	1763	Nottingham	Rockingham	
Nottingham	1722	1722		Rockingham	
Nottingham West *(see Hudson)*					
Number 1 *(see Chesterfield & Mason)*					
Number 2 *(see Wilton)*					
Number 4 *(see Alstead & Charleston)*					
Number 5 *(see Hopkinton)*					
Number 6 *(see Henniker)*					
Number 7 *(see Hillsborough)*					
Number 9 *(see Lempster)*					
Odell *(unincorporated)*				Coos	
Orange	1769	1790		Grafton	Cardigan, Bradford, Middletown, & Lipscomb
Orford	1761	1761		Grafton	
Ossipee	1785	1785		Carroll	New Garden
Oxford *(see Marlborough)*					
Packersfield *(see Nelson)*					
Palmer's Town *(see Meredith)*					
Paulsborough *(see Milan)*					
Peeling *(see Woodstock)*					
Pelham	1746	1746		Hillsborough	
Pembroke	1728	1759		Merrimack	Lovewell's Town, Suncook, & Buckstreet
Pemigewasset *(see Franklin)*					
Penacook *(see Concord)*					
Percy *(see Stark)*					
Perrystown *(see Sutton)*					
Peterborough	1737/8	1738		Hillsborough	
Peterborough Slip *(see Temple)*					
Piermont	1764	1764		Grafton	
Pinkham's *(unincorporated)* Grant				Coos	
Pinkham *(unincorporated)* Notch				Coos	
Piscataqua *(see Portsmouth)*					

Town	Estab'd	Named	Parent	County/Probate	Aliases
Pittsburg	1840	1840		Coos	Indian Stream Republic
Pittsfield	1782	1782	Chichester	Merrimack	
Plainfield	1761	1761		Sullivan	
Plaistow	1761	1761	Haverhill, MA	Rockingham	
Plymouth	1763	1762		Grafton	New Plymouth
Preston *(see Columbia)*					
Poplin *(see Fremont)*					
Portsmouth	1631	1653		Rockingham	Strawbery Banke & Piscataqua
Protectworth *(see Springfield)*					
Randolph	1772	1824		Coos	Durand
Raymond	1764	1764	Chester	Rockingham	Freetown
Richmond	1735	1752		Cheshire	Sylvester, Canada
Rindge	1736/7	1768		Cheshire	Rowley, Canada
Robiestown *(see Weare)*					
Rochester	1722	1722		Strafford	
Rollinsford	1849	1849	Somersworth	Strafford	
Rowe's Corner *(see Hooksett)*					
Rowley, Canada *(see Rindge)*					
Roxbury	1812	1812	Marlborough	Cheshire	
Rumford *(see Concord)*					
Rumney	1761	1761		Grafton	
Rye	1726	1726	Portsmouth	Rockingham	
Ryetown *(see Warner)*					
Salem	1750	1741		Rockingham	No. Parish of Methuen, MA
Salisbury	1736/7	1768		Merrimack	Baker's Town, Stevenstown, & Gerrishtown
Sanbornton	1748	1748		Belknap	
Sandown	1756	1756		Rockingham	
Sandwich	1763	1763		Carroll	
Sargent's *(unincorporated)* Purchase				Coos	
Saville *(see Sunapee)*					
Seabrook	1768	1768	Hampton Falls	Rockingham	Dist. of So. Hampton
Second College *(unincorporated)* Grant				Coos	
Sharon	1791	1738	Peterborough	Hillsborough	
Shelburne	1769	1769		Coos	
Somersworth	1754	1754	Dover	Strafford	
So. Hampton	1742	1742	Amesbury & Salisbury, MA	Rockingham	
Springfield	1769	1794		Sullivan	Protectworth
Stark	1774	1832		Coos	Percy
Stevenstown *(see Salisbury)*					
Stewartstown	1770	1799		Coos	

Town	Estab'd	Named	Parent	County/Probate	Aliases
Stoddard	1752	1774		Cheshire	Monadnock No. 7 & Limerick
Stonington *(see Northumberland)*					
Strafford	1820	1774 or earlier		Strafford	
Stratford	1762	1773		Coos	Woodbury
Stratham	1715/6	1716		Rockingham	
Strawberry Banke *(see Portsmouth)*					
Success *(unincorporated)*	1773			Coos	
Sugar Hill		1962	Lisbon	Grafton	
Sullivan	1787	1787		Cheshire	
Sunapee	1768	1850		Sullivan	Saville & Wendell
Suncook *(see Pembroke)*					
Surry	1769	1769		Cheshire	
Sutton	1749	1784		Merrimack	Perrystown
Swanzey	1733	1753		Cheshire	
Sylvester, Canada *(see Richmond)*					
Tamworth	1766	1766		Carroll	
Temple	1750	1750		Hillsborough	Peterborough Slip
Thompson & Meserve's Purchase *(unincorporated)*				Coos	
Thornton	1763	1763		Grafton	
Tilton	1869	1869	Sanbornton	Belknap	
Timberlane Parish of Haverhill, MA *(see Hampstead)*					
Trecothick *(see Ellsworth)*					
Troy	1815	1815	Marlborough	Cheshire	
Tuftonborough	1750	1750		Carroll	
Twitcheville *(see Harrisville)*					
Tyngsborough *(see Manchester)*					
Unity	1753	1764		Sullivan	Buckingham
Upper Ashuelot *(see Keene)*					
Wakefield	1749	1774		Carroll	Ham's-town, East-town, & Watertown
Walpole	1736	1761		Cheshire	Bellowstown
Warner	1735/6	1774		Merrimack	New Amesbury, Jennestown, Waterloo, & Ryetown
Warren	1763	1764		Grafton	
Washington	1735/6	1776		Sullivan	Monadnock No. 8, New Concord & Camden
Waterloo *(see Warner)*					
Watertown *(see Wakefield)*					
Waterville Valley	1829	1976		Grafton	Waterville

Town	Estab'd	Named	Parent	County/Probate	Aliases
Weare	1735	1764		Hillsborough	Beverly, Canada, Halestown, Robiestown, & Wearestown
Wearestown (see Weare)					
Webster	1860	1860	Boscawen	Merrimack	
Wendell *(see Sunapee)*					
Wentworth	1766	1766		Grafton	
Wentworth Location	1797	1881		Coos	
Westmoreland	1735/6	1735		Cheshire	Great Meadow
Whitefield	1774	1774		Coos	
Wilmot	1807	1807	Mt. Kearsarge Gore	Merrimack	
Wilton	1749	1762		Hillsborough	No. 2
Winchester	1733	1773		Cheshire	
Windham	1741/2	1741		Rockingham	
Windsor	1798	1798		Hillsborough	Campbell's Gore
Wolfeborough	1759	1759		Carroll	
Woodbury *(see Stratford)*					
Woodstock	1763	1840		Grafton	Peeling & Fairfield

NEW HAMPSHIRE

With settlements at Dover by 1628 and Portsmouth in 1631, N.H. ranks among the oldest states in New England. Through the first half of the 18th century, settlements were confined to the coastal region and the area around Nashua, and growth was slow. From 1642 to 1679, N.H. was governed by Mass. Under Benning Wentworth (governor 1741-67), many townships were granted in what is now Vermont, and settlement of inland N.H. proceeded rapidly after the French and Indian Wars. In 1764 the Conn. River was established as N.H.'s western boundary. The province was divided into five counties in 1769, to take effect in 1771 (Strafford, however, did not function until 1773). In 1776 a provisional constitution was adopted, and in 1788 N.H. was the ninth colony to ratify the Constitution. The 19th century saw settlement of the northern part of the state and, with the coming of the Industrial Revolution, growth of mill towns such as Manchester and Nashua. About the time of the Civil War, large numbers of French-speaking Québecois began to settle in N.H., joining a predominantly Yankee and Scots-Irish mix. Today, about a third of the state's population have French-Canadian surnames.

As in Mass., N.H.'s vital records were long kept by the towns, and land and probate records by the counties. Almost all pre-Revolutionary records are available in Concord at the NEW HAMPSHIRE HISTORICAL SOCIETY, STATE LIBRARY, DIVISION OF RECORDS MANAGEMENT AND ARCHIVES, or BUREAU OF VITAL RECORDS AND HEALTH STATISTICS.

STATE HOLIDAYS PECULIAR TO NEW HAMPSHIRE – REPOSITORIES MAY BE CLOSED – CALL

Fast Day [4th Mon in Apr] is *no longer* celebrated; Martin Luther King Day *not* celebrated, but repositories *may* or *may not* be closed for Civil Rights Day [same date]

VITAL RECORDS

Official records of all births, marriages, and deaths occurring in each N.H. town or city are kept by the clerk, who sends copies to the BUREAU OF VITAL RECORDS AND HEALTH STATISTICS (see below). The original records of every town, up to about 1850, have been microfilmed, along with an every-name index (not including Exeter); these films are available at the STATE LIBRARY and NEHGS. An alphabetic card-file, prepared from the state copies of town and city VRs, has also been filmed through 1900; this, too, is available at NEHGS.

STATE OF NEW HAMPSHIRE – BUREAU OF VITAL RECORDS AND HEALTH STATISTICS

Hazen Drive	[603] 271-4654	Rte 93 to Exit 14; E on Rte 202
Concord, NH 03301	& -4650	(Loudon Rd), ½ mi; left at
		light & sign for NH State Office Park
Mon-Fri 8:30am-4pm		E; follow signs to Health & Human
		Services Bldg.

Volunteers staff the Vital Records Room, retrieve all records, and explain policies; closed for the day if no volunteers are available. Photocopies, $.50/page (non-certified) or $10/page (certified); by mail, $10/search; two film readers. **HOLDINGS**: births to 1901, deaths, marriages, and divorces to 1938 (coverage best after *ca.* 1880). To see later records, one must demonstrate a "direct and tangible" interest. N.B., after (roughly) the 1880s, births, marriages, and deaths were published in annual town reports (Manchester was an exception). Large communities discontinued this practice at various points after 1900, but most small towns still publish their vital events (in a short form).

FEDERAL CENSUS

The DIVISION OF RECORDS MANAGEMENT AND ARCHIVES (see LIBRARIES – CONCORD) has original U.S. census schedules 1850-80; also 1840 for Rockingham, Merrimack, and Strafford Counties. Printed copies of 1790 and 1800, films of 1800-80, and printed indexes are available at the STATE LIBRARY. The NEW HAMPSHIRE HISTORICAL SOCIETY LIBRARY has the printed versions of 1790 and 1800, a photocopy of 1800, and printed indexes. All federal censuses (1800-1920) are available from the NATIONAL ARCHIVES (see NEW ENGLAND chapter). All federal censuses of N.H. are also available at NEHGS.

STATE CENSUS

N.H. has never conducted a state census. However, editions of the provincial rate (*i.e.*, tax) lists for 1732 and 1742 are available at genealogical libraries; the original is at the DIVISION OF RECORDS MANAGEMENT AND ARCHIVES.

PROBATE AND LAND

BELKNAP COUNTY

64 Court Street
Laconia, NH 03246

Courthouse at X of Rtes 3 & 106, downtown Laconia; accessible *via* Lakes Region Transit (Laconia's bus system).

Register of **Probate**   [603] 524-0903   See above.
Mon-Fri 8am-4pm

Free and open to public; staff copying, $1/page (wills) or $.50/page (all other documents); mail inquiries answered, as staffing permits. **HOLDINGS**: probates, 1841 to present.

Register of **Deeds**   [603] 524-0618   See above.
Mon-Fri 8:30am-4pm

Free and open to public; deed-books on open shelves; copies, $2/deed up to 4 pages, $.50/each additional page. **HOLDINGS**: deeds, 1840 to present. Also has typed copies of Strafford County deeds pertaining to Belknap County land, 1765-1840.

CARROLL COUNTY

P.O. Box 419 / 95 Water Village Road (Route 171)
Ossipee, NH 03864-0419

Rtes 16 or 28 to Ossipee Village; W 1 mi on Rte 171 to Carroll County Administration Bldg. No public transit.

Register of **Probate**   [603] 539-4123
Mon-Fri 8:30am-4:30pm

Free and open to public; records retrieved by staff; staff copying, $1/page (wills) or $.50/page (all other documents); *simple* mail inquiries accepted (not for record searches), billing for copies as above. **HOLDINGS**: probates, 1840 to present; Kardex.

Register of **Deeds**   [603] 539-4872   Same address & directions as probate
P.O. Box 163   & -4265   (see above).
Ossipee, NH 03864-0163

Mon-Fri 9am-5pm

Free and open to public; copies, $1/page; *simple* mail inquiries accepted (no record searches), billing for copies as above, plus $1 for document certification; plan copies, $2.50/small, $5/large. **HOLDINGS**: deeds, 1840 to present; grantor/grantee indices, writs of attachment, federal-tax liens, old-age-assistance liens, real-estate-tax liens, plans (survey maps), and daybooks back to 1866.

CHESHIRE COUNTY

Register of **Probate**	[603] 357-7786	Central Sq at corner of
12 Court Street		Court & Winter Sts.
Keene, NH 03431		

Mon-Fri 8am-4:30pm

Free and open to public; staff copying, $1/page (wills) or $.50/page (all other documents); brief mail inquiries accepted (at cost of copies). **HOLDINGS**: probates, 1771 to present.

Register of **Deeds**	[603] 352-0403	1 block from probate office
33 West Street	& -7678 (FAX)	(see above).
Keene, NH 03431		

Mon-Fri 8:30am-4:30pm

Free and open to public; staff copying, $1/page; mail requests must be pre-paid (call ahead to find out how many pp.); mail inquiries accepted for one indexing period only (may be anything from 1 to 10 years); certification, $2/document (by mail or in person). **HOLDINGS**: deeds, 1771 to present.

COOS COUNTY

55 School Street, Suite 103	Rte 3, 150 yds N of town center,
Lancaster, NH 03584	behind library and park.

Register of **Probate**	[603] 788-2001	See above.
Mon-Fri 8am-4pm		

Free and open to public; staff copying, $.50/page; mail inquiries accepted. **HOLDINGS**: probates (on open shelves) 1887 to present (earlier records lost in fire).

Register of **Deeds**	[603] 788-2392	See above.
Mon-Fri 8am-4pm		

Free and open to public *by appointment* (1 week in advance); copies, $2/page. **HOLDINGS**: deeds, 1803 to present (some from 1700s); 7 volumes of Grafton County deeds for Coos County land.

GRAFTON COUNTY

North Haverhill, NH 03774	Courthouse on Rte 10.

Register of **Probate**	[603] 787-6931	See above.
Mon-Fri 8am-4pm		

Free and open to public; pre-1900 records must be viewed in books or at State Archives; staff copying, up to $1/page. **HOLDINGS**: probates, 1773 to present; card index.

Register of **Deeds**	[603] 787-6921	See above.
Mon-Fri 7:30am-4:30pm		

Free and open to public; staff copying only, $1/page; certification, $2/document. **HOLDINGS**: deeds, 1771 to present – first 360 volumes must be viewed on film.

HILLSBOROUGH COUNTY

Register of **Probate**	[603] 882-1231	From Everett Tpk, E on Amherst St
30 Spring Street / P.O. Box P	[603] 424-7844	to Main St, S. Main St; left on E. Hollis
Nashua, NH 03061		St; left on Spring St; 1 block to court-
		house, next to P.O.
Mon-Fri 8am-4pm		

Free and open to public; reasonable mail inquiries accepted; self-service copying, $.25/page; by staff, $.50/page (staff copying of *wills*, $1/page). **HOLDINGS**: probates, 1771 to present. N.B., the probate court at 300 Chestnut Street, Manchester is for *hearings only* – no records, no research.

Registry of **Deeds**	[603] 882-6933	Everett Tpk to Exit 5E (Rte 111);
19 Temple Street	& -7527 (FAX)	at X of 111 & Spring St, go straight
Nashua, NH 03060-3472		1 block past stop sign. Metered
		parking on left; enter bldg at rear.
Mon-Fri 8am-4pm		

Free and open to public; staff copying, $1/page (plus postage if mailed); mail requests *citing volume and page* accepted. **HOLDINGS**: deeds, 1771 to present; original books to 1950, plus indexes, in basement vault; 1950+, on 1st floor; 1981+ on optical retrieval system; *all* volumes on film, but originals may be consulted; probate index; plans also available.

MERRIMACK COUNTY

163 North Main Street		Rte I-93 to Exit 14 to Main; right
Concord, NH 03301		at light. Next to Bank of NH and
		Stewart Nelson Plaza.

Register of **Probate**	[603] 224-9589	See above.
Mon-Fri 8am-4:30pm		

Free and open to public; copying – self-service or staff, rates are identical – $1/page (wills) or $5/document (inventories and accounts); service by mail (rates same). **HOLDINGS**: probates, 1823 to present; card index; originals may be consulted.

Registry of **Deeds**	[603] 228-0101	See above.
Mon-Fri 8am-4:30pm		
no copying after 4:15pm		

Mail: P.O. Box 248 / Concord, NH 03302-0248

Free and open to public; staff copying, $1/page (deeds), $5/plan; mail service available (no staff research) at above rates plus postage. **HOLDINGS**: deeds, 1823 to present; all records on film for public use and sale; index on CD, 1960-96, for use and sale; documents on CD, 1974 to present, for use and sale. N.B., for film, CD, or on-line price list, send SASE.

ROCKINGHAM COUNTY (kept and continued the pre-1771 N.H. provincial records)

Rockingham County Courthouse
#10 Route 125
Brentwood, NH 03833

Rte 101 to 125S, 6 mi on right **OR**
Rte 111 to 125N, 3 mi on left.

Register of **Probate**　　　　[603] 642-7117　　　　See above.
Mon-Fri 8am-4pm

Mail: P.O. Box 789 / Kingston, NH 03848

Free and open to public; film reader/printer and self-service copying, both $.25/page; no mail inquiries. **HOLDINGS**: probates, 1771 to present (film), 1918 to present (originals). Originals, 1760-1918, are at the DIVISION OF RECORDS MANAGEMENT AND ARCHIVES.

Registry of **Deeds**　　　　[603] 642-5526　　　　See above.
Mon-Fri 8am-4pm

Mail: P.O. Box 896 / Kingston, NH 03848

Free and open to public; copies: of *plans*, off film, $1.50/page; off originals, $3/each; *all other* documents, $1/page. Mail service at above rates plus postage (prepaid); 36 readers. **HOLDINGS**: deeds and index, 1643 to present (film); plans on aperture cards. N.B., volumes 1-100 are customarily called the 'provincial deeds;' volumes 101+, 'Rockingham deeds.'

STRAFFORD COUNTY

Justice and Administration Building
P.O. Box 799 / County Farm Road
Dover, NH 03820

Spaulding Tpk to Exit 9; follow
signs to Bldg.

Register of **Probate**　　　　[603] 742-2550　　　　See above.
Mon-Fri 8am-4:30pm

Free and open to public; staff copying, $.50/image. **HOLDINGS**: probates, 1773 to present, on film (earlier in Rockingham County); originals may *not* be consulted; film is of *contemporary copybooks only* to *ca.* 1900. Book index to pre-1900 records; post-1900 index on cards.

Register of **Deeds**　　　　[603] 742-1741　　　　See above.
Mon-Fri 8:30am-4:15pm

Free and open to public; staff copying, $1/page; 1 film reader, 1 reader/printer; *limited* mail inquiries accepted. **HOLDINGS**: deeds, 1773 to present; computerized index to 1970.

SULLIVAN COUNTY

14 Main Street / P.O. Box 417
Newport, NH 03773

Rte 10 to Newport bldg, on E side of
Main.

Register of **Probate**　　　　[603] 863-3150　　　　See above.
Mon-Fri 8am-4:30pm

Free and open to public. Staff copying, $.50/page. **HOLDINGS**: probates, 1827 to present; all in vault, staff access only; early indexes by first letter of surname only.

    Register of **Deeds**   [603] 863-2110   See above.
    Mon-Fri 8am-4pm

Free and open to public. Staff copying, $1/first page, $.50/each additional, plus postage if by mail. **HOLDINGS**: deeds, 1827 to present.

CEMETERY RECORDS

The NEW HAMPSHIRE HISTORICAL SOCIETY (see under LIBRARIES) has a large collection of gravestone inscriptions, arranged by town. For a list of their holdings, see the Winter 1975 and Spring 1980 issues of *Historical New Hampshire.* See also NEW HAMPSHIRE OLD GRAVEYARD ASSOCIATION (under SOCIETIES).

CHURCH RECORDS

Originals are usually found at the church itself. When a church was discontinued, its records may have been deposited with a state organization, transferred to neighboring churches, or kept in private hands. Many churches have deposited their early records with the NEW HAMPSHIRE HISTORICAL SOCIETY (see under LIBRARIES). Local libraries, also, may have church records.

Original and microfilmed Quaker records for most of New England are at the RHODE ISLAND HISTORICAL SOCIETY (see under LIBRARIES – PROVIDENCE), with films at NEHGS in Boston (see under NEW ENGLAND).

MILITARY RECORDS

The DIVISION OF RECORDS MANAGEMENT AND ARCHIVES (see under LIBRARIES) has records of the French and Indian Wars, with a name index. These were printed in the *Adjutant General's Report, 1866*, vol. 2, and the *New Hampshire Provincial and State Papers*, vols. 5, 6, 14, and 16. The Division also has Revolutionary records, which were published in the *New Hampshire Provincial and State Papers*, vols. 14-17 and 30, and Civil War records – alphabetical by surname – published by the Adjutant General in *Revised Register of Soldiers and Sailors of New Hampshire in the War of the Rebellion* (1895). All this material is also available at NEHGS in Boston.

Pension records for Revolutionary soldiers and sailors are at NARA in Washington, D.C., and may be requested with proper forms. The pension *applications* are on microfilm at NARA's Waltham and Pittsfield facilities (see NEW ENGLAND chapter). The NEW HAMPSHIRE HISTORICAL SOCIETY has a 71-volume alphabetical typescript covering N.H. veteran pensioners; NEHGS has a microfilm copy.

IMMIGRATION AND NATURALIZATION

See this section in the CONNECTICUT chapter.

Direct entry of foreign nationals into N.H. has been almost solely from Canada; most relevant immigration records therefore fall under the auspices of the St. Albans District, which covers the entire U.S./Canadian border (see NEW ENGLAND – NARA – WALTHAM). St. Albans records begin in 1895; earlier passage across the border was essentially unregulated and unrecorded. Records of *ship-passenger* arrivals – *via* Portsmouth – from 1820 on (but with gaps) are also at NARA. Most maritime entry, of course, was by way of Boston or Portland.

See NARA also for N.H. naturalization records.

NEWSPAPERS

N.H.'s newspapers begin in 1756 with the Portsmouth *New-Hampshire Gazette*. The STATE LIBRARY has those 19th- and early 20th-century N.H. papers that have been filmed; many early *original* issues are at the NEW HAMPSHIRE HISTORICAL SOCIETY LIBRARY (see under CONCORD). (Microfilm of many old N.H. newspapers may also be found at the BOSTON PUBLIC LIBRARY.)

VRs have been extracted from N.H. newspapers and published in book form by: Otis G. Hammond, *Notices from the New Hampshire Gazette, 1765-1800* (1970: Lambertville, NJ, Hunterdon House); Scott Lee Chipman, *New England Vital Records from the Exeter News-Letter* [1831-58], 4 vols. (1993-4: Camden, ME, Picton Press); and David Colby Young and Robert L. Taylor, *Death Notices from Freewill Baptist Publications, 1811-1851* (1985: Bowie, MD, Heritage Books). (The latter denomination was strong in N.H. and Maine.)

For a detailed list of early American newspapers – with locations (possibly obsolete) of copies or sets – see Clarence S. Brigham, *History and Bibliography of American Newspapers, 1690-1820*, 2 vols. (1962: Hamden and London, Archon Books).

CIVIL AND CRIMINAL COURT RECORDS

The N.H. *Provincial* court files have been filmed, along with a card index to cases (by plaintiff and defendant), from 1638-1772 (when the Province was split into counties); these films may be found at the STATE ARCHIVES and NEHGS. The STATE ARCHIVES has *original* post-1771 county court files, up to a cutoff that varies from county to county; call the courthouses – which should have more recent files – for exact years. (See also Frank Mevers and Harriet S. Lacy, "Early Historical Records (*c.*1620-*c.*1817) at the New Hampshire State Archives," *Historical New Hampshire*, 31[1976]:108-18, for more on the Archives' court-records holdings.) The STATE LIBRARY, also, has film of post-1771 common pleas records for Rockingham, Strafford, Hillsborough, Cheshire, and Grafton counties.

See also Laura P. Hulslander, *Abstracts of Strafford County, New Hampshire, Inferior Court Records, 1773-1783* (1990: Bowie, MD, Heritage Books).

LIBRARIES

Almost all N.H. towns have public libraries, whose holdings vary greatly. Most have small collections, which may or may not include items of genealogical interest. Many are open 12 hours a week or less and undertake no research. For a national list of libraries and hours, see the *American Library Directory,* in most large libraries.

CONCORD – NEW HAMPSHIRE DIVISION OF RECORDS MANAGEMENT AND ARCHIVES

71 South Fruit Street   [603] 271-2236
Concord, NH 03301
Web: http://www.state.nh.us/state/archives.htm

Mon-Fri 8am-4:30pm

From S, N, or E: Rtes 93 to 89, Exit 2;
E 1 mi on Clinton St to flashing light
(Fruit); left on Fruit ¼ mi to sign for
State Office Park South. First bldg in
Park. From W: Rte 89 to Exit 2,
then as above.

Free admission; copies $.20/page (by mail, depending on document's condition or confidentiality); 2 film reader/printers. Payment: cash, or check/money order payable to State of New Hampshire. No interlibrary loan. **HOLDINGS**: provincial and state records; court records (including probate); town and county records; original federal censuses, 1850-80 (and 1840 for Merrimack, Rockingham, and Strafford Counties); Revolutionary and other military records. For a further description of holdings, see (under CIVIL AND CRIMINAL COURT RECORDS) Mevers and Lacy, "Early Historical Records;" and *Guide to Early Documents at the New Hampshire Records Management and Archives Center* (1981). New material, from crowded county courthouses and elsewhere, arrives monthly. N.B., the current *Guide* is at their Website (see above).

CONCORD – NEW HAMPSHIRE HISTORICAL SOCIETY LIBRARY

30 Park Street   [603] 225-3381
Concord, NH 03301   [603] 224-0463 FAX
Web: http://www.nhhistory.org/library.html
E-mail: NhhsLib@aol.com

Tue-Sat 9:30am-5pm

Rte 93N to Exit 14; left, 2 blocks W;
left on No. State St. State House on
right of street.

Air-conditioned, handicapped accessible; $5/day, non-members; some open stacks; staff copying, $.20/page, members; $.25, non-; film reader/printer, $.50/page. Mail requests for *brief* searches accepted, no research outside of building – first 15 minutes free, then $20/hour, plus copies. No interlibrary loan. **HOLDINGS**: 5,000 printed and manuscript genealogies (mainly northern New England); printed vital records; town, county, and state histories for all New England; pre-1900 N.H. newspapers (most on film); cemetery inscriptions; printed and manuscript maps; 1 million pages of well-indexed manuscripts from N.H. families; provincial probates and deeds (on film), 1650-1771; card index of 30,000 N.H. 'notables,' including current obits; 150,000 photos of N.H. scenes and people. N.B., finest library in state for N.H. genealogy, local history, and biography, and largest genealogical library in New England north of Boston. Their card catalog is now on-line at their website.

CONCORD – NEW HAMPSHIRE STATE LIBRARY

20 Park Street   [603] 271-2144 (Ref)   Rte 93 to Exit 14 (Bridge St); Rte 202W
Concord, NH 03301   1 block; left on No. Main St; right
                                             on Park. Metered parking.

Mon-Fri 8:30am-4:30pm

Free admission; some open stacks; copying, $.10/page; 2 film readers; 2 printers, $.25/page; mail requests for *brief* searches accepted (minimum copy fee $1); materials do not circulate. **HOLDINGS**: copies of most pre-1850 N.H. town records, with card index to all names appearing therein (except for Exeter); many county-court records and manuscript genealogies; federal censuses of N.H. (1790-1920); most 20th-century N.H. newspapers (film).

DOVER PUBLIC LIBRARY

73 Locust Street   [603] 743-6050   From Spaulding Tpk, Exit 8 (Silver St /
Dover, NH 03820   Rte 9) to downtown; library behind City
Web: http://www.dover.lib.nh.us   Hall, corner of Locust & Hale. Parking
                                             at rear.

Mon-Wed 9am-8:30pm; Fri -5:30pm
Sat -5pm (*summer*: Sat -1pm)

Free admission; self-service copying, $.10/page; 2 film readers, 1 fiche; mail inquiries accepted (brief questions or catalog-checking only – no research); materials do not circulate. **HOLDINGS**: one of state's best and largest collections of books and journals on N.H. genealogy and local history; many rare books and pamphlets on Dover-area history; Dover newspapers (film), 1825+; LDS's IGI fiche for New England and Québec. N.B., card catalog will be at above website in near future.

DURHAM – UNIVERSITY OF NEW HAMPSHIRE – DIMOND LIBRARY – SPECIAL COLLECTIONS DEPARTMENT

18 Library Way   [603] 862-2714   Rte 4 to Durham; follow signs to UNH
Durham, NH 03824   campus (on Main St, W of town center);
                                            Special Collections, 1st floor. Ample
Mon-Fri 8am-4:30pm   parking.

Free admission; copying, $.15/page; film readers; no staff research; materials do not circulate. **HOLDINGS**: extensive – New England genealogy and local history, N.H. history; Albert H. Lamson Library, owned by Piscataqua Pioneers and on deposit – inventory published in *Piscataqua Pioneers Register of Members and Ancestors, 1905-1981*, 4th rev. (1982), 226-59. (Inventory also online: http://www.izaak.unh.edu/specoll/piscapio.htm.) Dimond also has film of U.S. censuses for N.H., and many state and local newspapers.

EXETER PUBLIC LIBRARY

Founders Park   [603] 772-3101   From Rte 95 (N or S), Exit 2 to Rtes
Exeter, NH 03833   101W & 85S; along river to town ctr;
Web: http://www.exeternh.org   left at bandstand, over bridge; library at
                                             end of bridge on right.

Sat 10am-5pm (*mid-Jun to Labor Day*: -1pm)

Copying, $.10/page; genealogical materials do not circulate; limited staff assistance – call ahead if extensive help needed; limited mail-in genealogical searches by knowledgeable volunteers as time permits. If request too involved, researcher referred to professional. **HOLDINGS**: Rockingham County genealogy; N.H. town histories; *Exeter News-Letter* (film), 1831 to present; U.S. censuses of N.H. (selected counties; film), 1850-1910; likewise of Vermont, 1880-1910; pre-Columbian history collection of New England Antiquities Research Association.

HANOVER – DARTMOUTH COLLEGE LIBRARY

Hanover, NH 03755	[603] 646-2560 (Ref) & -2165 (Micro)	I-89 to Rte 10 or I-91 to Hanover; Baker Library (large, with bell tower) just N of green. Metered parking.
Mon-Fri 8am-10pm; Sat 9am-6pm; Sun 1-10pm		
Baker Stacks: Mon-Sun 8am-midnight	[603] 646-2567	*N.B., hours may vary when College not in session*
Special Collections: Mon-Fri 8am-4:30pm	[603] 646-2037	

Open to public; ID required for Baker Stacks; librarians undertake no research; genealogical mail-queries not answered unless relating to Hanover or Dartmouth individuals; 5 copiers, $.10/page; several film/fiche readers and reader/printers. **HOLDINGS**: genealogical resources relating to the College, Hanover, and surrounding N.H. and Vermont towns; N.H. and Vermont federal censuses; Hanover cemetery inscriptions; genealogical manuscript collections. Detailed guide to genealogy and family-history materials available free of charge at Information Desk in Baker Library.

KEENE PUBLIC LIBRARY

The Wright Room's collection of N.H. genealogies and town histories has been permanently moved to the Cheshire County Historical Society – [603] 352-1895.

MANCHESTER – AMERICAN-FRENCH GENEALOGICAL SOCIETY LIBRARY

4 Elm Street P.O. Box 6478 Manchester, NH 03108 **Web**: http://ourworld.compuserve.com	[603] 622-1554	I-293 to Queen City Exit; over bridge; right on Elm; right on W. Baker.
Wed, Fri 9am-9pm; Sat -4pm (*other hours by arrangement*)		

$5/day, non-members; self-service copying, $.15/page; film and fiche readers; 1 reader/printer, $.50/page. **HOLDINGS**: 9,000 volumes and 4,000 microforms on Canadian and American genealogy. Probably best library in New England for French-Canadian ancestry. (See also under NEW ENGLAND – SOCIETIES.)

MANCHESTER PUBLIC LIBRARY

405 Pine Street Manchester, NH 03104 **Web**: http://www.manchester.lib.nh.us	[603] 624-6550	I-93 to Exit 7 (Candia Rd); at end of ramp, straight across Candia to next light (Hanover St); right on Hanover. Before downtown, right on Pine; library on right, opposite Victory Park & next to Manchester Historical Society.
N.H. Room: Mon 8:30am-12:30pm & 5:30-8:30pm Tue-Thu 1:30-5:30pm; Fri, Sat 8:30am-5:30pm		

Free and open to public; copying, $.15/page; mail inquiries accepted ($5 fee plus cost of copies). **HOLDINGS**: N.H. and Manchester histories; some genealogies; Manchester directories, mid-1800s to present; local newspaper (in periodical room); some early VRs; some N.H. federal census records; maps and atlases (mostly for Manchester area).

PORTSMOUTH ATHENAEUM

Joseph P. Copely   [603] 431-2538
  Research Library
6-8 Market Square / Box 848
Portsmouth, NH 03802
E-mail: athenaeum@juno.com

Library & Randall Room: Tue, Thu 1-4pm; Sat 10am-4pm
Reading Room: Thu 1-4pm

Free and open to public; mail inquiries accepted (up to ½ or 1 hour of research); donations encouraged; copying at librarian's discretion, $.25/page. **HOLDINGS**: 40,000 volumes; 70+ manuscript collections; 600+ small manuscripts; microfilm; maps; newspapers; large photo collection. Focus on local/regional history, literature, and culture. Portraits, ship models, and artifacts in Reading Room. Randall Room: periodically changing exhibits reflective of local/regional interests. Many genealogies; manuscript and printed church records; graveyard information; vertical file on local families; town and state histories; and customs house records. N.B., Research Library on 3rd floor.

PORTSMOUTH PUBLIC LIBRARY

8 Islington Street   [603] 427-1540   I-95 (N or S) to Exit 7 to Market
Portsmouth, NH 03801   Sq (downtown); library at 2nd
Web: www.cityofportsmouth.com/library/library.htm   light (Congress St); Congress
     X's with Islington. Library on
Mon-Thu 9am-9pm; Fri -5:30pm; Sat -5pm   left; parking at rear & across
     street.

Free and open to public; copying, $.10/page (if fragile, $.25/page, only by Special Collections librarian); 2 film reader/printers, 1 fiche, $.25/page; no interlibrary loan; genealogical materials do not circulate; *brief* searches by mail accepted. Portsmouth History and Genealogy Room open same hours as library. Local historian on duty Tue, 9am-5:30pm. **HOLDINGS**: Portsmouth and surrounding area; 100+ maps of N.H. and Maine, 17th-20th century; Portsmouth newspapers (original or film), 1756 to present; Portsmouth VRs from 1699; church records, 1823-1917; city directories, 1821 to present; and town records, 1645-1822.

LDS FAMILY HISTORY CENTERS

Concord – 90 Clinton Street; [603] 225-2848; Wed, Thu 10am-2pm & 6:30-9pm; Sat 10am-2pm

Exeter – 55 Hampton Falls Rd.; [603] 778-2509; Wed, Thu 10am-2pm & 6:30-9pm; Sat 9am-4pm

Nashua – 110 Concord Street; [603] 594-8888; Tue 10am-2pm; Wed, Thu 10am-2pm & 6:30-9pm; Sat 10am-3pm

(For FHC holdings, see NEW ENGLAND chapter.)

SOCIETIES

AMERICAN-CANADIAN GENEALOGICAL SOCIETY (see NEW ENGLAND – SOCIETIES and NEW HAMPSHIRE – LIBRARIES – MANCHESTER)

NEW HAMPSHIRE HISTORICAL SOCIETY (see also under LIBRARIES – CONCORD)

30 Park Street   [603] 225-3381
Concord, NH 03301
Web: http://www.nhhistory.org

Founded 1823 to investigate, collect, preserve, and communicate whatever may relate to the history of N.H. and its people. Annual dues: $30/individual, $50/family. Annual meeting first Saturday in May. Publication: *Historical New Hampshire* (began 1944; semi-annual; comes with membership) – historical, not genealogical; queries not accepted. Submissions should result from original research and pertain to some aspect of N.H.'s past.

NEW HAMPSHIRE OLD GRAVEYARD ASSOCIATION (NHOGA)

Kim Sowles, Corresponding Secretary
7 Maple Court
Tilton, NH 03276

Founded 1975 to study N.H. cemeteries and gravestones for their artistic, historic, cultural, and genealogical value, and to help preserve N.H.'s old cemeteries. Annual dues: $3/individual, $5/institution. Three meetings per year; annual meeting in spring at various locations. Publishes *Rubbings* (newsletter; with membership) and *Graveyard Restoration Hand Book* ($1.50).

NEW HAMPSHIRE SOCIETY OF GENEALOGISTS (NHSOG)

P.O. Box 2316
Concord, NH 03302-2316
Web: http://www.tiac.net/users/nhsog
E-mail: pfwells@pop.mond.net

Founded in 1978 to educate in genealogical research technique, bring people interested in genealogy together, publish genealogical material, ensure public access to records, and promote records preservation. Membership: 600 individual, 50 household, 65 life. Annual dues: $20/individual, $30/household, $400/life. Quarterlies: *New Hampshire Genealogical Record* and *Newsletter* (both with membership). See website for membership, special publications, and 'New Hampshire Families in 1790.' Society maintains a 'Family Register,' covering individuals and families known to have resided in N.H. prior to 1901. Meets twice annually (Mar/Apr and Sep/Oct, usually in Concord area). Member of Federation of Genealogical Societies and New England Regional Genealogical Conference. Contact Society for complete information.

PISCATAQUA PIONEERS

Duncan D. Chaplin III,
   Assistant Registrar   [603] 269-4524 FAX
RFD 2 Box 568
Center Barnstead, NH 03225-9103
E-mail: asnack@worldpath.net

Founded in 1905 to secure and preserve records of the Piscataqua Valley pioneers and their Maine and N.H. descendants, and promote fellowship among members. Dues: $5/yr, $50/life ($5 initial fee). Annual meeting in Portsmouth, last Sat in July. Curator is in charge of applications and keeping up-to-date records of reference material in the Lamson Collection at UNH's Dimond Library (see under LIBRARIES – DURHAM). Copies of member applications obtainable from Dimond or LDS Family History Library (see NEW ENGLAND chapter). **HOLDINGS**: Society's collection housed in Special Collections division of Dimond Library; index lists books and manuscripts. Particular collection items available for research *via* written request to Library Staff; items then loaned for use within Special Collections section. Another index lists past and present members by surname of qualifying ancestor. Applications for membership must contain lineage form, and are available for viewing on microfilm. (There is no every-name index to applications.) The Genealogical Society of Utah has published (on film) the Piscataqua Pioneers' *Applications for Membership 1623-1775, Register of Members and Ancestors, 1905-1981*, and *Applications for Membership, 1978-1982*.

PERIODICALS

N.H.'s only statewide genealogical magazine is the ***NEW HAMPSHIRE GENEALOGICAL RECORD*** (quarterly), which ran originally from 1903 to 1910, fell into abeyance for eight decades, then resumed publication in 1990 (see under NEW HAMPSHIRE SOCIETY OF GENEALOGISTS). In addition, many N.H. counties have 'dedicated' genealogical journals of their own, which vary in quality.

For the genealogy of French-Canadians in N.H., see the ***AMERICAN-CANADIAN GENEALOGIST*** (quarterly), the official organ of the AMERICAN-CANADIAN GENEALOGICAL SOCIETY (see under NEW ENGLAND – SOCIETIES and LIBRARIES – MANCHESTER).

BOOKS AND ARTICLES

Belknap, Jeremy and **John Farmer**, *The History of New Hampshire*, 2 vols. (repr. ed., 1991: Bowie, MD, Heritage Books).

Chipman, Scott Lee, *New England Vital Records from the Exeter News-Letter*, vols. 1-5 (1993+: Camden, ME, Picton Press).

Copeley, William, *Index to Genealogies in New Hampshire Town Histories* (1988: Concord, New Hampshire Historical Society).

Dearborn, David C., "New Hampshire Genealogy: A Perspective," *NEHGR*, 130[1976]:244-58; also in Ralph J. Crandall, ed., *Genealogical Research in New England* (1984: Baltimore, Genealogical Publishing Co.).

Eichholz, Alice and **George F. Sanborn Jr.**, "New Hampshire," in *Ancestry's Red Book* (rev. ed., 1992: Salt Lake City, Ancestry Publishing).

Goss, Mrs. Charles Carpenter, *Colonial Gravestone Inscriptions in the State of New Hampshire* (1942: Baltimore, Clearfield Co.).

Green, Scott E., *Directory of Repositories of Family History in New Hampshire* (1993: Baltimore, Clearfield Co.).

Hanrahan, E. J., ed., *Hammond's Check List of New Hampshire History* (1971: Somersworth, New Hampshire Publishing Co.).

Haskell, John D., Jr. and **T. D. Seymour Bassett**, eds., *New Hampshire: A Bibliography of Its History* (1979: Boston, G. K. Hall).

Hunt, Elmer M., *New Hampshire Town Names and Whence They Came* (1971: Peterborough, NH, Noone House).

New Hampshire Provincial and State Papers, 40 vols. (1867-1943); vols. 1-9 have been repr. by Heritage Books, Bowie, MD. For good discussion of contents, see R. Stuart Wallace, "The State Papers, A Descriptive Guide," in *Historical New Hampshire*, 31[1976]:119-28.

Noyes, Sybil, Charles Thornton Libby, and **Walter Goodwin Davis**, *Genealogical Dictionary of Maine and New Hampshire* (repr. ed., 1972: Baltimore, Genealogical Publishing Co.).

Roberts, Richard P., *New Hampshire Name Changes 1768-1923* (1996: Bowie, MD, Heritage Books).

Sanborn, George Freeman, Jr. and **Melinde Lutz**, *Hampton New Hampshire Vital Records to the End of the Year 1900*, 2 vols. (1992 and 1998: Boston, NEHGS).

Towle, Laird C. and **Ann N. Brown**, *New Hampshire Genealogical Research Guide* (1983: Bowie, MD, Heritage Books).

Wentworth, William Edgar, *Vital Records, 1790-1829, from Dover, New Hampshire's First Newspaper* (1994: Camden, ME, Picton Press).

_____, *Journals of Enoch Hayes Place* (1998: Boston, NEHGS).

RHODE ISLAND

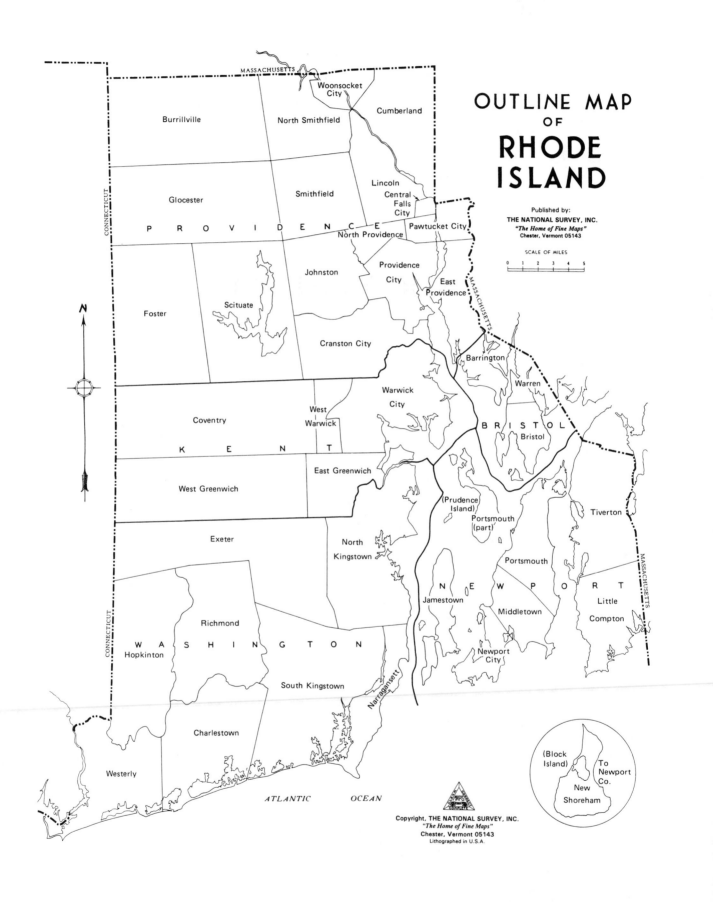

OUTLINE MAP
OF
RHODE ISLAND

Published by:
THE NATIONAL SURVEY, INC.
"The Home of Fine Maps"
Chester, Vermont 05143

SCALE OF MILES
0 1 2 3 4 5

MASSACHUSETTS

CONNECTICUT

Woonsocket City

Burrillville

North Smithfield

Cumberland

Lincoln

Central Falls City

Smithfield

Glocester

P R O V I D E N C E

Pawtucket City

North Providence

Johnston

Providence City

East Providence

MASSACHUSETTS

Foster

Scituate

Cranston City

Barrington

Warren

B R I S T O L

Bristol

Warwick City

West Warwick

Coventry

K E N T

East Greenwich

West Greenwich

(Prudence Island)

Tiverton

Exeter

North Kingstown

Portsmouth (part)

Portsmouth

MASSACHUSETTS

N E W P O R T

Jamestown

Middletown

Little Compton

Richmond

W A S H I N G T O N

Hopkinton

Newport City

South Kingstown

Narragansett

Charlestown

Westerly

ATLANTIC   OCEAN

(Block Island)

To Newport Co.

New Shoreham

Copyright, **THE NATIONAL SURVEY, INC.**
"The Home of Fine Maps"
Chester, Vermont 05143
Lithographed in U.S.A.

COUNTIES

County	Formed	Parent(s)	Seat
Bristol	1746/7	Bristol County, MA	Bristol
Kent	1750	Providence	E. Greenwich
Newport	1703	-----	Newport
Providence	1703	-----	Providence
Washington	1729	Newport	W. Kingston

N.B.: all Rhode Island vital, probate, and land records are kept and held by the *towns*; the only records kept by the counties are court and federal census records. The superior courts, at the county seats, hold recent records; early court records are now at the JUDICIAL RECORDS CENTER in Pawtucket.

TOWNS

Town	Estab'd	Parent(s)	County	Aliases	Town Hall
Attleboro Gore *(see Cumberland)*					
Barrington	1717	MA, 1747	Bristol	Warren ('til 1747)	Warren
Block Island *(see New Shoreham)*					
Bristol	1681	MA, 1747	Bristol	Mt. Hope	
Burrillville	1806	Glocester	Providence		Harrisville
Central Falls	1895	Lincoln	Providence		
Charlestown	1738	Westerly	Washington		
Conanicut *(see Jamestown)*					
Coventry	1741	Warwick	Kent		
Cranston	1754	Providence	Providence		
Cumberland	1747	MA, 1747	Providence	Attleboro Gore	
Dedford *(see E. Greenwich)*					
E. Greenwich	1677		Kent	Dedford (1686-9)	
E. Providence	1862	MA, 1861	Providence	Rehoboth & Seekonk	
Exeter	1742/3	N. Kingstown	Washington		
Feversham *(see Westerly)*					
Foster	1781	Scituate	Providence		
Glocester	1731	Providence	Providence		Chepachet
Haversham *(see Westerly)*					
Hopkinton	1757	Westerly	Washington		
Jamestown	1678		Newport	Conanicut	
Johnston	1759	Providence	Providence		
Lincoln	1871	Smithfield	Providence		Central Falls
Little Compton	1682	MA, 1747	Newport		
Middletown	1743	Newport	Newport		
Mt. Hope *(see Bristol)*					
Narragansett	1901	S. Kingstown	Washington		
Newport	1639		Newport		

Town	Estab'd	Parent(s)	County	Aliases	Town Hall
New Shoreham	1661		Washington	Block Island (1664-72)	Block Island
N. Kingstown	1641		Washington	Rochester (1686-9)	Wickford
(Kingstown from 1641 'til 1723 when name was changed to N. Kingstown)					
N. Providence	1765	Providence	Providence		Centredale
(see also Pawtucket)					
N. Smithfield	1871	Smithfield	Providence	Slater (1871)	Slatersville
Pawtucket	1828	MA, 1747	Providence	part of N. Providence (1874)	
Pocasset *(see Portsmouth)*					
Portsmouth	1638		Newport	Pocasset ('til 1639)	
Providence	1636		Providence		
Rehoboth *(see E. Providence)*					
Richmond	1747	Charlestown	Washington		Wyoming
Rochester *(see N. Kingstown)*					
Scituate	1731	Providence	Providence		N. Scituate
Seekonk *(see E. Providence)*					
Smithfield	1731	Providence	Providence		Georgiaville
(early records in Central Falls)					
Slater *(see N. Smithfield)*					
S. Kingstown	1723	Kingstown	Washington		Wakefield
Tiverton	1694	MA, 1747	Newport		
Warren	1747	MA, 1747	Bristol	Barrington, Swansea, & Rehoboth, MA; part of Bristol (1873)	
(see also Barrington)					
Warwick	1643		Kent	Shawomet ('til 1648)	Apponaug
Westerly	1669		Washington	Misquamicut (1669); Feversham or Haversham (1686-9)	
W. Greenwich	1741	E. Greenwich	Kent		
W. Warwick	1913	Warwick	Kent		
Woonsocket	1867	Cumberland & Smithfield	Providence		

N.B., in 1747, Barrington, Bristol, Cumberland, Little Compton, Tiverton, and Warren were ceded by Mass. (E. Providence, in 1862.) Pre-1747 county court, probate, and land records for the first group of towns are in Taunton, Mass.; all VRs, however – including those from Mass. days – are in the town halls. The RHODE ISLAND HISTORICAL SOCIETY has vital and probate records for almost all Rhode Island towns.

RHODE ISLAND

Genealogical research in Rhode Island can be interesting and enjoyable. There is a wealth of primary source material available for study – much of it well-indexed and in good condition. Because the state is geographically small, it is possible to travel easily from one end to the other to examine records firsthand. Most libraries and other institutions welcome researchers and willingly provide assistance. Mail requests are usually answered, and referrals given to other possible sources of information. The RHODE ISLAND HISTORICAL SOCIETY library in Providence is highly recommended as the place to start, as its collection is the most extensive in the state.

STATE HOLIDAYS PECULIAR TO RHODE ISLAND – REPOSITORIES MAY BE CLOSED – CALL

VJ [Victory over Japan] Day [mid-Aug]

VITAL RECORDS

<u>1636 to 1850</u>: see James N. Arnold, *Vital Record of Rhode Island, 1636-1850*, 21 vols. (1891-1912), and A.G. Beaman, *Rhode Island Vital Records*, new series, 17 vols. (1975-87), available at NEHGS and many other major libraries.

<u>1850 to 1853</u>: available only at town clerk's office.

<u>1853 to present</u>:

Rhode Island Department   [401] 222-2811   Near State House.
   of Health
Division of Vital Records
3 Capitol Hill, Room 101
Providence, RI 02908-5097

Mon-Fri 8:30am-4pm

Open to public; service by mail; $15/search (of two years at a time; fee includes copy, if record is found. $10/each extra copy; $.50/each additional year searched. Check or money order payable to General Treasurer, State of Rhode Island.). **HOLDINGS**: records of birth, marriage (begin 1897), and death (begin 1947), to present. N.B., the RHODE ISLAND HISTORICAL SOCIETY library has an index to births, marriages, and deaths, 1853-90. The RHODE ISLAND STATE ARCHIVES has birth and marriage records, 1853-96, and death records, 1853-1946.

FEDERAL CENSUS

Federal census returns for Rhode Island are available at the RHODE ISLAND STATE ARCHIVES (see under LIBRARIES – PROVIDENCE), the NATIONAL ARCHIVES (see NEW ENGLAND chapter), and the RHODE ISLAND HISTORICAL SOCIETY (see under LIBRARIES – PROVIDENCE).

STATE CENSUS

Three Rhode Island colonial censuses (1774, 1777, and 1782) have been published (see under BOOKS AND ARTICLES). State censuses were also taken in 1865, '75, and '85, and 1905, '15, '25, and '35. The RHODE ISLAND HISTORICAL SOCIETY library has films of 1865 (with index), '75, and '85. The RHODE ISLAND STATE ARCHIVES has the originals, 1865-1935. Ann S. Lainhart's *State Census Records* (1992) fully describes the information in each of these censuses (see under BOOKS AND ARTICLES).

PROBATE AND LAND

Like VRs, these are in the town halls. Early records of some 'daughter' towns may be in the town halls of their 'parents' (see list of TOWNS, above).

CEMETERY RECORDS

Edwin W. Connelly's *List of Historical Cemeteries in Rhode Island* (1970) gives, for each town, all state-designated 'historical' cemeteries and all other known burial grounds, along with their owners, locations, conditions, and numbers of graves and veterans.

David W. Dumas's 8-page *Rhode Island Grave Records: A Bibliography* (1977) discusses general sources and then lists, for each town, specific printed or manuscript transcriptions. Copies of both guides are at the RHODE ISLAND HISTORICAL SOCIETY library and a few other libraries in the state.

John Sterling, of the ASSOCIATION FOR GRAVESTONE STUDIES (see under NEW ENGLAND – CEMETERY RECORDS) has undertaken to document and transcribe all historical Rhode Island cemeteries. His growing database is at the RHODE ISLAND HISTORICAL SOCIETY library on computer, and at NEHGS. This project, now listing over 400,000 names, has produced several books of cemetery maps and transcriptions as well, which also describe the condition, material, and style of the stones (see under BOOKS AND ARTICLES).

CHURCH RECORDS

By and large, each church or synagogue maintains its own records, and should be contacted individually. One very dated source is *Guide to Church Vital Statistics Records in the State Of Rhode Island: A Supplement to the Guide to Public Vital Statistics*, published in 1942 by the WPA. This volume is at the RHODE ISLAND HISTORICAL SOCIETY library and possibly others. More recent information may be available at the RHODE ISLAND STATE ARCHIVES.

Original Quaker (Friends) records for much of New England are at the RHODE ISLAND HISTORICAL SOCIETY library; the NEWPORT HISTORICAL SOCIETY has Quaker records for Newport and Portsmouth. *All* Rhode Island Quaker records are on film at the RIHS and some other libraries.

MILITARY RECORDS

For *Colonial Wars*, see Howard Chapin, *Rhode Island in the Colonial Wars* [King George's War, 1740-48] (1920) and *Rhode Island in the Colonial Wars* [Old French and Indian Wars, 1755-62] (1918).

For the *Revolution*, see Benjamin Cowell, *Spirit of '76 in Rhode Island* (1850), and manuscripts at the RHODE ISLAND STATE ARCHIVES and RHODE ISLAND HISTORICAL SOCIETY (both under LIBRARIES – PROVIDENCE).

For both *Revolution* and *Colonial Wars*, see also Joseph Jenks Smith, *Civil and Military List of Rhode Island, 1747-1800* (1900).

For the *War of 1812* and *Mexican War*, see *Ibid., Civil and Military List of Rhode Island, 1800-1850* (1901), and *New Index* (1907).

For the *Civil War*, see Brig. Gen. Elisha Dwyer, *Annual Report of the Adjutant General of the State of Rhode Island and Providence Plantations for the Year 1865*, 2 vols. (1893-5), an official register of Civil War soldiers serving from Rhode Island.

IMMIGRATION AND NATURALIZATION

See this section in the CONNECTICUT chapter.

The NATIONAL ARCHIVES AND RECORDS ADMINISTRATION's Waltham, Mass. facility (see NEW ENGLAND chapter) has Providence ship-passenger arrivals, 1820-67 and 1911-43. Rhode Island's many settlers of French-Canadian origin would, in most cases, have passed from Canada to the U.S. by land; see the discussion of the St.-Albans-District border-crossing records (which start in 1895: earlier passage across the border was unregulated and unrecorded), also at NARA – WALTHAM.

Finally, NARA has Rhode Island naturalizations, 1842-1950.

NEWSPAPERS

Far and away the best collection of early Rhode Island newspapers (originals and film) is at the RHODE ISLAND HISTORICAL SOCIETY LIBRARY; holdings start as early as 1732, with the *Rhode Island Gazette*. Out of state, the BOSTON PUBLIC LIBRARY has a significant collection of Rhode Island newspapers on film.

Volumes 12-21 of Arnold's *Vital Record of Rhode Island* (see under BOOKS AND ARTICLES) list alphabetized notices of marriages and deaths reported in Rhode Island newspapers, mid-1700s to mid-1800s.

CIVIL AND CRIMINAL COURT RECORDS

Records to 1704 are in print (see Fiske, Jane Fletcher, under BOOKS AND ARTICLES). All colonial and state court records, 1645-1900, are at:

RHODE ISLAND SUPREME COURT JUDICIAL RECORDS CENTER

1 or 5 Hill Street	[401] 222-3249	I-95S to Exit 27; right at 2nd
Pawtucket, RI 02860	& -3552 (FAX)	light (Pine St); after 2nd light, right on Hill **OR** I-95N to Exit
Mon-Fri 8:30am-4:30pm (*summer*: -4pm)		27; left at 2nd light (Pine); after 3rd light, right on Main St, 1st right on Hill.

Free and open to public; appointment desired one or more days ahead; copying, $.15/page. **HOLDINGS**: <u>Archives</u> – civil and criminal court (1671-1905), divorce (1749-1905), and naturalization records (1793-1905 and 1917-80); <u>Records Center</u> – civil and criminal court and divorce records (both, 1905-90). (For 20th-century divorces, call Family Court first [(401) 222-3340] for case number.) The LDS has filmed the early naturalization records. N.B., the holdings of the Archives consist mainly of record books – which contain case summaries – and file papers. Bristol and Kings/Washington County files suffered severe water and mold damage; access to these may be restricted due to fragility.

LIBRARIES

Most Rhode Island towns have public libraries. Holdings vary greatly. For a list, with hours, consult the *American Library Directory* (in most large libraries).

EAST GREENWICH FREE LIBRARY

82 Peirce Street	[401] 884-9510	I-95S to Rte 4 Exit; immediate left; 1st
East Greenwich, RI 02818	& -3790 (FAX)	Exit to E. Greenwich. Bldg 1 block
E-mail: egrlib@ri.ultranet.com		uphill from, & parallel to, Main St.
Web: http://www.ultranet.com/~egrlib		

Mon-Thu 10am-8pm; Fri, Sat -4pm

Free and open to public; copying, $.15/page; 1 fiche reader; 1 film reader/printer; materials do not circulate; no interlibrary loan. **HOLDINGS**: 600 volumes; Rhode Island genealogy; East Greenwich families; a few manuscripts; cemetery records, including Rhode Island Cemetery Database.

NEWPORT HISTORICAL SOCIETY LIBRARY

82 Touro Street	[401] 846-0813	Next to Touro Synagogue. Onstreet
Newport, RI 02840		parking.

Tue-Fri 9:30am-4:30pm; Sat -noon

Free and open to public; copying, $.30/page; 2 film readers; 1 reader/printer, $.50/page; mail inquiries accepted; materials do not circulate; interlibrary loan by photo- or microcopy. **HOLDINGS**: surviving pre-Revolutionary Newport town records (vital; land and probate); church records; southeastern New England, Rhode Island, and Newport genealogies; correspondence; manuscripts (logs, diaries, *etc.*); newspapers; obituaries; hereditary society publications; genealogical journals; city directories. Emphasis on Newport County.

NEWPORT PUBLIC LIBRARY

300 Spring Street	[401] 847-8720	Rte 24 to Rte 114 (turns into W. Main
Newport, RI 02840		Rd, which turns into Broadway); thru
		Washington Sq to Thames St; past PO;
Sep-May: Mon 12:30-9pm; Tue 9:30am-9pm		left on Brewer St – leads straight into
Fri, Sat -6pm; Sun 1-5pm		parking lot.
Jun-Aug: Mon 11am-8pm; Tue-Thu 9am-8pm		
Fri, Sat -6pm		

Free and open to public; copying, $.15/page, film/fiche copies, $.25/page; 4 film and 4 fiche readers, 2 reader/printers; limited mail inquiries accepted. **HOLDINGS**: mainly Newport (and some Rhode Island) genealogies; census; some filmed land and probate records.

PROVIDENCE – BROWN UNIVERSITY – JOHN HAY LIBRARY

Prospect Street
Providence, RI 02912
E-mail: rock@brown.edu

[401] 863-2146
& -2093 (FAX)

Metered on-street parking.

Mon-Fri 9am-5pm

Free and open to public, no research fee; must present ID; staff copying, $.15/page; 1 film reader/printer, $.20/page; limited service by mail (photocopy/microfilm requests only); materials do not circulate; interlibrary loan. **HOLDINGS**: Revolutionary pension applications and supporting documents (each volume has separate index); early Rhode Island records (mostly books, but some 17th- and 18th-century newspapers, and documents, deeds, and correspondence); published genealogies; family papers; manuscript information on Brown University grads (in university archives). N.B., library catalog available *via* telnet or Web at library.brown.edu.

PROVIDENCE – KNIGHT MEMORIAL LIBRARY

275 Elmwood Avenue
Providence, RI 02907

[401] 455-8102

Rte 95 to Elmwood Exit. Next to United Camera. Free parking.

Mon-Wed 9am-8pm; Thu noon-8pm; Fri -5:30pm; Sat 9am-5:30pm
(*Jul 4 to Labor Day*: closed Sat)

Copying, $.25/page; mail inquiries accepted (minimal research only); materials do not circulate; no interlibrary loan. **HOLDINGS**: James N. Arnold Collection, donated in 1920s, at that time the best genealogical collection in Rhode Island: several hundred family and local histories; many Rhode Island gravestone inscriptions (also on film at PROVIDENCE PUBLIC LIBRARY); some "family notes;" and an indexed scrapbook of newspaper clippings. Other Arnold papers are at the RHODE ISLAND HISTORICAL SOCIETY.

PROVIDENCE ATHENAEUM

The Athenaeum's 'Rhode Island genealogy and local history collection' was transferred *in toto* to the RHODE ISLAND HISTORICAL SOCIETY (second listing below) in 1998.

PROVIDENCE PUBLIC LIBRARY

225 Washington Street
Providence, RI 02903

[401] 455-8000

Near Civic Center, next to Police Station. Parking difficult.

Mon-Thu 9am-8pm; Fri, Sat -5:30pm
Sun 1-5pm (*May-Sep only*)

Copying, $.15/page; 2 film readers; 6 reader/printers, $.75/page; mail-order copying; limited mail inquiries accepted; materials do not circulate. **HOLDINGS**: *Alphabetical Index of the Births, Marriages and Deaths Recorded in Providence, 1636-1945,* 30 vols.; Arnold's *Vital Record of Rhode Island*; Providence directories, 1824 to present; index to *Providence Journal* – many entries for prominent Rhode Islanders.

PROVIDENCE – RHODE ISLAND HISTORICAL SOCIETY LIBRARY

121 Hope Street   [401] 331-8575   Rte 195E to Exit 3 (Gano St); right on
Providence, RI 02906   Gano; left on Power St to Hope. On-
Web: http://www.RIHS.org   street parking.

Tue-Sat 9am-5pm; Sun noon-4pm
Manuscripts & Graphics: by appointment only

Free admission; card issued after registration form completed; purses, briefcases, large envelopes, *etc.* must be checked in locker; copying, $.15/page; 6 film readers; 3 reader/printers; genealogical mail queries answered at $35/hr, includes first 20 copies; list of researchers sent on request; materials do not circulate; no interlibrary loan. **HOLDINGS**: published and manuscript genealogical collection; most Rhode Island town records and newspapers on film; Quaker (Friends) New England yearly meeting records – which include many VRs – 1600s-1900s (172 reels); Revolutionary pension records; Rhode Island federal and state censuses (with 1880, 1900, and 1920 Soundexes, and index to 1865 state census); Rhode Island Cemetery Database (over 370,000 records); Rhode Island VRs, 1636 to 1900; most complete in-state collection of Rhode Island city directories.

PROVIDENCE – RHODE ISLAND STATE ARCHIVES

337 Westminster Street   [401] 222-2353   Near Public Library. Metered on-street
Providence, RI 02903   parking; lot on corner reserves places
                                            for Archives.

Mon-Fri 8:30am-4:30pm

Free admission; ID required; materials do not circulate; copying, $.15/page; 3 film readers; 3 reader/printers; service by mail (only copies and postage charged). **HOLDINGS**: federal and state censuses; military records (including colonial); petitions to General Assembly; correspondence; vital records (births and marriages, 1853 to 100 years ago [currently 1899]; deaths, 1853 to 50 years ago [currently 1949]); name indexes for colonial notarial records and petitions to the General Assembly; card catalog and index of Revolutionary and Civil War files. Most material has been filmed by LDS. "Guide to Genealogical Resources" available on site.

WESTERLY PUBLIC LIBRARY

44 Broad Street   [401] 596-2877   Downtown Westerly, next to Wilcox
P.O. Box 356   Park. On-street parking and city lots.
Westerly, RI 02891   Amtrak Sta 3 blocks away.

Library: Mon-Wed 9am-9pm; Thu, Fri -6pm; Sat -4pm; Sun, noon-4pm
Genealogy Room: Mon, Wed-Fri 10am-4pm; Sat -noon (*volunteer staff – call ahead*)

Copying, $.15/page; 4 reader/printers, $.15/page; only basic (1-name) mail queries answered (out-of-staters: $10, plus copies and postage); materials do not circulate; no interlibrary loan. **HOLDINGS**: Rhode Island and Conn. genealogies; many unique genealogies for Westerly area (including some Conn. towns); clippings; manuscripts; local newspaper index; Westerly vital records.

WOONSOCKET – AMERICAN-FRENCH GENEALOGICAL SOCIETY LIBRARY

78 Earle Street [401] 765-6141 In basement of First Universalist
Woonsocket, RI 02895 Church, off Social St, behind Senior
E-mail: afgs@ids.net Citizens Ctr. Ample parking.
Web: http://www.ids.net/afgs/afgshome.html

Mon noon-5pm; Tue 1-10pm; 1st & 3rd Sat (*Sep-Jun*) 10am-4pm

Members only, though visitors welcome once for free – each later non-member visit, $5. Copying, $.25/page. Film and fiche copies, $1/page. **HOLDINGS**: 2,300 reels of film (from Drouin Institute of Montreal) covering Québec, part of Ontario, La., Mich., Mass., New Brunswick, Nova Scotia, Wis., and Rhode Island; VRs for Rhode Island, N.H., and Maine (marriage index, 1892-1966, on CD). Will soon have lending library for members, offering 4,300 fiche (Loiselle Index, Drouin – Women, and parish registers, including all Québec). See also under SOCIETIES.

WOONSOCKET – UNION SAINT JEAN-BAPTISTE BIBLIOTHEQUE MALLET

Cumberland Street [401] 769-0520 x 143 Next to Ste. Ann's Church.
Box F
Woonsocket, RI 02895

Wed 9am-12:30pm; Thu, Fri 8:30am-3:30pm

Free and open to public; appointment desired, 1 week ahead; copying, $.05/page; 1 film reader; mail inquiries accepted (research, $10/hr, non-members; plus $10/certified copy; donation suggested for *small* research request); limited in-house help with research; materials do not circulate; no interlibrary loan. **HOLDINGS**: French-Canadian genealogy; 13 New England French newspapers (1909-42; film); vertical file on French-Canadians in U.S.; photos; parish histories.

LDS FAMILY HISTORY CENTER

Warwick – 1000 Narragansett Parkway; [401] 463-8150; Wed, Fri 10am-2pm & 7-9pm; Thu 7-9pm; Sat 10am-4pm

(See NEW ENGLAND chapter for FHC holdings.)

SOCIETIES

AMERICAN-FRENCH GENEALOGICAL SOCIETY (AFGS) (see also under LIBRARIES – WOONSOCKET)

78 Earle Street [401] 726-0254
P.O. Box 2113
Pawtucket, RI 02861-0113

Founded in 1978 "to discover, preserve, and study Franco-American heritage" … with an emphasis on French Canada, not France. All interested parties are welcome to join. Dues: $30/year/individual; $10 for each additional family member; $360/life/individual. Meets second Saturday of month, year-round.

Publications: *Je me souviens* (despite title, in English), spring and fall, 120 pages; *AFG NEWS*, a five-issues-a-year newsletter. Both available through membership. Back issues $3.50/each (bound).

RHODE ISLAND GENEALOGICAL SOCIETY (RIGS)

P.O. Box 433
Greenville, RI 02828

Founded in 1975 to bring together genealogists, historians, and others interested in accurate research; encourage preservation and publication of records; and conduct workshops. Membership open to all: $16/year/individual, $24/couple. Meets 4-6 times a year at various locations. Journal: *Rhode Island Roots* (quarterly, from 1975; only with membership); Jonathan Galli, CGRS, editor; queries, up to 30 words, $3 for members; $5, non-; articles welcome; index, 1975-9, $3.75. Mail inquiries accepted (from members only) – volunteers perform simple searches. You may also contact RIGS for a list of researchers, with some of whom you may be able to arrange for more extensive research; the Society, however, cannot be responsible for their work.

RHODE ISLAND JEWISH HISTORICAL ASSOCIATION

130 Sessions Street   [401] 331-1360
Providence, RI 02906

Mon-Fri 9am-1:30pm

Founded in 1951 "to procure, collect, and preserve books, records, *etc.*, and any historical material relating to the history of the Jews of RI; to encourage and promote the study of such history … and to publish information as to such history." Membership open to all, $25/year. One annual spring meeting, one interim winter meeting – both at Jewish Community Center, Elmgrove Avenue, Providence. Journal: *Rhode Island Jewish Historical Notes* (from 1954) – free with membership, otherwise $12.50/current issue, $10/back issue (may be photocopy); Judith Weiss Cohen, editor. Queries accepted. Librarian will undertake some research. Copying, $.20/page.

SOCIETY OF MAYFLOWER DESCENDANTS IN RHODE ISLAND

Mrs. Harold P. Williams,   [401] 467-7594
   Secretary
35 Hodsell Street
Cranston, RI 02910

Founded in 1901 "to perpetuate the memory of … and to publish genealogical and historical information relating to the pilgrims." Members must be able to prove descent from a 1620 Mayflower passenger; $18/year. Four meetings per year, location varies. Journal: *Mayflower Newsletter* (from 1958; members only); Mrs. Earl L. Berwick, editor.

PERIODICALS

RHODE ISLAND GENEALOGICAL REGISTER (owner: Mrs. Alden G. Beaman; editor: Nellie B. Mosher)

P.O. Box 1414
Ashburn, VA 20146-1414
E-mail: rigr@erols.com

Independent annual (from 1979); publishes will abstracts for all Rhode Island towns incorporated before 1850. Volume 16 is index (to testators only). Also features deeds, Court of Common Pleas abstracts, cemetery records, town council minutes, Rhode Island families, and people who left Rhode Island. $35-50/volume.

RHODE ISLAND ROOTS (see under RHODE ISLAND GENEALOGICAL SOCIETY).

BOOKS AND ARTICLES

Arnold, James N., ed., *The Narragansett Historical Register* (repr. ed., 1994: Bowie, MD, Heritage Books).

_____, *Vital Record of Rhode Island: 1636-1850*, 21 vols. (1891-1912: Providence, Narragansett Publishing Co.).

Austin, John O., *Genealogical Dictionary of Rhode Island* (rev. ed., 1969: Baltimore, Genealogical Publishing Co.).

Bartlett, John R., *Census of the Inhabitants of the Colony of Rhode Island and Providence Plantations 1774* (1969: Baltimore, Genealogical Publishing Co.).

Beaman, Alden G., *Rhode Island Vital Records*, new series, 17 vols. (1976: Princeton, MA, the author).

Chamberlain, Mildred M., *Rhode Island 1777 Military Census* (1985: Baltimore, Genealogical Publishing Co.).

Farnham, Charles W., "Rhode Island Colonial Records," *Rhode Island History*, 29[1970]:36-45.

Fiske, Jane Fletcher, "Genealogical Research in Rhode Island," *NEHGR*, 136[1982]:173-219; also in Ralph J. Crandall, ed., *Genealogical Research in New England* (1984: Baltimore, Genealogical Publishing Co.).

_____, *Gleanings from Newport Court Files, 1659-1783* (1998: Boxford, MA, private). Available from author, c/o NEHGS.

_____, *General Court of Trials 1671-1704* (1998: Boxford, MA, private). Available from author, c/o NEHGS.

Holbrook, Jay Mack, *Rhode Island 1782 Census* (1979: Oxford, MA, Holbrook Research Institute).

Lainhart, Ann S., *State Census Records* (1992: Baltimore, Genealogical Publishing Co.), 99-101.

Lamar, Christine, *A Guide to Genealogical Materials in the Rhode Island Historical Society Library* (1984).

MacGunnigle, Bruce Campbell, *East Greenwich, Rhode Island Historical Cemetery Inscriptions* (1991: East Greenwich, East Greenwich Preservation Society).

_____, *Rhode Island Freemen, 1747-1755* (1977: Baltimore, Genealogical Publishing Co.).

McAleer, Althea H., **Beatrix Hoffius**, and **Deby Jecoy Nunes**, *Graveyards of North Kingstown, Rhode Island* (1992: North Kingstown, the first author).

Parks, Roger N., ed., *Rhode Island: A Bibliography of Its History* (1983: Hanover, NH, University Press of New England).

Sperry, Kip, *Rhode Island Sources for Family Historians and Genealogists* (1986: Logan, UT, Everton Publishers).

Sterling, John E., and **Bill Eddleman**, *Coventry, Rhode Island Historical Cemeteries* (1998: Baltimore, Gateway Press).

_____ (alone), *Exeter, Rhode Island Historical Cemeteries* (1994: Baltimore, Gateway Press).

_____, *Warwick, Rhode Island Historical Cemeteries* (1997: Baltimore, Gateway Press).

Taylor, Maureen, ed., *Register of Seamen's Protection Certificates from the Providence, Rhode Island Customs District, 1796-1870* (1995: Providence, Clearfield Co.).

_____, *Rhode Island Passenger Lists: Port of Providence, 1798-1808; 1820-1872; Port of Bristol and Warren, 1820-1871* (1995: Baltimore, Genealogical Publishing Co.).

_____, *Runaways, Deserters and Notorious Villains from Rhode Island Newspapers* (1994: Camden, ME, Picton Press).

VERMONT

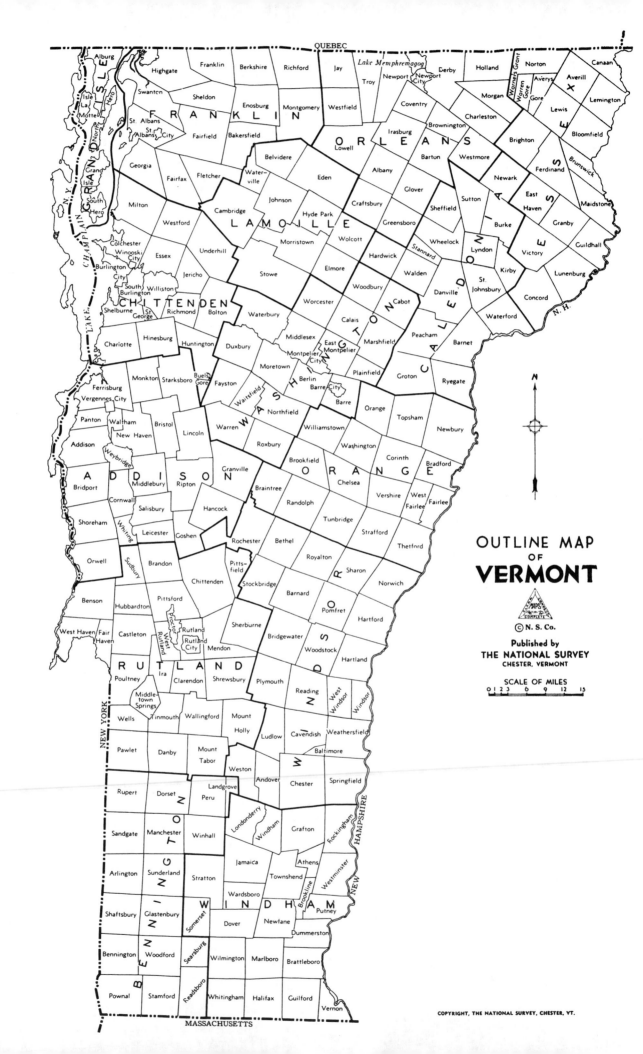

OUTLINE MAP
OF
VERMONT

© N. S. Co.

Published by
THE NATIONAL SURVEY
CHESTER, VERMONT

SCALE OF MILES
0 1 2 3   6   9   12   15

COUNTIES

County	Formed	Parent(s)	Probate Districts
Addison	1785	Rutland	Addison (& Fairhaven, 1824-1962; absorbed New Haven district, 1958)
Bennington	1778	--------	Bennington & Manchester
Caledonia	1792	Orange	Caledonia
Chittenden	1787	Addison	Chittenden
Essex	1792	Orange	Essex
Franklin	1792	Chittenden	Franklin
Grand Isle	1802	Franklin	Grand Isle
Lamoille	1835	Chittenden, Washington, Orleans, & Franklin	Lamoille
Orange	1781	Cumberland	Orange (was Bradford & Randolph 'til 1994)
Orleans	1792	Orange	Orleans
Rutland	1781	Bennington	Rutland & Fair Haven
Washington *(called Jefferson County until 8 Nov 1814)*	1810	Addison, Caledonia, Chittenden, & Orange	Washington
Windham	1781	Cumberland	Marlboro & Westminster
Windsor	1781	Cumberland	Windsor & Hartford

New York Counties:

County	Formed	Parent(s)	Probate Districts
Albany	1764	(NY)	Albany (NY)

(All of Vermont added to county in this year – included only present southern Bennington County from 12 Mar 1772 to 15 Jan 1777, when Vermont claimed independence)

| Charlotte | 1772 | Albany (NY) | Washington (NY) |

(Eliminated in 1777 by Vermont's independence; remnant became Washington County [NY] on 2 Apr 1784)

| Cumberland | 1766 | Albany (NY) | Marlboro |

(Eliminated in 1777)

Gloucester	1770	Albany (NY)	Orange
(Eliminated in 1777)			

Annexed by Vermont:

From:	*Held*:	*To*:	*Historians' name for tract*:
Grafton (NH) (southwestern section)	11 Jun 1778 to 12 Feb 1779	… state	"The First Eastern Union" (16 towns)
Charlotte (NY) (southern part only)	26 Jun 1781 to 22 Feb 1782	… Rutland	"Western Union" (14 towns)
Cheshire (NH) (northern part only)	11 Apr 1781 to 23 Feb 1782	… Windsor	"Eastern Union" called Washington County, wholly in present-day NH; 35 towns
Grafton (NH) (southern part only)	11 Apr 1781 to 23 Feb 1782	… Windsor	"Eastern Union"
Grafton (NH) (northwestern border)	11 Apr 1781 to 23 Feb 1782	… Orange	"Eastern Union"

TOWNS

The following information was taken from several sources, including the *Vermont Yearbook* and *Vermont Place Names* (see BIBLIOGRAPHY). NEHGS has the 1939-41 *Inventories of Town, Village and City Archives* for those towns distinguished, below, by **bold type**. Towns followed by "*" are 'unorganized' – administered by their county, they have no government of their own. 'Gores' or 'grants' are in the same boat.

Town	Estab'd	Parent(s)	County	Probate District	Aliases
Adamant *(part of Calais)*					
Addison	1761		Addison	Addison	
Albany	1782		Orleans	Orleans	Lutterloh
Alburg	1781		Grand Isle	Grand Isle	Grand Isle
Amsden *(part of Weathersfield)*					
Andover	1761		Windsor	Windsor	
Arlington	1761		Bennington	Manchester	Tory Hollow
Ascutney *(part of Weathersfield)*					
Athens	1780		Windham	Westminster	
Averill*	1762		Essex	Essex	
Averill Village *(part of Norton)*					
Avery's Gore	1791		Essex	Essex	
Bakersfield	1791		Franklin	Franklin	
Baltimore	1793	Cavendish	Windsor	Windsor	
Barnard	1761		Windsor	Hartford	
Barnet	1763		Caledonia	Caledonia	
Barre	1781		Washington	Washington	Wildersburgh

Town	Estab'd	Parent(s)	County	Probate District	Aliases
Barton	1789		Orleans	Orleans	Providence
Bartonsville *(part of Rockingham)*					
Basin Harbor *(part of Ferrisburgh)*					
Beebe Plain *(part of Derby)*					
Beecher Falls *(port of entry in Canaan)*					
Bellows Falls *(part of Rockingham)*					
Belmont *(part of Mt. Holly)*					
Belvidere	1791		Lamoille	Lamoille	
Bennington	1749		Bennington	Bennington	Hoosick
Benson	1780		Rutland	Fair Haven	
Berkshire	1781		Franklin	Franklin	
Berlin	1763		Washington	Washington	
Bethel	1779		Windsor	Hartford	
Billymead *(see Sutton)*					
Binghamville *(part of Fletcher)*					
Bloomfield	1762		Essex	Essex	Mineshead
Bolton	1763		Chittenden	Chittenden	
Boltonville *(part of Newbury)*					
Bondville *(part of Windhall)*					
Bradford	1770		Orange	Bradford	Mooretown
Braintree	1781		Orange	Randolph	
Brandon	1761		Rutland	Rutland	Neshobe
Brattleboro	1753		Windham	Marlboro	
Breadloaf *(part of Ripton)*					
Bridgewater	1761		Windsor	Hartford	
Bridport	1761		Addison	Addison	
Brighton	1781		Essex	Essex	Random (1832)
Bristol	1761		Addison	Addison	Pocock
Brookfield	1781		Orange	Randolph	
Brookline	1794		Windham	Westminster	
Brooksville *(part of New Haven)*					
Brownsville *(part of W. Windsor)*					
Brownington	1790		Orleans	Orleans	
Brumley *(see Peru)*					
Brunswick	1761		Essex	Essex	
Buel's Gore	1780		Chittenden	Chittenden	
Burke	1782		Caledonia	Caledonia	
Burlington	1763		Chittenden	Chittenden	
Cabot	1780		Washington	Washington	
Calais	1781		Washington	Washington	
Caldersburgh *(see Morgan)*					
Cambridge	1781		Lamoille	Lamoille	
Cambridgeport *(part of Rockingham)*					
Canaan	1782		Essex	Essex	
Carthage *(see Jay)*					
Castleton	1761		Rutland	Fair Haven	
Cavendish	1761		Windsor	Windsor	
Centerville *(part of Hyde Park)*					
Charleston	1780		Orleans	Orleans	Navy

Town	Estab'd	Parent(s)	County	Probate District	Aliases
Charlotta *(see Charlotte)*					
Charlotte	1762		Chittenden	Chittenden	Charlotta
Chelsea	1781		Orange	Randolph	Turnersburgh
Chester	1754		Windsor	Windsor	Flamstead
Chimney Point *(part of Addison)*					
Chippenhook *(part of Clarendon)*					
Chiselville *(part of Sunderland)*					
Chittenden	1780		Rutland	Rutland	Philadelphia
Clarendon	1761		Rutland	Rutland	
Clarendon Springs *(part of Clarendon)*					
Coit's Gore *(see Waterville)*					
Colbyville *(section of Waterbury)*					
Colchester	1763		Chittenden	Chittenden	
Cold River *(part of Rutland)*					
Concord	1780		Essex	Essex	
Corinth	1764		Orange	Bradford	
Cornwall	1761		Addison	Addison	
Coventry	1780		Orleans	Orleans	Orleans
Craftsbury	1781		Orleans	Orleans	Minden
Cuttingsville *(part of Shrewsbury)*					
Danby	1761		Rutland	Rutland	
Danville	1786		Caledonia	Caledonia	
Derby	1779		Orleans	Orleans	
Derby Line *(incorporated part of Derby)*					
Dewey's Mills *(part of Hartford)*					
Dorset	1761		Bennington	Manchester	
Dover	1810		Windham	Marlboro	
Draper *(see Wilmington)*					
Dummerston	1753		Windham	Marlboro	
Duncansborough *(see Newport)*					
Duxbury	1763		Washington	Washington	
E. Haven	1790		Essex	Essex	
E. Montpelier	1781	Montpelier	Washington	Washington	
Eden	1781		Lamoille	Lamoille	
Elmore	1781		Lamoille	Lamoille	
Ely *(part of Fairlee)*					
Emerson *(part of Rochester)*					
Enosburg	1780		Franklin	Franklin	
Enosburg Falls *(incorporated part of Enosburg)*					
Essex	1763		Chittenden	Chittenden	
Essex Junction *(incorporated part of Essex)*					
Evansville *(part of Brownington)*					
Fairfax	1763		Franklin	Franklin	
Fairfield	1763		Franklin	Franklin	
Fair Haven	1779		Rutland	Fair Haven	
Fairlee	1761		Orange	Bradford	
Fayston	1782		Washington	Washington	
Felchville *(part of Reading)*					
Ferdinand*	1761		Essex	Essex	

Town	Estab'd	Parent(s)	County	Probate District	Aliases
Ferrisburgh	1762		Addison	Addison	
Flamstead *(see Chester)*					
Fletcher	1781		Franklin	Franklin	
Florence *(part of Pittsford)*					
Forestdale *(part of Brandon)*					
Franklin	1789		Franklin	Franklin	Huntsburgh
Gallup Mills *(part of Victory)*					
Gassetts *(part of Chester)*					
Gaysville *(part of Stockbridge)*					
Georgia	1763		Franklin	Franklin	Hell's Gate
Gilman *(part of Lunenburg)*					
Glastenbury*	1761		Bennington	Bennington	Glossenbury
Glossenbury *(see Glastenbury)*					
Glover	1783		Orleans	Orleans	
Gordon Landing *(part of Grand Isle)*					
Goshen	1792		Addison	Addison	
Goshen Gore *(see Stannard)*					
Grafton	1754		Windham	Westminster	Thomlinson
Granby	1761	Rutland	Essex	Essex	
Grand Isle	1779		Grand Isle	Grand Isle	
Graniteville *(part of Barre)*					
Granville	1781		Addison	Addison	Kingston
Green River *(part of Guilford)*					
Greensboro	1781		Orleans	Orleans	
Groton	1789		Caledonia	Caledonia	
Guildhall	1761		Essex	Essex	
Guilford	1754		Windham	Marlboro	
Halifax	1750		Windham	Marlboro	
Hammondsville *(part of Reading)*					
Hancock	1781		Addison	Addison	
Hanksville *(part of Huntington)*					
Hardwick	1781		Caledonia	Caledonia	Little Chicago
Harwich *(see Mt. Tabor)*					
Harmonyville *(part of Townshend)*					
Hartford	1761		Windsor	Hartford	
Hartland	1761		Windsor	Hartford	
Hartland Four Corners *(part of Hartland)*					
Harvey *(part of Danville)*					
Healdville *(part of Mt. Holly)*					
Heartwellville *(part of Readsboro)*					
Hell's Gate *(see Georgia)*					
Highgate	1763		Franklin	Franklin	
Hinesburg	1762		Chittenden	Chittenden	
Hinsdale *(see Vernon)*					
Holden *(part of Chittendon)*					
Hoosick *(see Bennington)*					
Hortonia *(part of Hubbardton & Mt. Holly)*					
Hortonville *(part of Mt. Holly)*					
Holland	1779		Orleans	Orleans	

Town	Estab'd	Parent(s)	County	Probate District	Aliases
Houghtonville *(part of Grafton)*					
Hubbardton	1764		Rutland	Fair Haven	
Hungerford *(see Sheldon)*					
Huntington	1763		Chittenden	Chittenden	
Huntsburgh *(see Franklin)*					
Hyde Park	1781		Lamoille	Lamoille	Skins
Hydeville *(part of Castleton)*					
Ira	1781		Rutland	Rutland	
Irasburg	1781		Orleans	Orleans	
Island Pond *(part of Brighton)*					
Isle La Motte	1779		Grand Isle	Grand Isle	
Jacksonville *(incorporated part of Whitingham)*					
Jamaica	1780		Windham	Westminster	
Jay	1792		Orleans	Orleans	Carthage
Jeffersonville *(part of Cambridge)*					
Jericho	1763		Chittenden	Chittenden	
Johnson	1792		Lamoille	Lamoille	
Jonesville *(part of Richmond)*					
Kansas *(part of Sunderland)*					
Kelly Stand *(part of Sunderland)*					
Kellyvale *(see Lowell)*					
Kent *(see Londonderry)*					
Kent's Corner *(part of Calais)*					
Killington *(part of Sherburne)*					
Kingston *(see Granville)*					
Kirby	1807		Caledonia	Caledonia	
Lake Bomoseen *(part of Castleton)*					
Lake Dunmore *(part of Salisbury)*					
Landgrove	1780		Bennington	Manchester	
Larrabee's Point *(boatslip in Shoreham)*					
Leicester	1761		Addison	Addison	
Lemington	1762		Essex	Essex	Orange
Lewis*	1762		Essex	Essex	
Lewiston *(part of Norwich)*					
Lincoln	1780		Addison	Addison	
Little Chicago *(see Hardwick)*					
Littleton *(see Waterford)*					
Londonderry	1780		Windham	Westminster	Kent
Lowell	1791		Orleans	Orleans	Kellyvale
Ludlow	1761		Windsor	Windsor	
Lunenburg	1763		Essex	Essex	
Lutterloh *(see Albany)*					
Lyndon	1780		Caledonia	Caledonia	
Lyndonville *(incorporated part of Lyndon)*					
Maidstone	1761		Essex	Essex	
Mallets Bay *(part of Colchester)*					
Manchester	1761		Bennington	Manchester	
Mansfield	1763 *(annexed to Stowe in 1848)*				
Marlboro	1751		Windham	Marlboro	

Town	Estab'd	Parent(s)	County	Probate District	Aliases
Marshfield	1782		Washington	Washington	
McIndoe Falls *(part of Barnet)*					
Mendon	1781		Rutland	Rutland	Medway & Parkerstown
Mechanicsville *(part of Hinesburg & Mt. Holly)*					
Medway *(see Mendon)*					
Middlebury	1761		Addison	Addison	
Middlesex	1763		Washington	Washington	
Middletown Springs	1784		Rutland	Rutland	
Miles Pond *(part of Concord)*					
Mill Village *(part of Vershire & Rutland)*					
Milton	1763		Chittenden	Chittenden	
Minden *(see Craftsbury)*					
Mineshead *(see Bloomfield)*					
Missisquoi *(see Troy)*					
Monkton	1762		Addison	Addison	
Monroe *(see Woodbury)*					
Montgomery	1789		Franklin	Franklin	
Montpelier	1781		Washington	Washington	
Mooretown *(see Bradford)*					
Moretown	1763		Washington	Washington	
Morgan	1780		Orleans	Orleans	Caldersburg
Morristown	1781		Lamoille	Lamoille	
Morrisville *(part of Morristown)*					
Morse's Line *(port of entry for Canadian & US Customs & Immigration in Franklin)*					
Moscow *(part of Stowe)*					
Mt. Holly	1792	Wallingford, Ludlow & Jackson's Gore	Rutland	Rutland	
Mt. Tabor	1761		Rutland	Rutland	Harwich 'til 1803
Navy *(see Charleston)*					
Neshobe *(see Brandon)*					
Newark	1781		Caledonia	Caledonia	
Newbury	1763		Orange	Bradford	
Newfane	1753		Windham	Marlboro	
New Haven	1761		Addison	Addison	
New Huntington *(see Huntington)*					
Newport	1802		Orleans	Orleans	Duncansborough
Northfield	1781		Washington	Washington	
N. Hero	1779		Grand Isle	Grand Isle	Two Heros
Norton	1769		Essex	Essex	
Norwich	1761		Windsor	Hartford	
Oakland *(part of Georgia & St. Albans)*					
Orange	1781		Orange	Randolph	
Orange *(see Lemington)*					
Orleans *(incorporated part of Barton)*					

Town	Estab'd	Parent(s)	County	Probate District	Aliases
Orleans *(see Coventry)*					
Orwell	1763		Addison	Addison	
Panton	1761		Addison	Addison	
Parkerstown *(see Mendon)*					
Passumpsic *(part of Barnet)*					
Pawlet	1761		Rutland	Fair Haven	
Peacham	1763		Caledonia	Caledonia	
Perkinsville *(part of Weathersfield)*					
Peru	1761		Bennington	Manchester	Brumley
Philadelphia *(see Chittenden)*					
Pittsfield	1781		Rutland	Rutland	
Pittsford	1761		Rutland	Rutland	
Plainfield	1787		Washington	Washington	Whitelaw; St. Andrews Gore; Goshen Gore #2
Pleasant Valley *(part of Cambridge)*					
Plymouth	1761		Windsor	Windsor	Saltash
Pocock *(see Bristol)*					
Pomfret	1761		Windsor	Hartford	
Pompanoosuc *(part of Norwich)*					
Post Mills *(part of Thetford)*					
Poultney	1761		Rutland	Fair Haven	
Pownal	1760		Bennington	Bennington	
Proctor	1886	Rutland & Pittsford	Rutland	Rutland	
Proctorsville *(part of Cavendish)*					
Prosper *(part of Woodstock)*					
Providence *(see Barton)*					
Putnamville *(part of Middlesex)*					
Putney	1753		Windham	Westminster	
Quechee *(part of Hartford)*					
Randolph	1781		Orange	Randolph	
Random *(see Brighton)*					
Rawsonville *(part of Jamaica)*					
Reading	1761		Windsor	Windsor	
Readsboro	1764		Bennington	Bennington	
Richford	1780		Franklin	Franklin	
Richmond	1792		Chittenden	Chittenden	
Ricker Mills *(part of Groton)*					
Ripton	1781		Addison	Addison	Riptown
Riverside *(part of Jericho)*					
Riverton *(part of Berlin)*					
Robinson *(part of Rochester)*					
Rochester	1781		Windsor	Hartford	
Rockingham	1752		Windham	Westminster	
Roxbury	1781		Washington	Washington	
Royalton	1769		Windsor	Hartford	
Rupert	1761		Bennington	Manchester	

Town	Estab'd	Parent(s)	County	Probate District	Aliases
Rutland	1761		Rutland	Rutland	
Ryegate	1763		Caledonia	Caledonia	
St. Albans	1763		Franklin	Franklin	
St. Andrews Gore *(see Plainfield)*					
St. George	1763		Chittenden	Chittenden	
St. Johnsbury	1786		Caledonia	Caledonia	
Salisbury	1761		Addison	Addison	
Saltash *(see Plymouth)*					
Sandgate	1761		Bennington	Manchester	
Saxtons River *(incorporated part of Rockingham)*					
Searsburg	1781		Bennington	Bennington	
Shady Rill *(part of Middlesex)*					
Shaftsbury	1761		Bennington	Bennington	
Sharon	1761		Windsor	Hartford	
Sheffield	1763		Caledonia	Caledonia	
Shelburne	1763		Chittenden	Chittenden	
Sheldon	1763		Franklin	Franklin	Hungerford
Sherburne	1761		Rutland	Rutland	Killington
Shoreham	1761		Addison	Addison	
Shrewsbury	1761		Rutland	Rutland	
Simonsville *(part of Andover)*					
Skins *(see Hyde Park)*					
Somerset*	1761		Windham	Marlboro	
S. Burlington	1864	Burlington	Chittenden	Chittenden	
S. Hero	1779		Grand Isle	Grand Isle	
Springfield	1761		Windsor	Windsor	
Stamford	1753		Bennington	Bennington	
Stannard	1867 *(but Goshen Gore #1 from 1798)*		Caledonia	Caledonia	Goshen Gore #1
Starksboro	1780		Addison	Addison	
Stevens Mills *(part of Richford)*					
Stockbridge	1761		Windsor	Hartford	
Stowe	1763		Lamoille	Lamoille	Mansfield
Strafford	1761		Orange	Bradford	
Stratton	1761		Windham	Marlboro	
Sudbury	1763		Rutland	Fair Haven	
Sunderland	1761		Bennington	Manchester	
Sutton	1782		Caledonia	Caledonia	Billymead 'til 1812
Swanton	1763		Franklin	Franklin	Taftsville *(part of Woodstock)*
Talcville *(part of Rochester)*					
Thetford	1761		Orange	Bradford	
Thomlinson *(see Grafton)*					
Thompson's Point *(part of Charlotte)*					
Tice *(part of Holland)*					
Tinmouth	1761		Rutland	Rutland	
Topsham	1763		Orange	Bradford	
Tory Hollow *(see Arlington)*					

Town	Estab'd	Parent(s)	County	Probate District	Aliases
Townshend	1753		Windham	Westminster	
Troy	1801		Orleans	Orleans	Missisquoi
Tunbridge	1761		Orange	Randolph	
Turnersburg (see Chelsea)					
Two Heroes (see N. Hero)					
Tyson (part of Plymouth)					
Underhill	1763		Chittenden	Chittenden	
Union Village (part of Thetford)					
Vergennes	1788		Addison	Addison	
Vernon	1753		Windham	Marlboro	Hinsdale
Vershire	1781		Orange	Bradford	
Victory	1781		Essex	Essex	
Waitsfield	1782		Washington	Washington	
Waits River (part of Topsham)					
Walden	1781		Caledonia	Caledonia	
Wallingford	1761		Rutland	Rutland	
Wallace Pond (part of Canaan)					
Waltham	1796		Addison	Addison	
Wardsboro	1780		Windham	Marlboro	
Warner's Grant	1787		Essex	Essex	
Warren	1780		Washington	Washington	
Warren's Gore	1782		Essex	Essex	
Washington	1781		Orange	Randolph	
Waterbury	1763		Washington	Washington	
Waterford	1780		Caledonia	Caledonia	Littleton
Waterville	1824	Coit's Gore, Belvidere, & Bakersfield	Lamoille	Lamoille	Coit's Gore
Weathersfield	1761		Windsor	Windsor	
Websterville (part of Barre)					
Wells	1761		Rutland	Fair Haven	
Wells River (part of Newbury)					
W. Fairlee	1797		Orange	Bradford	
W. Haven	1792		Rutland	Fair Haven	
W. Rutland	1886	Rutland	Rutland	Rutland	
W. Windsor	1761	Windsor	Windsor	Windsor	
Westfield	1780		Orleans	Orleans	
Westford	1763		Chittenden	Chittenden	
Westford (see Westmore)					
Westminster	1752		Windham	Westminster	
Westmore	1781				
Williamstown	1780		Orange	Randolph	
Williamsville (part of Newfane)					
Williston	1763		Chittenden	Chittenden	
Wilmington	1751		Windham	Marlboro	Draper
Windham	1795		Windham	Westminster	
Windsor	1761		Windsor	Windsor	
Winhall	1761		Bennington	Manchester	
Winooski	1922	Colchester	Chittenden	Chittenden	

Town	Estab'd	Parent(s)	County	Probate District	Aliases
Wolcott	1781		Lamoille	Lamoille	
Woodbury	1781		Washington	Washington	Monroe
Woodford	1753		Bennington	Bennington	
Woodstock	1761		Windsor	Hartford	
Worcester	1763		Washington	Washington	Worster
Worster *(see Worcester)*					

N.B., all named subsections of towns have been listed and cross-referenced, except for names that include the official town name – *e.g.*, East Wallingford is part of Wallingford and Lower Cabot is part of Cabot; they are therefore not listed separately.

<u>VERMONT</u>

Vermont is the youngest New England state. Permanent settlements first arose around Ft. Dummer (now Dummerston) in 1724, and blossomed in the 1760s under grants issued by N.H. This long-disputed region was placed under the jurisdiction of New York by the crown in 1764, as part of Albany County. The eastern slope of the Green Mountains was split into two counties, Gloucester to the north (in 1768) and Cumberland to the south (in 1770). The western side was made part of northern New York's Charlotte County in 1772. In 1777, however, settlers formed the independent state of Vermont, under which the eastern half was Cumberland County, the western, Bennington. During the struggle for independence, several towns along Vermont's borders formed the so-called Eastern and Western Unions. These N.H. and New York towns briefly allied themselves with Vermont in 1781-2. Vermont's large counties were quickly subdivided; the names Cumberland and Gloucester were soon historical footnotes. Vermont joined the Union in 1791 as the fourteenth state.

Settlers from southern and western N.H., central and western Mass., Conn., and Rhode Island generally set down east of the Green Mountains; those hailing from between the Conn. and Hudson Rivers moved into western Vermont. There were also special pockets of settlement, such as Scots farmers from southwest of Glasgow who established Barnet and Ryegate in 1772, and Italians who settled around the quarry towns of Proctor and Barre. Other European immigrant groups were as likely to enter Vermont *via* Canada (especially the ports of Québec City and Montréal) as Boston or New York. This is especially true of Irish settlers between 1820 and 1860. And from earliest days – but in larger numbers after the Civil War – many French-Canadians moved into Vermont from Québec.

In Vermont, as in Conn. and Rhode Island, the basic governmental unit is the town, where original vital records and deeds were and are kept. Probate records, however, were kept in 'districts;' court records, by the counties. One's best research strategy is to go to Middlesex and Montpelier first. The GENERAL SERVICES CENTER repository in Middlesex houses microfilm copies of most town and district records to about 1850. It also has a film of the state-transcribed vital records cards, from 1760. The capital, Montpelier, only seven miles southeast of Middlesex, is home to two major libraries and all other state agencies.

STATE HOLIDAYS PECULIAR TO VERMONT – REPOSITORIES MAY BE CLOSED – CALL

Bennington Battle Day [usually observed Mon or Fri nearest Aug 16];
not usually closed for Ethan Allen Day

VITAL RECORDS

Vital records have been kept in Vermont from the earliest permanent settlement, about 1760. All original records are maintained by the town or city, and can be viewed at the clerk's office. In smaller towns, offices may have limited hours or even be in the clerk's home; it is always best to call ahead. A useful free guide to addresses, hours, and phone numbers is *Town Clerks of Vermont*, printed annually by the Secretary of State, 26 Terrace Street, Redstone Building, Montpelier, VT 05609-1103.

The present 'vital records' registration law was enacted in 1857, requiring that all births, marriages, and deaths be recorded by the clerk in the town of occurrence. In 1919, a system of centralized registration was established – each clerk was to transcribe, and send to the state, copies of all town records of past vital events, as well as all data from pre-1871 gravestones. Most towns complied, but researchers are urged to consult the original town books to check for omissions or transcribing errors in the state copy. A microfilm of the state copies – covering births, marriages, deaths, and gravestones – is available at NEHGS (see NEW ENGLAND chapter). In Vermont itself, 'state' vital records are held at one of two locations, depending on date of occurrence, as follows.

From 1760 to 10 Years Ago:

STATE OF VERMONT – GENERAL SERVICES CENTER

Route 2	[802] 828-3286	I-89N to Exit 9; follow signs to Rte 2.
Middlesex, VT	& -3701	Right at 1st stop sign. Bldg on right
	& -3710 (FAX)	behind State Police HQ.
Mon-Fri 8am-4pm		

Mail: Public Records Division / Drawer 33 / Montpelier, VT 05633-7601

Film/fiche readers; 2 staff-operated reader/printers, $.50 to $2.50/copy, depending on size (8½ x 11" up to 18 x 24"); vital records, $7/certified copy (includes $3 search fee); mail inquiries accepted (no extensive genealogical research). Mail requests for vital records must specify one or two blocks of dates (see below). Land/probate/town records research: $3/fifteen mins. All mail requests must include check/money order and SASE. Vital- and divorce-record request forms available. Only certified records can be mailed. FAX service available for some records at additional $2/page. **HOLDINGS**: all town, vital, land, probate, and naturalization records. Vital and divorce records (film), 1760 to 10 years before present. Vitals are alphabetized by name for five separate time-frames (1760-1870; 1871-1908; 1909-44; 1945-54; 1955-78), and for one year at a time, 1979+. (The original state vital-records cardfile is now closed to researchers.) Most town (including land), probate, and civil-court records, through 1850, on film. Scattered U.S. and Canadian censuses, and Barbour's Conn. VRs.

Past 10 Years:

DEPARTMENT OF HEALTH – VITAL RECORDS

108 Cherry Street *or*	[802] 863-7275	I-89 to Exit 14W; straight past
P.O. Box 70		University of Vermont; Main St;
Burlington, VT 05602		right on So. Winooski Av; left on
		Pearl St; 2 blocks; left; bldg on left.
Mon-Fri 8am-4pm (*except holidays*)		

Staff retrieves 5 records at a time; certified copies, $7 each; service by mail. **HOLDINGS**: vital and divorce records for past decade ('old year' transferred to General Services Center each Jan).

FEDERAL CENSUS

Vermont's returns begin with the 1790 census, actually taken in 1791, when it was admitted as the fourteenth state. All federal returns, 1791-1920 – including Soundexes for 1880, 1900, and 1920 – are on microfilm at the NARA facilities (see NEW ENGLAND chapter). The original state returns, 1850-80, are available by special request at the VERMONT DEPARTMENT OF LIBRARIES: REFERENCE AND LAW SERVICES (see under MONTPELIER). Federal returns for Vermont, 1791-1910, including Soundexes, are also at NEHGS.

STATE CENSUS

Vermont has never taken a state census. However, in 1771 New York took a head-of-household census of Cumberland and Gloucester Counties (the eastern half of what became Vermont). For Gloucester County (northeast Vermont), see *Documentary History of the State of New York*, 4[1851]:432-33. For Cumberland (southeast Vermont), see "Antiquarian Documents" from the Brattleboro *Eagle* of 20 Jan 1850 (typescript at the VERMONT HISTORICAL SOCIETY). See also Jay Mack Holbrook, *Vermont 1771 Census* (1982).

PROBATE

Vermont has 14 counties but 18 probate districts (4 southern counties have 2 districts each). There are plans to merge the two double districts into one per county over the next few years. Each probate court holds estates, trust estates, guardianships, name changes, adoptions, and relinquishments. The two latter categories are confidential for 100 years. No Vermont probate court has film readers or printers. However, the pre-1850 probate records are on film at the GENERAL SERVICES CENTER in Middlesex, and NEHGS.

N.B., all Vermont courthouses have fireproof safes, as required by state law; all have card indexes, as well. Recording in docket books ceased in Jul 1997.

ADDISON COUNTY

Addison **Probate** Court	[802] 388-2612	US Rte 7N to Middlebury (Court
7 Mahady Court		St). Approaching 3rd light, keep to
Middlebury, VT 05753		far right. Courthouse on corner.
		Right at light to Mahady; driveway
Mon-Fri 8am-4:30pm		at courthouse rear.

Staff copying, $.25/page; limited mail inquiries; appointment desired; early afternoon best for visits. **HOLDINGS**: Addison probate files, 1853 to present (earlier destroyed by fire); New Haven District files (1824-1957); card index.

N.B., New Haven and Addison Districts merged in 1958.

BENNINGTON COUNTY was established in 1778 – earlier records are in Charlotte County (now part of Washington County) and Albany County, New York.

TWO BENNINGTON COUNTY PROBATE DISTRICTS

Bennington District – Bennington, Glastenbury, Pownal, Readsboro, Searsburg, Shaftsbury, Stamford, and Woodford.

Manchester District – Arlington, Dorset, Landgrove, Manchester, Peru, Rupert, Sandgate, Sunderland, and Winhall.

Bennington District   [802] 447-2705   On Rte 7, 1 block S of Rte 9.
   Probate Court
207 South Street / P.O. Box 65
Bennington, VT 05201-0065

Mon-Fri 9am-noon & 1-4:30pm

Staff copying; card index. **HOLDINGS**: Bennington District probate files, 1778 to present.

Manchester District   [802] 362-1410   On Rte 7A in Manchester Village,
   Probate Court   across from Old Equinox House.
Route 7A / P.O. Box 446
Manchester, VT 05254

Mon-Fri 8am-noon & 1-4:30pm

Staff copying, $.25/page; mail inquiries accepted; card index. **HOLDINGS**: Manchester District probate files, 1778 to present; card index; some records filmed by LDS.

CALEDONIA COUNTY

Caledonia District   [802] 748-6605   At X of Rtes 2 & 5 in St. Johnsbury.
   Probate Court
27 Main Street / P.O. Box 406
St. Johnsbury, VT 05819

Mon-Fri 8am-4:30pm

Staff copying; please phone for appointment. **HOLDINGS**: probate files, early 1790s to present; card index.

CHARLOTTE COUNTY (see BENNINGTON COUNTY; Washington and Albany Counties, New York; and New York State Archives in Albany)

CHITTENDEN COUNTY

Chittenden **Probate** Court　　[802] 651-1518　　On Rte 2 at corner of Main & Church
175 Main Street / P.O. Box 511　　　　　　　　Sts, downtown; big granite bldg.
Burlington, VT 05402

Mon-Fri 8:30am-4pm

Staff copying. Pre-1900 records in storage; call ahead for retrieval. **HOLDINGS:**　probate files, 1795 to present; card index.

CUMBERLAND COUNTY (see WINDHAM COUNTY – MARLBORO DISTRICT)

ESSEX COUNTY

Essex District　　　　　　[802] 723-4770　　In Municipal Bldg on Main St.
　Probate Court
Main Street / P.O. Box 426
Island Pond, VT 05846

Mon-Fri 8:30am-noon & 1-3:30pm

Staff copying, $.25/page; mail inquiries accepted (minimum fee, $1). **HOLDINGS:**　probate files, 1791 to present (volume 28 missing); card index.

FRANKLIN COUNTY

Franklin District　　　　　[802] 524-7948　　On Taylor Park, 1 block E of Rte 7.
　Probate Court
Church Street
St. Albans, VT 05478

Mon-Fri (*by appointment only*)

Open to public but patrons must climb high ladders; no photocopying. **HOLDINGS:**　probate files, 1791 to present; card index.

GLOUCESTER COUNTY (see ORANGE COUNTY – RANDOLPH DISTRICT)

GRAND ISLE COUNTY

Grand Isle District　　　　[802] 372-8350　　In gray marble bldg on Main St (Rte 2).
　Probate Court
Route 2 / P.O. Box 7
North Hero, VT 05474

Mon-Fri 8am-4:30pm

Staff copying, $.10/page; appointment preferred, 2 days' notice; mail inquiries accepted. **HOLDINGS:** probate files, early 1800s to present; card index.

LAMOILLE COUNTY

Lamoille **Probate** Court   [802] 888-3306   In brick bldg, town ctr.
Hyde Park, VT 05665

Mon-Fri 8am-12:30pm & 1-4:30pm

Staff copying. **HOLDINGS**: probate files, 1837 to present; card index.

ORANGE COUNTY

TWO ORANGE COUNTY PROBATE DISTRICTS

Randolph District – Braintree, Brookfield, Chelsea, Orange, Randolph, Tunbridge, Washington, and Williamstown.

Bradford District – Bradford, Corinth, Fairlee, Newbury, Strafford, Thetford, Topsham, Vershire, and W. Fairlee.

N.B., the Randolph and Bradford Districts merged in 1994, under the Orange District.

Orange District   [802] 685-4870   Courthouse on Rte 110.
     Probate Court
RR #1, P.O. Box 30
Chelsea, VT 05038

Mon-Fri 8am-4:30pm

Free and open to public; staff copying, $.25/page; certified copies, $5; mail inquiries accepted (cost of copies, $1 minimum). **HOLDINGS**: probate files, 1760s to present, for *all* Orange County; 1760s-81 – all that's extant – for Gloucester County (NY/VT); pre-1900 docket books may be viewed; card index.

ORLEANS COUNTY

Orleans District   [802] 334-3366   Main St is Rte 5.
     Probate Court
83 Main Street
Newport, VT 05855

Mon-Fri 8am-noon & 1-4pm

Staff copying; card index. **HOLDINGS**: probate files, 1796 to present. For pre-1850 data, only docket books may be consulted (*i.e.*, original papers will not be pulled).

RUTLAND COUNTY

TWO RUTLAND COUNTY PROBATE DISTRICTS

Rutland District – Brandon, Chittenden, Clarendon, Danby, Ira, Mendon, Middletown Springs, Mt. Holly, Mt. Tabor, Pittsfield, Pittsford, Rutland, Sherburne, Shrewsbury, Tinmouth, Wallingford, and W. Rutland.

Fair Haven District – Benson, Castleton, Fair Haven, Hubbardton, Pawlet, Poultney, Sudbury, Wells, and W. Haven.

Rutland District **Probate** Court 83 Center Street Rutland, VT 05701	[802] 775-0114	S on Rte 7 to Center; courthouse on corner of Center & Court Sts – brick bldg opposite Rutland Public Library.

Mon-Fri 8am-4:30pm

Staff copying. **HOLDINGS**: probate files, 1780s to present; card index.

Fair Haven District **Probate** Court Fair Haven, VT 05743	[802] 265-3380	In Municipal Bldg, No. Park Place.

Mon-Fri 8am-noon & 1-4pm

Copying, $.25/page; appointment desirable; mail inquiries accepted. **HOLDINGS**: probate files, *ca.* 1790 to present; card index.

WASHINGTON

Washington District **Probate** Court State and Elm Streets / P.O. Box 15 Montpelier, VT 05602	[802] 828-3405	I-89 to Exit 8; left on Taylor St; cross bridge; right on State.

Mon-Fri 7:45am-noon & 1-4:30pm (*except* Fri -4)

Self-service copying. **HOLDINGS**: probate files, 1811 to present; card index.

WINDHAM COUNTY

TWO WINDHAM COUNTY PROBATE DISTRICTS

Marlboro District – Brattleboro, Dover, Dummerston, Guilford, Halifax, Marlboro, Newfane, Somerset, Stratton, Vernon, Wardsboro, Whitingham, and Wilmington.

Westminster District – Athens, Brookline, Grafton, Jamaica, Londonderry, Putney, Rockingham (including Bellows Falls), Townshend, Westminster, and Windham.

Marlboro District **Probate** Court West River Road / P.O. Box 523 Brattleboro, VT 05302	[802] 257-2898	Rte 30, 2 mi N of town in Brattleboro Professional Ctr.

Mon-Fri 8am-noon & 1-4:30pm (*see note below*)

Staff copying, $.25/page (mail: $1 minimum). **HOLDINGS**: probate files, 1781 to present; card index. Early originals (to 1896) in storage – only docket books available for viewing (some early volumes in poor condition, may not be copied).

N.B., court may be unable to accommodate all researchers during morning (hearings) hours – generally open for research during afternoon.

Westminster District **Probate** Court 39 "The Square" / P.O. Box 47 Bellows Falls, VT 05101	[802] 463-3019	At X of Rtes 5 & 12; 2nd floor.

Mon-Fri 8am-noon & 1-4:30pm

Staff copying, $.25/page (mail: $1 minimum); appointment desirable, day or more in advance; mail inquiries accepted (for *availability* of record only, not content). **HOLDINGS**: probate files, 1781 to present. Early originals fragile; recorded volumes must be used.

WINDSOR COUNTY

T W O W I N D S O R C O U N T Y P R O B A T E D I S T R I C T S

Windsor District: Andover, Baltimore, Cavendish, Chester, Ludlow, Plymouth, Reading, Springfield, Weathersfield, W. Windsor, Weston, and Windsor.

Hartford District: Barnard, Bethel, Bridgewater, Hartford, Hartland, Norwich, Pomfret, Rochester, Royalton, Sharon, Stockbridge, and Woodstock.

N.B., Scott Andrew Bartley plans 1999 publication of a consolidated index to both districts, to 1899.

Windsor District **Probate** Court Route 106 or P.O. Box 402 North Springfield, VT 05150	[802] 886-2284 & -2285 (FAX)	4 mi from town ctr on Rte 106N, in Cota Fuel Bldg; on right, coming from town.

Mon-Fri 8am-noon & 1-4:30pm

Staff copying, $.25/page; mail inquiries accepted; appointment desirable, 1-2 days ahead. Usually closed, Tue morning, for hearings. **HOLDINGS**: probate files, late 1780s to present; card index. Pre-1900 originals in storage – must use recorded volumes.

Hartford District [802] 457-1503 In town ctr, facing Green.
    Probate Court
On the Green / P.O. Box 275
Woodstock, VT 05091

Mon-Fri 8am-noon & 1-4:30pm

Staff copying; mail inquiries accepted. **HOLDINGS**: probate files, 1783 to present. Pre-1864 originals burned – only recorded volumes available.

LAND

From the early 1780s, jurisdiction and maintenance of original Vermont land records (*i.e.*, ownership and transfer; deeds), has rested with the town clerk. Previously, deeds were kept by the county. However, land records for the whole state up to 1980 are available on film at the GENERAL SERVICES CENTER. These records are available *via* any LDS Family History Center, including NEHGS. For records after 1980, the relevant town clerk's office must be consulted.

CEMETERY RECORDS

The **VERMONT OLD CEMETERY ASSOCIATION (VOCA)** is dedicated to the restoration and preservation of old and abandoned cemeteries. Transcriptions are sparse but VOCA will share any information in their records for a given town. (Address *requests* to VOCA Archives, c/o Arthur Hyde, RR #1, P.O. Box 10, Bradford, VT 05033; address *correspondence* to Charles E. Marchant, P.O. Box 132, Townshend, VT 05353.) Membership (annually, $5; or $20 for 5 years) includes a quarterly newsletter on current cemetery restoration and transcription projects. VOCA's 1991 *Burial Grounds of Vermont* (485 pages; available from VERMONT HISTORICAL SOCIETY's gift shop) gives directions to all known Vermont cemeteries, as well as their age, condition, and number of plots. Also helpful is the *Index to Known Cemetery Listings in Vermont*, 3rd ed. (1995; at VHS gift shop), by Joann H. Nichols and Patricia L. Haslam. Margaret R. Jenks has transcribed all Rutland County cemeteries; copies available from author (24 Mettowee Street, Granville, NY 12832-1037).

The GENEALOGICAL SOCIETY OF VERMONT publishes cemetery records in its quarterly, *Vermont Genealogy* (formerly *Branches and Twigs*). The VERMONT HISTORICAL SOCIETY and NEHGS have many cemetery transcriptions, some by the DAR.

CHURCH RECORDS

Vermont church records – including baptisms, marriages, burials, and rosters of membership – are usually found locally, in church offices, parsonages, homes of church clerks, or town-office vaults. Occasionally, records for given denominations are sent to regional or national repositories, often outside the state. In 1938-42, the WPA inventoried Vermont church records. Although the goal was to find and describe all such records, only three books were published (copies at NEHGS):

- *Inventory of the Church Archives of Vermont: Churches of Hinesburg: A Preliminary Publication* (1939).
- *Directory of Churches and Religious Organizations in the State of Vermont* (1939).
- *Inventory of the Church Archives of Vermont, No. 1. The Diocese of Vermont Protestant Episcopal* (1940).

Some unpublished WPA inventories are at the GENERAL SERVICES CENTER. Though out of date, these inventories are helpful in discovering what records *were* available, and where. From 1970-75, the Vermont chapter of the National Society of Colonial Dames tried to find church records not located by the WPA. Their list can be found at the GENERAL SERVICES CENTER.

VERMONT <u>BAPTIST</u> STATE CONVENTION

89 North State Street *or*   [603] 643-4201
P.O. Box 2403
Concord, NH 03302-2403

The Vermont Baptist Convention joined the American Baptist Churches of New Hampshire on 1 Jan 1990 to become the American Baptist Churches of Vermont and New Hampshire. Their main office is in Concord, N.H.; local church clerks are encouraged to deposit early records there. Inquiries *re*: the various Baptist denominations may also be referred to the American Baptist Historical Society, 1106 Goodman Street, Rochester, NY 14620-2532. For a good history, see Henry Crocker, *History of the Baptists in Vermont* (1913).

ARCHIVES OF THE ROMAN <u>CATHOLIC</u> DIOCESE OF BURLINGTON

351 North Avenue   [802] 658-6110   I-89 to Exit 14W (Williston Rd,
Burlington, VT 05401   becomes Main St); Main to Lake
                                                   Champlain; right on Battery St to North
Tue-Thu 9am-5pm (*appointment preferred*)   Av.

Mail-in inquiries answered, but genealogical questions in most cases referred to appropriate parish, which should have records. A few early record books; indexed, but give little genealogical information, *e.g.* place of birth. Referrals possible only if town, or at least county, and approximate date can be provided. In the early 19th century priests from Canada and Mass. served Vermont Catholics, often carrying their records with them; present whereabouts of such records is generally unknown. The Archives holds inactive records, from 1853, of the Diocese of Vermont, including the papers of deceased bishops and priests, parish and institutional historical files, *etc.*, as well as a variety of non-sacramental parish record books. For a good collection of brief historical sketches of individual parishes, see *Diocese of Burlington 1853-1953: One Hundred Years of Achievement by the Catholic Church in the Diocese of Burlington, Vermont* (1953).

<u>CONGREGATIONAL</u> (see UNITED CHURCH OF CHRIST)

<u>EPISCOPAL</u> DIOCESAN CENTER

5 Rock Point Road   [802] 863-3431   From I-89, Exit 14W (Williston Rd)
Burlington, VT 05401   [802] 860-1562 FAX   becomes Main St; right on Battery St
                                                   to North Av; left on Institute Rd; right
Mon-Fri 9am-4pm (*summer hrs may vary;*   thru gates to 2nd bldg – 1-story brick,
call 24 hrs ahead)   on left.

Free and open to public; mail inquiries answered within a week (copying charges – $.10/page – may apply). **HOLDINGS**: Vermont Episcopal records, 1790 to present, including: confirmations (1854 to present); records of closed congregations (once restricted); Bishops' papers – especially of Hopkins Hall; records of Society for the Preservation of the Gospel in Foreign Parts; records of Trustees and other bodies, including the Vermont Episcopal Institute. For a good history, see *The Documentary History of the Protestant Episcopal Church in the Diocese of Vermont, Including the Journals of the Conventions from the Year 1790 to 1832* (1870).

TROY ANNUAL CONFERENCE OF THE UNITED <u>METHODIST</u> CHURCH

P.O. Box 560   [518] 584-8214
Saratoga Springs, NY 12866

Useful for clergy during their time in the Conference. **HOLDINGS**: journals of Vermont Methodist Conference and Methodist Episcopal Church, and yearbooks of Troy Conference. Conference archives are at GREEN MOUNTAIN COLLEGE LIBRARY

VERMONT CONFERENCE OF THE <u>UNITED CHURCH OF CHRIST</u> (<u>CONGREGATIONAL</u>)

285 Maple Street   [802] 864-0248   I-89 to Exit 14W; thru 3 closely spaced
Burlington, VT 05401   lights to Main St; Univ of VT campus
                                                                      on right (4th light). At next light, left on
Mon-Fri 8:30am-4:30pm   So. Willard St; Maple is 1st right, down-
                                                                      hill; sign on lawn, at left.

Free and open to public; mail inquiries accepted; copies free at this time. **HOLDINGS**: no church records – chief service to genealogists is information as to a minister's time and place of service. Contact local churches and CONGREGATIONAL LIBRARY (Boston) for locations of church records; the above office *may* be able to direct you to the right addresses and phone numbers, though that is not their essential role. A handy guide: John M. Comstock, *The Congregational Churches of Vermont and Their Ministry, 1762-1942* (1942).

FOR ADDRESSES OF OTHER DENOMINATIONS, SEE *VERMONT YEARBOOK,* PUBLISHED YEARLY BY THE NATIONAL SURVEY, CHESTER, VT 05143 ([802] 875-2133 [FAX])

<u>MILITARY RECORDS</u>

Vermont Adjutant General   [802] 828-3381   I-89 to Exit 8; left at 2nd light; cross
Veterans' Affairs Office   bridge; right at 1st light. Office just
120 State Street   beyond State Office Bldg (houses Motor
Montpelier, VT 05620-4401   Vehicle Dept); small white house, rear.

Mon-Fri 7:30am-4pm (*appointment desired, one week in advance*)

Free and open to public; copies free, but donation to Vermont Memorial Cemetery requested; mail inquiries answered. **HOLDINGS**: printed rosters; card file for ongoing 'Graves of Veterans' project; veterans' service files, Revolution onward; some State Militia and National Guard files from beginning to 1950; all National Guard '201' files (personal) are at Military Personnel Records Office, Camp Johnson, Colchester, VT 05446-3004. Most pre-1920 records, *e.g.* muster and pay rolls, *etc.*, were destroyed by fire. Fortunately, Revolutionary records were published in John E. Goodrich, ed., *Rolls of the Soldiers in the Revolutionary War, 1775 to 1783* (1904), and War-of-1812 records in Herbert T. Johnson, ed., *Roster of Soldiers in the War of 1812-1814* (1933, rep. 1995). 20th-century files are not open to public. However, staff makes every effort to answer *WRITTEN* questions, if not subject to Privacy Act of 1974.

N.B., see also Maj. Gen. Carleton Edward and Sue (Gray) Fisher, *Soldiers, Sailors and Patriots of the Revolutionary War – Vermont* (1992) and Byron N. Clark, *A List of Pensioners of the War of 1812* [Vermont] (1904, rep. 1969). Registrations for WWI service are at town clerks' offices.

IMMIGRATION AND NATURALIZATION

See this section in the CONNECTICUT chapter.

Direct entry of foreign nationals into Vermont has been solely from Canada; relevant immigration records therefore fall under the auspices of the St. Albans District, which covers the entire U.S./Canadian border (see NEW ENGLAND – NARA – WALTHAM). St. Albans records begin in 1895; earlier passage across the border was essentially unregulated and unrecorded.

See NARA also for Vermont naturalization records.

NEWSPAPERS

The two best places to go for Vermont newspapers (which begin in 1780) are (1) the State Law Library (see under LIBRARIES – MONTPELIER – VERMONT DEPARTMENT OF LIBRARIES: REFERENCE AND LAW SERVICES) and (2) the University of Vermont's BAILEY-HOWE LIBRARY (see under LIBRARIES – BURLINGTON). The State Law Library has the largest existing collection of hard copies of early Vermont newspapers; is coordinating Vermont's participation in a federally-funded 50-state effort to ID and inventory all such; and will also be the official repository for microfilm copies of the same. Out of state, Mass.'s BOSTON PUBLIC LIBRARY has a broad range of early Vermont newspapers on film, though most holdings cover fairly short periods.

Marsha H. Rising is now abstracting VRs (1783-1810) from the Burlington *Gazette*; expect publication in 2000.

CIVIL AND CRIMINAL COURT RECORDS

Since earliest days, Vermont has had both a Supreme Court, and a courthouse in the 'shire town' of each county. These are: *Addison* – Middlebury; *Bennington* – Bennington; *Caledonia* – St. Johnsbury; *Chittenden* – Burlington; *Essex* – Guildhall; *Franklin* – St. Albans; *Grand Isle* – N. Hero; *Lamoille* – Hyde Park; *Orange* – Chelsea; *Orleans* – Newport; *Rutland* – Rutland; *Washington* – Montpelier; *Windham* – Newfane; and *Windsor* – Woodstock. The Supreme Court has handled civil and criminal cases, petitions, and the like, across the state and at all levels of gravity; the county courts handle only more local and less serious matters – all murder cases or other capital offenses, for example, are sent to the Supreme Court.

The records of Vermont's Supreme Court have been – and are still being – published in *Vermont Reports*, available at some large libraries, including the VERMONT DEPARTMENT OF LIBRARIES: REFERENCE AND LAW SERVICES (see under LIBRARIES – MONTPELIER); the early records of the county courts, on the other hand, are in the process of being relocated to the GENERAL SERVICES CENTER in Middlesex (see under VITAL RECORDS). (More recent records, of course, are at the courthouses themselves.) Not all Vermont counties have yet sent their old records to Middlesex; those that have, have adopted different cutoff years; call the relevant courthouse for further information.

LIBRARIES

Vermont has over 200 public libraries, whose holdings vary greatly. Most have small collections, which may include items of genealogical interest. Many are open 12 hours a week or less and can undertake no research. For a list, with hours, consult the *Vermont Library Directory* at any large Vermont library, or the *American Library Directory* in most large libraries. For an online list of web-searchable Vermont catalogs, see http://www.dol.state.vt.us.

ARLINGTON – MARTHA CANFIELD MEMORIAL FREE LIBRARY

P.O. Box 267 Arlington, VT 05250-0267	[802] 375-6307	Rte 7 to Exit 3 to Arlington Village; library ¼ mile E, near schools.

Tue 9am-5pm, *& by appointment*

Free and open to public; copying service. **HOLDINGS**: "Vermontiana" (Dr. George Russell Collection); good genealogical collection for Arlington, Sandgate, and Sunderland.

ARCHIVES OF BARRE HISTORY at ALDRICH PUBLIC LIBRARY

6 Washington Street Barre, VT 05641 **E-mail**: Barre@dol.state.vt.us **Web**: http://www.uvm.edu/~histpres/VHN/vtiana/aldrich.html	[802] 479-7550	On US Rte 302 at X with Rte 14; corner of Elm St.

Mon, Fri noon-5pm; Thu 10am-5pm; Sat -4pm (*summer*: -1pm)

Copying, $.15/page; reader/printer, $1/page; mail inquiries accepted (first 15 minutes free, then $10/hour). **HOLDINGS**: Vermont reference, plus information on Barre families; good collection of Barre photos – individuals, families, and community groups, local buildings and industries; complete run of Barre city directories.

BENNINGTON – GENEALOGICAL AND HISTORICAL LIBRARY / BENNINGTON MUSEUM

West Main Street Bennington, VT 05201 **Web**: http://www.neinfo.net, http://www.bennington.com/museum	[802] 447-1571 [802] 442-8305 FAX	W. Main is also Rte 9, *aka* Molly Stark Trail.

Nov-May: Mon, Thu, Sat 11am-5pm; *Jun-Oct*: Mon-Sat 11am-5pm

Librarian on duty Mon, Thu, and Sat; volunteers, other days; copying, $.10/page; film reader; mail inquiries accepted (donation requested). *Museum* open 9am-5pm every day of year except Thanksgiving, Christmas, and New Year's, but *library* days and hours only as above; materials do not circulate; mail queries preferred to phone-calls. The Museum fee – $5/day; $4.50/day, senior citizens – is charged for library use; $25 annual membership confers unlimited museum and library privileges. **HOLDINGS**: local, state, and regional historical and genealogical information compiled by patrons, scholars, and staff; New England and New York federal census indexes, 1790-1850; The *New England Historical and Genealogical Register*, with indexes; the 200-volume *American Genealogical and Biographical Index*; the *Boston Transcript* and *Hartford Times* genealogical columns, with indexes; many early southern New England VRs; 2,000 published family histories (mainly New England); vertical file on regional families; regional biographies; Revolutionary and Civil War rosters and other military data for the New England states and New York; index to early inhabitants of Bennington and nearby towns; correspondence files; Vermont town, county, and state histories; Hemenway's *Vermont Historical Gazetteer*; the Day Papers (25 indexed scrapbooks of newspaper clippings, 1870-1916); the Harwood Diaries (1805-37, indexed); regional cemetery records; Bennington church records (including Old First); early maps, atlases, and municipal directories; the 1880s Aldrich histories and Child directories of Vermont counties. List of local researchers-for-hire available on request.

BRATTLEBORO – BROOKS MEMORIAL LIBRARY

224 Main Street   [802] 254-5290   Next to Municipal Ctr. Parking at rear,
Brattleboro, VT 05301   near library entrance.
Web: http://www.state.vt.us/
    vhs/lhs/windham.htm#Brattleboro2

Mon, Wed, Thu 9am-9pm; Fri -6pm; Sat -5pm (*summer*: -noon)

Copying, $.10/page; 1 reader/printer, $.25/page; limited staff research; mail answered; must sign at desk for key to locked room; materials do not circulate. **HOLDINGS**: basic genealogical references for New England, emphasizing Vermont and Mass.; 3,000 photos of late 19th- and early 20th-century Windham County; federal censuses, 1800-1920; two Brattleboro newspapers on film; small family-history collection. Separate room for local history.

BURLINGTON – FLETCHER FREE LIBRARY

235 College Street   [802] 863-3403   I-89 to Exit 14W; right on So. Union
Burlington, VT 05401   St; left on College.
Web: http://www.state.vt.us/vhs/
    lhs/chitten.htm#Burlington

Mon, Tue, Thu, Fri 8:30am-6pm; Wed -9pm; Sat 9am-5:30pm; Sun noon-5:45pm (*Sep-May only; call ahead to verify hours*)

Copying, $.15/page; reader/printer, $.25/page; materials circulate for card-holders only (fee for Burlington non-residents, $25/year); local history collection in closed stacks, available only when librarian on duty; limited research by mail. **HOLDINGS**: miscellaneous genealogical collection (several hundred books), including Vermont military rosters; *New England Historical and Genealogical Register* (full run); index to Burlington VRs, 1789-1833, and Burlington marriages, 1830-63. Local history collection, including Burlington city directories and annual reports from about 1870; Vermont town and county histories; Beers' atlases; Hemenway's *Vermont Historical Gazetteer*; and *Burlington Free Press* on film, 1848 to date.

BURLINGTON – UNIVERSITY OF VERMONT – BAILEY-HOWE LIBRARY

University of Vermont   [802] 656-2138   N on Rte 2 betw I-89 & downtown
Burlington, VT 05405   Burlington; library E of common.
Web: http://www.sageunix.uvm.edu/page2.html

school term only: Mon-Thu 8am-11:45pm; Fri -9:45pm; Sat 9am-9:45pm; Sun -11:45pm (*Sep-May*: 2-5pm) (*call ahead to verify hours*)

Copying, $.05/page; 15+ film readers; photocopying service available; good staffing; no genealogical research except quick check of specific items – list of researchers available on request; materials loaned to students, faculty, staff, and guest borrowers (applications available at library); interlibrary loan using standard ILL forms. **HOLDINGS**: large collection of Vermontiana; some on other New England states; much Canadian local history and genealogy; some family histories; newspapers on film, including *Burlington Free Press*, with indexes, 1848-95 and 1959 to present (including marriage and death notices).

Special Collections of the   [802] 656-2138
    University of Vermont Lib'y. & -4038 (FAX)
E-mail: edow@zoo.uvm.edu
Web: http://sageunix.uvm.edu/~sc (*collection overview*)

school terms: Mon-Thu 9am-9pm; Fri -5pm; Sat, Sun 1-5pm
summer & intersession: Mon-Fri 9am-5pm

Copying subject to staff approval; limited interlibrary loan. **HOLDINGS**: Wilbur Collection of Vermontiana and large manuscript collection; Vermont Baptist records; records of several Burlington-area churches; account books; diaries; letters; town reports; some Vermont Old Cemetery Association (VOCA) transcriptions; many Burlington school records; records of a number of Vermont organizations, businesses, and societies, including the Vermont Medical Society; photos. N.B., phone or write ahead if planning to use manuscripts – many stored off-campus.

MIDDLEBURY – SHELDON MUSEUM (SWIFT-STEWART RESEARCH CENTER)

1 Park Street   [802] 388-2117   Park & Main Sts near X of Rtes 125 &
Middlebury, VT 05753   30, just W of Rte 7; bldg faces small
Web: http://www.ruralvermont.com/   park.
    vermontweathervane/96.8august/history.html

Tue-Fri 1-5pm; Tue, Thu 6-9pm (*Oct-Apr; hours vary – please call ahead*)

Staff copying, $.25/page; materials do not circulate; mail inquiries accepted (donations requested). **HOLDINGS**: Addison County history – town histories; family and business papers; organizational records; Middlebury newspapers; scrapbooks; letters; and photos. Some indexes.

MONTPELIER – VERMONT DEPARTMENT OF LIBRARIES: REFERENCE AND LAW SERVICES

109 State Street   [802] 828-3268   I-89 to Exit 8; left on Bailey (Rte 2);
Montpelier, VT 05609   cross bridge; right on State; in Supreme
E-mail: dol_ill_mail@dol.state.vt.us   Court Bldg to right of Capitol.

Mon-Fri 7:45am-4:30pm

Free and open to public; circulates for Vermont residents; self-service copying, $.10/page (paid *after* making copies); staff copying, $.50/page; reader/printer, $.10/page; all correspondence answered; limited research; interlibrary loan (send standard ILL forms to Reference and Law Services, as above). **HOLDINGS**: largest collection of Vermont newspapers in state (repository for U.S.-newspaper microfilming project); Vermont federal census returns, 1791-1920, with 1880, 1900, and 1920 Soundexes (plus state copies of originals, 1850-80 – closed except by special permission); state-government publications; "Vermontiana" – "a major collection of books, periodicals, pamphlets, documents, *etc.* about Vermont, its history, including county and town histories, its people and its culture."

MONTPELIER – VERMONT STATE ARCHIVES

26 Terrace Street   [802] 828-2308   I-89 to Exit 8; left at 2nd light on Bailey
Redstone Building   Av, up hill; left at fork. Bldg at hilltop
Montpelier, VT 05609-1103   on left.
Web: http://www.sec.state.vt.us
   (*home page with link to statewide records database*)

Mon-Fri 7:45am-4:30pm

Staff copying – first 9 pages free; 10+, $.04/page; no loans; all inquiries answered (30-minute research limit; extra time, $.23/minute; will check name index, search for and mail relevant material). **HOLDINGS**: Vermont State Papers, in manuscript, with 1740-1850 name index; Hagerman Index (1800+); Nye Index (to names in many 1770-1840 records); gubernatorial and legislative records; 18th- and 19th-century legislative petitions; and state reports.

MONTPELIER – VERMONT HISTORICAL SOCIETY LIBRARY

109 State Street Pavilion   [802] 828-2291   I-89 to Exit 8; left at light; cross bridge;
   Office Building   right at light on State (Rte 2). Brick
Montpelier, VT 05609-0901   Victorian after Capitol; large verandah.
E-mail: vhs@vhs.state.vt.us
Web: http://www.vt.state.us/vhs

Tue-Fri 9am-4:30pm; 2nd Sat (*Jun-Sep*) -4pm; Mon (*Labor Day-Columbus Day*) -4:30pm (*call ahead to verify hours*)

$5 donation – in lieu of admission – suggested for non-members. Part of VERMONT HISTORICAL SOCIETY, which also maintains museum. Copying: members, $.15/page, non-, $.20; plus postage ($.75 for 25 pages, $3 minimum); genealogical mail inquiries accepted ($12 flat fee); materials not generally loaned. **HOLDINGS**: largest genealogical collection in state, covering all New England; large manuscript collection; library of the Vermont Society of Colonial Dames, including *American Genealogical and Biographical Index* and *Barbour Index to Connecticut Vital Records*; LDS Family Search CDs.

POULTNEY – GREEN MOUNTAIN COLLEGE – GRISWOLD LIBRARY

1 College Circle   [802] 287-8225   Rte 4W to Exit 4 (Poultney/Castleton
Poultney, VT 05764-1199   & -8099 (FAX)   Corners); S on Rte 30, 7 mi to Poultney;
E-mail: griswold@greenmtn.edu   right on Main St.

Mon-Thu 8am-10:30pm; Fri -5pm; Sat 1-5pm
Sun -10:30pm; *summer*: Mon-Fri 8am-4pm

Free and open to public. Mail inquiries answered; records searched as time permits. **HOLDINGS**: Troy Methodist Conference archives; Conference journals and yearbooks; vertical files for each church in Conference; Welsh collection; and – in separate 'WAGS' room, free, by appointment only ([802] 287-8309) – Welsh-American Genealogical Society records.

RUTLAND FREE LIBRARY

10 Court Street   [802] 773-1860   From So. Main St (Rte 7), W on
Rutland, VT 05701-4058   & -1861   Center St. Corner of Center &
E-mail: rutland_free@dol.state.vt.us   Court.

Mon-Wed 9am-9pm; Thu-Fri -5:30pm; Sat -5pm (*closes at 5:30pm, Tue, in summer*)

Free and open to public; copying, $.15/page; 2 film readers, 1 reader/printer; *limited* mail-in research requests accepted, but low priority – postage and per-hour fees may apply; *extensive* research referred to local genealogist. **HOLDINGS**: federal census film for Rutland County (1791-1920) and the rest of Vermont (-1850); Rutland *Herald* from 1794; *Barbour Index to Connecticut Vital Records*; DAR lineage books; Walton's registers; Hemenway's *Vermont Historical Gazetteer;* town reports from 1880; directories; Beers' atlases; printed and filmed Vermont and New England histories and genealogies.

SAINT JOHNSBURY ATHENAEUM

30 Main Street   [802] 748-8291   I-91 to Exit 21; 1 mi to Main; library
St. Johnsbury, VT 05819-2289   atop hill.
E-mail: stjathenaeum@dol.state.vt.us

Mon, Wed 10am-8pm; Tue, Thu, Fri -5:30pm; Sat 9:30am-4pm

Free and open to public; copying, $.20/page; mail inquiries accepted (answered when volunteers available). **HOLDINGS**: Vermont town histories, maps, gazetteers; complete run of *Caledonia Record* on film (no printer), in-house index to same, to 1985.

VERGENNES – BIXBY MEMORIAL LIBRARY

258 Main Street   [802] 877-2211   On N side of Rte 22 in town ctr.
Vergennes, VT 05491
Web: http://www.state.vt.us/vhs/lhs/addison.htm#Vergennes

Mon, Fri 12:30-8pm; Tue, Thu -5pm; Wed 10am-5pm

Copying, $.15/page; 1 film reader; staff research limited to quick checks; interlibrary loan on standard ILL forms. **HOLDINGS**: Vermontiana; small genealogical collection; local newspapers on film (some from 1850); DAR *Patriot Index*; war rosters; Hemenway's *Vermont Historical Gazetteer*.

WOODSTOCK – NORMAN WILLIAMS PUBLIC LIBRARY

Woodstock, VT 05091   [802] 457-2295   I-89 to Rte 4 (Woodstock); library on Green.

Mon-Fri 10am-5pm; Tue, Wed 7-9pm
Sat 10am-4pm (*summer*: 9am-3pm)

Free and open to public; small local-history room in basement. **HOLDINGS**: complete run of the *Vermont Journal* (Windsor), and *Vermont Standard* (Woodstock).

LDS FAMILY HISTORY CENTER

Berlin – 244 Hersey Road; [802] 229-0482; Wed, Thu 10am-4pm; Thu 6:30-9:30pm; Sat 10am-3pm

SOCIETIES

GENEALOGICAL SOCIETY OF VERMONT (GSV)

P.O. Box 1553
St. Albans, VT 05478-1006
Web: http://ourworld.compuserve.com/homepages/induni_n_j

Founded in 1971; over 1,000 members; preserves and disseminates genealogically important Vermont records, encourages compilation of Vermont genealogies, and brings together people with common Vermont research interests. $20 yearly includes *Vermont Genealogy* (1996 to present, replacing *Branches & Twigs,* 1972-95), a quarterly of primary records, methodological articles, compiled genealogies, book reviews, *etc.*, and a quarterly *Newsletter*. GSV has also published two volumes of an ongoing *Vermont Families in 1791* project, as well as the VRs of several towns (Putney, Georgia, and Rockingham). Meets twice yearly (May and October) at various Vermont sites.

VERMONT HISTORICAL SOCIETY (see address under LIBRARIES – MONTPELIER)

Founded in 1838; keeps a library, museum, and administrative offices. $12/year includes a quarterly, *Vermont History*, and a newsletter (neither genealogical).

PERIODICAL

Vermont's only statewide genealogical journal is **VERMONT GENEALOGY** (formerly *Branches and Twigs*; quarterly; see under GENEALOGICAL SOCIETY OF VERMONT).

BOOKS AND ARTICLES

Bartley, Scott Andrew, *Vermont Families in 1791*, 2 vols. (1992 and 1997: Camden, ME, Picton Press and St. Albans, VT, Genealogical Society of Vermont).

_____ and **Alice Eichholz**, "Vermont," *Ancestry's Red Book* (rev. ed., 1992: Salt Lake City, Ancestry Publishing).

Bassett, T. D. Seymour, *Vermont: A Bibliography of Its History* (1981: Boston, G. K. Hall).

Batchellor, Albert Stillman, ed., *The New Hampshire Grants: Being Transcripts of the Charters of Townships and Minor Grants of Land Made by the Provincial Government of New Hampshire, Within the Present Boundaries of the State of Vermont, from 1749 to 1764* (1895: Concord, NH, E. N. Pearson). Same as vol. 26 of *New Hampshire State Papers*.

Hanson, Edward W., "Vermont Genealogy: A Study in Migration," *NEHGR*,133[1979]:3-19; also in Ralph J. Crandall, ed., *Genealogical Research in New England* (1984: Baltimore, Genealogical Publishing Co.).

Hemenway, Abby Maria, *Vermont Historical Gazetteer*, 5 vols. (1867-91: Burlington, the author, and other cities and publishers) and index (1923: Rutland, Tuttle Publishing Co.).

Holbrook, Jay Mack, *Vermont 1771 Census* (1982: Oxford, MA, Holbrook Research Institute).

Hyde, Arthur L. and **Frances P.**, *Burial Grounds of Vermont* (1991: Bradford, Vermont Old Cemetery Association).

Leppman, John A., "A Bibliography for Vermont Genealogy," *Vermont Genealogy*, 3[1998]:17-26, 128-36, 4[1999]:17-30 (*to be continued*).

National Survey Co., *Vermont Yearbook* (annual: Chester, VT, National Survey Co.).

Nichols, Joann H. and **Patricia L. Haslam**, *Index to Known* [*i.e.*, published] *Cemetery Listings in Vermont,* 3rd ed. (1995: Montpelier, Vermont Historical Society).

O'Callaghan, Edmund B., ed., *The Documentary History of the State of New York* (1851: Albany, Weed, Parsons & Co.). Vol. 4 has over 500 pages documenting the struggle between New York and N.H. for jurisdiction over Vermont.

Potter, Constance, "St. Albans Passenger Arrival Records," *Prologue*, 22[1990-91]:90-3.

Rollins, Alden M., *Vermont Warnings Out*, 2 vols. (1995 and 1997: Camden, ME, Picton Press).

Secretary of State, *State Papers of Vermont*, 22+ vols. (1918-91+: Montpelier, Office of the Secretary of State).

Stilwell, Lewis D., *Migration from Vermont* (1948: Montpelier, Vermont Historical Society).

Swift, Esther M., *Vermont Place-Names: Footprints of History* (1977 and 1996: Camden, ME, Picton Press and Brattleboro, Greene Press).